KNOCKING

FROM THE INSIDE

A MEMOIR VEILED IN NUMBERS

Jacquii Leveine

Afrodite Art
New York

ACKNOWLEDGMENTS

Grateful acknowledgment is given for permission to reprint from:

Numbers and You: A Numerology Guide for Everyday Living by Lloyd Strayhorn. Copyright © 1980, 1987, 1997 by Lloyd Strayhorn. Published by Ballantine Books, an imprint of the Random House Publishing Group.

Card Reading for Today! by Danny Tarot. Copyright © 2020 by Danny Tarot. Published on Facebook (www.facebook.com/1Dannytarot/).

Design by Jacquii Leveine

ISBN: 978-1-7347416-0-5

Printed in the United States of America.

This divinely-influenced creation you behold,
Pays homage to my ancestors and their gifts bestowed,
My angels who guided me along my life's path,
My mother who inspired me to cultivate and share my craft,
My girlfriends who wailed the sistahood blues,
My male companions who've unknowingly been my muse,
My coaches and mentors who modeled the successful climb,
And all the psychics whose prophecies have led me to this exact space in time.

To everyone who's interacted with this work via thought, word, or deed, I thank you. May all the eyes capturing my deepest thoughts and minds tapping into my bookish abundance be sated with spiritual sustenance.

"Because at the end of the day, the miracle comes from within. You are your own miracle worker."

~ *Chris Ochun Capone*

INTRODUCTION

"We don't speak, we hustle. We are the meek with muscle. We are the huh--"

I'M AN EXILE SETTLED IN A COLONY OF VOICELESS HUSTLERS. My compatriots and I live on nebulous grounds located between consciousness and insensibility. I was banished to this land because at some point within the last nine years of my life I became a deaf mute.

Not the kind of deaf mute who involuntarily lives in stark silence with a landscape of experiences built upon sight, smell, and touch. That still would be too real, vibrantly full of excitement as the senses are heightened with new textures, bouquets, and expansive horizons.

No, this is the type of deaf mute disability that's self-inflicted. Somewhere along my path I rendered myself speechless, missing out on the colors of life that reside in sound--the sound of my own voice. My voice lost its joyous resonance. In turn, I lost my unabashed honesty. I lost my courage. I lost my fearlessness. I lost my sense of adventure. I lost myself!

It's almost as if I was sleepwalking the days by, in and out of wake. I'd awake to deal with the needs and wants of others or to ensure that my societal obligations were met. I'd sleep on *my* desires, *my* dreams, *my* truths, and *my* inner voice. In introspective reflection, my inner voice has been stifled for quite some time. I'm surprised and grateful it hasn't yet abandoned me, having been neglected for so long.

Instead, it stayed with me during times when I doubted it most, sometimes allowing me to go deeper into some dark and dangerous lessons and other times beckoning me to follow it out of the abyss. Despite either of the paths chosen at any given time, it was always there to protect me. Not fully understanding and realizing my gift of what I now know is inner-sight, I didn't always trust it. I didn't trust myself. So, I ignored many red flags.

There isn't one root cause for my catatonic state. Rather, the causes are an amalgamation of sundry slights and self-disregard intricately woven into a complex, beautifully-flawed tapestry which hangs heavily over the core of my soul, concealing the real me. The real, authentic me that dwells in an unwavering acceptance of the dualities in right and wrong, beautiful and ugly, dark and light, yin and yang.

Sleepwalking triggered me to choose sides. If I was beautiful, I couldn't stand to look at the ugly. If I represented the light, I could never be dark. Of course, I was always in the right. No need to mention that other word because it was nonexistent in my disillusioned world ... *WRONG!*

Spiritual teacher Iyanla Vanzant would have referred to me as one of her *neck-down dead* clients. Meaning that I was devoid of real feelings from the heart. I intellectualized emotions of happiness, sadness, and pain, but from the neck down, I was numb. I was emotionally dead. I was out of touch with my life's pulse which resides in my heart and my stomach.

Throughout my twenties I walked around holding my breath, taking life in in short spurts and constricted sneezes, wondering why my cheeks were covered with pimples and my ribcage ached. I didn't know how to breathe down into the pit of my stomach, extending my ribs outwards, allowing my diaphragm to move up and down freely, engaging the central nervous system, standing in confidence and awareness. I thought sneezing softly was proper, poised, and royal. The raucousness of my naturally loud sneeze would frighten, overwhelm, and embarrass me.

Today I know I'm all these things--soft, proper, poised, royal, and raucously loud ... on purpose.

Life is such that we no longer ask direct questions. I can avouch that I rarely come out and expose my true self, nor do I ask too much of others because I fear I may be treading on emotional landmines. Instead, I ask enough questions to tease a premature hunger.

When that hunger cries out for fulfillment, I resolve it to a partial feeding of my own incomplete perceptions. The spoonful, however, is never quite enough; for as a loveless lady, I often find myself limiting my mind and inner vision to whatever I *want* to know, accept, and see and exclude all else as irrelevant.

The story I'm about to tell is of my *own* truth. Although I encourage your perusal, it's more for me than it is you, a self-analysis which I hope will assist me in identifying past pathologies or patterns within my present and past lives. Consider it an open book examination of will and faith. It won't be pretty. Nor will it fit perfectly in a neat, shiny box. I aim for honesty and objectivity as I stand outside myself looking in like an astral traveler who's fully awake.

This narrative spans over a nine-year period from my thirty-fourth earth day through my forty-third. It's essential to note that I began to write these events approximately four months into my forty-second year on this physical plane. Depending on the time I finish channeling my written memoirs, I may very well be forty-three, completing the full nine-year interval, making my way into the next.

Through this journey upon which I'll again embark, I've come to learn and lean on the teachings of numerology. By dissecting my birthday and birthname, I intend to delineate a nine-year, numerological roadmap that demystifies two plaguing questions: Why do I consistently attract *this* type of man? How is my romantic partner a reflection of me?

I go by Jacquii Leveine. Jacqueline Noelle Leveine is the name my soul entered into a written contract with at inception. I was born on April 20, 1976. I'm an eleven life path.

As an eleven, I'm the poster child for Luke 12:48 verse, *To whom much is given, much is required.* I operate on a higher-octave vibration than my lower base number two. My eleven life path calls on me to be a healer of people and mankind through words, the arts, and creative channels. As an old soul who's amassed a great deal of spiritual wisdom from past incarnations, I'm one of the universe's *wounded healers*.

The significance of the nine-year duration is in direct correlation to the second pinnacle cycle of my life path. There are four pinnacle cycles. Each cycle represents a time of profound transformation as I move from one phase of maturation to another. My first pinnacle cycle represented my youth, the cultivation of the *I* as my persona was shaped.

My second pinnacle, one of personal growth and honoring obligations, is preparing me for future life events through the perfection of my craft. My third pinnacle will emphasize my expansion of knowledge into new fields, home or abroad. The fourth pinnacle cycle will be a period of reflection, encouraging me to use the wisdom gained from my spiritual experiences to influence the tides of humanity on a grander level.

Each pinnacle cycle represents a life lesson and its corresponding challenge to be mastered within that specified timeframe. As an eleven life path, these are my four pinnacle cycles. I'll initiate my ascent from the windmills of my mind by propelling myself into the lesson and challenge of the second.

Pinnacle One	Pinnacle Two	Pinnacle Three	Pinnacle Four
Ages 0 – 34	Ages 35 – 43	Ages 44 – 52	Ages 53 – 81
Lesson	Lesson	Lesson	Lesson
6	7	4	9
Challenge	Challenge	Challenge	Challenge
2	3	1	1

You see, in the former years of my second pinnacle, I lacked the spiritual awareness to ascertain my seven lesson number as a means to develop my inner spiritual acuity, tap into my intuition and learn to trust myself. I didn't understand, nor did those in my circle, why I shunned social gatherings to spend time in quiet introspection, learning about metaphysics and the mysteries of the universe. This lesson summons me to probe deeper into questions pertaining to my life's purpose and direction, connect to the Divine through prayerful meditation, and perfect my craft.

Similarly, my three challenge number dares me to recognize my feelings and communicate them through various modes of self-expression, allowing me to speak my truth. The struggle within the three challenge is my use of self-criticism and self-doubt as tools that stifle my creativity and sense of identity.

Within each pinnacle is the personal year cycle. Personal year cycles begin at birth and cycle through nine-year intervals throughout my lifetime. Each year, from January to December, there's a personal year number indicating the lessons, opportunities, and experiences I'll come upon.

This book is broken down in parts. Each part represents a year of my life and the events which have transpired therein. Since this is a self-analysis, each year will correlate to my personal year number and its overarching vibration.

I begin this reflective quest at the end of my first pinnacle cycle which is a nine personal year of completion and endings. Each part thereafter will be within the second pinnacle cycle starting on the one personal year of new beginnings. I figure the most comprehensive way for me to understand my life experiences is for me to look at the numerical influences governing that specific period of time.

I look forward to the learnings, self-discoveries, and revelations that will be unearthed once all is said and done. For now, let's start at the beginning, which in this case, is all about endings.

Jacquii Leveine

2010 – END OF FIRST PINNACLE

$$4 + (2 + 0) + (2 + 0 + 1 + 0)$$
$$4 + 2 + 3 = 9$$

Nine Personal Year

Completion, dreams fulfilled, endings, inspiration, long distance travel. This cycle symbolizes a completion of sorts, either in your personal or business affairs. Your capacity to let go of persons, habits, negative circumstances, or conditions that you've outgrown will be strong. Develop the humanitarian side of your nature, learn to give more of yourself to others without expecting payment in return. Cosmically, you'll be rewarded if you do.[1]

---

[1] (Strayhorn, 1997)

"I need a bitter man.
One who understands,
That too much loving makes you hard.
Only then will I let down my guard.
Send me a bitter man.
One without a plan,
To make me his wife or his life.
Cause he's used to the heartache and strife."

1

CHILDBEARING IS AN OVERRATED PASTIME RESERVED FOR THE OBTUSE AND lonesome.

That was my spiritless New Year's declaration. Leaving no time for the fulfillment of lofty resolutions, January began with the conception of life. It should have been a joyous milestone marked by a celebration of fertility, showered with overwhelming maternal love and affection for the fetus growing inside me. Instead, it was a trimester consisting of a series of lonely, drunken nights consumed in a Merlot-induced stupor, curled up on my living room couch.

I never had a penchant for Merlot, but the heartburn was increasingly unbearable. It was the only sedative capable of soothing the incessant, annoying ache in my chest. I reconciled the discomfort by visually caressing the notion of a beautiful cinnamon-flavored baby girl with hair reaching her ripe shoulders.

Considering her father's own hair fell down to his ass and mine, although worn in a Caesar, was a wavy mix of East Indian, South Asian, and Carib, chances were great that my premonition was accurate. I had envisioned a *Dougla* baby version of myself.

In dark solitude I spent many nights debating her fate while her father Collin traversed his daytime hustle at the barbershop and his nighttime hustle between thick thighs and street life highs. He was my señor blues, a wondering, wandering guy with no one gal to lay his head by. I often asked myself why a woman would subject herself to such misery for the sake of birthing someone else? My honesty sounds crude, I know.

"You're selfish!" Collin would frequently say to me. "How can you be such a beautiful woman and not want to share that with a child of your own?"

I'd say I was a woman of the world and didn't see the value of limiting myself with mundane lifetime obligations. Over this we'd argue for many nights. He'd go to sleep angry and I'd be flippantly indifferent. That was my twenty-four-year-old self rebelling against his twenty-seven-year-old self. He already had a son from a previous relationship and I didn't feel any urgency.

Ten years later I'd find myself lying alone waiting for him to bring me a shrimp roti. Each night this would seem like hours upon eternity. I was simply too tired from carrying the additional weight, too foggy with pregnancy brain, and too gassy to cook.

I loathed every minute of the wait. I hated being dependent upon a man whom I was smarter than. I came to learn that pregnancy didn't fill my heart with a flood of adoration for Collin. Rather, it amplified my existing feelings of dislike and disdain for him to a heightened hormonal state. It wasn't always like this, though. There was a time when we were sincerely, and happily, into each other in a crazed, viscerally impulsive kind of way.

Collin fell in love with me when I was twenty and still had my hair locs. We first saw each other at my friend Fabian's barbershop where he worked as a barber. He was new to America, fresh from Trinidad and Tobago and I was a fiery Trini descendant who wore purple, yellow, and blue hair down to the middle of my back during a time when *dreadlocks*, a misnomer, was considered taboo, ripped jeans, and a pierced nose.

He'd sing the lyrics to all the roots and culture reggae tunes that played while he'd ogle me, sneakily, under half closed eyelids. His eyes were magical. They were big, beautiful, probing, and bright like those of the spider Charlotte in the book *Charlotte's Web*. He was tall, about six feet, three inches, which always made him bend to get into and out of doorways and often made him extremely clumsy with anything surrounding him.

He was dark-skinned. A deep brown the color of cocoa beans. My girlfriends would ofttimes refer to him as the *nice looking darkie*. He was handsome. His features where neatly contained, with a small nose, full lips, and a gap-toothed smile concealed by a singular gold tooth. He was stylish.

I had a proclivity for fashion and putting clothes together in such a way that only I could wear. Like me, he had a style that others couldn't execute tastefully. I was seeing my boyfriend Noah at the time, and he and I were in a groove. So, our sightings would be brief. I'd go on to my man, and he'd go on to his wife.

As life would have it, my father passed in March of 1998. He was hit by a truck on the Priority Bus Route in Trinidad, which is a public transit roadway reserved for use only by buses, maxi taxis, and emergency vehicles. The accident severed his hip bone. He was healing slowly.

Unwilling to be an invalid for the remainder of his life, depending on my mother to be his caretaker, my father convinced the doctor to release him from the hospital under the guise of returning home. My father seized his early release as an opportunity to party and drank a whole gallon of Johnny Walker in commemoration of his fifty-fifth birthday.

The alcohol, coupled with the prescribed blood pressure medication, caused a heart attack, and my father died. The death was ruled a natural one. Trinidadians celebrate and surrender everything to the mercy of a bottle of rum, so no suspicion would ever be cast upon his death. I ruled it a suicide. He took the easy way out and chose not to fight, to confront his demons and come out the victor. For that, I was bitterly angry.

We were never close. In fact, I hated my father. He was a strange, tacit giant who hardly spoke but prophesized like a Buddha; hardly consoled, but mocked me like a toddler; hardly laughed with his family but was full of jokes with others outside us.

He was one of the misunderstood. I was too young and egotistical to realize that sometimes in this earthly incarnation the parent is really the spiritual student, and the child is the spiritual teacher. I regretted that I didn't employ the actions my intuition begged of me to make things right between us. He left me a legacy of guilt.

As the saying goes, death, be it physical or symbolic, comes in threes. First was the death of my father; shortly after, Noah and I parted ways simply because we'd outgrown each other; and I, on impulse, decided to discard the old me to reinvent the new. I changed my first name to Jacquii.

Born Jacqueline, my mother first shortened my name to Jacquie as a nickname. I completed my full schooling as Jacquie Noelle Leveine. But upon my graduation from college, I added a unique variation to its spelling by discarding the *e* and adding an extra *i* to get Jacquii. Three months after my twenty-second birthday I officiated the name change through the court system in front of a judge, published it in a local newspaper, and reflected the new name on all my legal documentation. In essence, I initiated my own death and rebirth.

I continued on, in vowed silence and rebellion, to cut my hair off. I went to Fabian's shop and had him cut the majority of my locs into a closed-cropped curly afro, tapered and edged to perfection with six locs remaining in the front cascading along the side of my face, asymmetrically from shortest to longest. Once again, yours truly was pioneering a new look. I was styling between two worlds, occupying the past and future, unwilling to acquiesce to either.

I saw Collin watching me in stifled mourning under his captivating eyes, as he couldn't understand why I'd cut off my hair that had grown so long and beautiful. It wasn't his business to understand. With that new look I left the shop and his purview. Eventually, I cut all my hair off into a Caesar. Inspired by then singing group Zhané, I had found home on my head.

For two years I moved between barbers trying to find the right cut and fit. As a result of too many late barber appointments, barber no-shows, and my favorite hairbrush being stolen by my then barber never to be relinquished, I ended up in Collin's chair. He had since moved from

Fabian's shop and found shelter in a shop on one of the busiest Caribbean streets in the heart of Brooklyn, Church Avenue.

Our courtship started out simple and sweet. He was patient. He was a great storyteller who had a way of drawing a visual picture with characters and dialogue so vivid it placed me in the middle of the scene. He had a sincere appreciation for life. He enveloped me with his humor, his transparency, and his eyes. Those eyes would indeed entangle me in his web, and oh, what a tangled web we weave when first we learn to diss Eve!

It was supposed to be about sex--that's all. "It's just a fuck thing," I declared to my girls. "I'll make him my fuck buddy, let him take the edge off."

A few months in I'd find myself cooking for him, making what Trinis called provisions--yams, dasheen, cassava, sweet potato, plantain topped with Callaloo, stew pigeon peas with pumpkin, and fried shark or curry king crab legs. Yes, your girl was going in! Not only would I cook these meals, I'd hand deliver them to the shop, where he worked, during the day, in front of the other barbers.

There were days when he'd sit on the back porch of my parents' home while I picked okra, tomatoes, and cucumbers from the back garden to prepare his meal. He'd talk, I'd laugh. He'd show me how to pick the okras before they got too big, too ripe, and too hard. He fancied that part of me. I was a city girl with a country girl's upbringing.

I catered to my man because that's what I grew up seeing in my home. I never had a problem with it. It made me feel like a woman, wanted and special. My heart would sing when he ate my meals with pure joy on his face, questioning if I really cooked or had someone else do it. We'd have beach hangs at Riis on the Rockaway Peninsula in the summer nights, he and I, with my *cousin* Tamia and his boy Lester. It was heaven.

The womanizing became an issue. I had severed my previous relationships prior to becoming involved with Collin, but he was still married. He claimed that he and his wife weren't compatible and didn't see eye to eye. He said they argued constantly, and many nights she forbade him from leaving the house by laying her body on the ground in front of the door, like a barricade.

I was aware of his wife. Quite frankly, I didn't give a damn. It was the arrogance of youth. I felt unstoppable and fearless. He'd demonstrated on several different occasions his lack of respect for his union by choosing to spend his anniversary with me or taking me out on days he'd promise to be with her. There were days that she'd come to the shop and see me at his station, not needing a haircut, and would ask me to ask him to come outside to speak to her.

On one particular day we sat in the shop on the bench next to each other, skin to skin. She was a beautiful, voluptuous woman. She complimented me on my Marciano Guess jeans, I told her where she could buy them, and we continued on in silence with a world of thoughts telepathically transmitting between us. Overwhelmed by the incredibility of the situation, I called Tamia.

"Girl, I'm in the barbershop, and you won't believe who I'm sitting next to right now."

"Don't tell me it's Collin's wife?" Tamia asked, gasping in amazement.

"Girl, if I only turn my face to the left, I could kiss her," I replied all in earshot of his wife.

I was disrespectful! For me it was about nothing more than power--the power to control a man and render him so weak that he'd allow me to reign supreme over his castle as, technically, the mistress. I was his Empress, a hypocorism he'd given me. I was clearly queen and what I wanted or said went--unequivocally--no questions asked.

It was an ambush of sovereignty, and I enjoyed every minute of it. I relished in the adrenaline rush, the danger, and the risk of it all. In short, I was reckless. I had no regard for his wife's feelings, but let's be clear. I was no homewrecker! Their home was in complete spiritual disarray way before I entered the equation. My presence merely illuminated an already existing breakdown in communication, connection, and trust. There were others! That was my main problem. It was one thing to have a wife and a mistress, but concubines? Hell no!

I found myself hunting him during my down time. After two years, I decided to leave my job with Verizon as a cable splicing technician. I left with a Master of Arts from Teacher's College, Columbia University in tow, courtesy of the company's financing.

With this newfound freedom, it was customary for me to pop into the barbershop on any random day at any given time, interrogating the barbers about his whereabouts. Of course, I didn't expect them to divulge his location, but they knew to call him advising I was on the lookout. Shortly thereafter, I'd receive my call; however, it became much worse when he started to drive.

I always had a car, so transport was solely on me. Not being able to track his movements when I wanted would send me into a bit of a manic fit. There was one girl in particular who really unnerved me. Her mannerisms were too much like mine. I'd come into the shop to get my hair cut or shaped up and she'd be hanging over his station in similar fashion as I. Her name was Geena. He claimed she was his *friend*, and they'd just *smoke* together. My intuition, or spirit, as I now refer to it, told me otherwise.

One night I drove to the barbershop to see him, but he wasn't there. I drove around the corner making my way back home and saw his car parked on Snyder Avenue, in front of the *smoking friend's* house. In a calculated rage, I called my partner in crime, Tamia.

"Girl, what are you getting into tonight?"

"Nothing, I'm just here," Tamia replied.

"Well, I just went to the shop to see Collin and he's not there. I'm driving around the corner and his car is in front of Geena's house. I'm about to park up and sit this shit out. You down?"

"I'm not doing anything right now, so come scoop me up," she said, excited about the night's new adventure.

I picked Tamia up from the block since we lived across the street from each other. Tamia and I had grown together since the age of eight and six respectively. Although there was no blood relation between us, we'd forged a childhood connection that aligned us as "cousins" of a kindred sort.

We went to the closest Dunkin Donuts, bought some tea and a box of donuts, and prepared ourselves for a stakeout.

Getting back to the perpetrator's location, I parked my then 2001 Nissan Maxima directly in front of his car. The windows of my car had 30% tints, so we had the visual advantage. We rolled the front seats all the way back, put on some stakeout music, sipped tea, ate donuts, and waited in the cut.

About four hours later, closer to 11:00 p.m., Collin came strolling down the block. This wasn't just any kind of stroll. This was a stroll somewhere between a skip and a bop. He was in a euphoric state of mind. During those times I was famous for wearing long vintage leather peacoats and high-heeled knee-high leather boots.

I opened that car door like a SWAT team swooping down on its suspect. In the fury of my movements, my leather coat flew up into the air like Nicholas Cage's in the movie *Face Off*. I ran up on him so quickly it took some time for his brain to transition from experiencing pure happiness to processing absolute shock.

"Eh heh! Yeah! I caught your ass! Explain what you were doing at that chick's house now!"

"Jacquii, you really stalked me out here tonight? You really parked your car up to stalk me?" he asked, ducking his head down to get a clearer look through the tinted windows. "And you brought your soldier with you too?" The argument would continue for the balance of the night, carrying on into days of me giving him the silent treatment.

There were other similar instances of me running his car off the road in drag racing fashion. I was a terror, and he loved every minute of it.

"You're silky and sugary!" he'd often tell me. "You don't even know how much sugar you have between your legs."

I didn't. I couldn't experience myself the way he did, but I could use it to my benefit. My vagina had him hooked, just like his penis had me. I guess we didn't have anything else to blame but the sugar factory.

My life took a turn for the serious when I started to work for the New York City Department of Education as a technology teacher. I began working in 2002 and found myself moving quickly up the ranks. After two years, I was out of the classroom and into a staff development position. I worked on getting an Advanced Master of Arts from Hunter College in Education Administration.

In turn, my relationship with Collin was becoming too redundant for the modern woman and we parted ways as friends. I'd still go to him for haircuts, but the sexual nature of our relationship ended. At the ripe age of twenty-eight, I was dabbling in the pool of a white-collar suitor. Although this relationship had its own share of womanizing woes, it felt good to have a partner with whom I could be equally yoked.

He was way beyond me in his profession, but I had earned his respect outside the bedroom. I was experiencing a life of new possibilities, wooed by candle-lit dinner parties, Broadway shows, Sunday brunch, political debates, catered meals, and spa-quality bubble baths.

This too lasted about four years on and off. Like before, there were others. I couldn't continue in the same vein, and this suitor wasn't built or bred for the daytime drive-bys and late-night stakeouts. I had to conduct myself like the lady I was quickly becoming. I was remaking myself into upwardly mobile elegance and thus had to employ other strategies of self-preservation. I simply left. That relationship, although I mention it here briefly, shaped me quite a bit during my first pinnacle cycle. I had acquired a taste for the "silk, satin, Manhattan, intelligent spiel" and it was insatiable.

When I left, I did so for the familiar. It's easy to fall into old rhythms and patterns because they're already worn and molded in exactitude like hand in glove. At age thirty-three, I had four degrees, my final one from New York University. I was making six figures as a Senior Project Manager. I was driving an Infiniti G35 after crashing my Maxima in a freak accident on the Belt Parkway. I moved from my place of eight years in Ditmas Park, Brooklyn to a swanky Crown Heights condominium, paying double the rent I was paying previously. It was apartment 2E!

"This apartment is fresh J! I can see myself in something like this," said my older brother Lucas as he and his then girlfriend Keisha helped me set up my TV for a cable appointment the next day. He walked over to the balcony which faced the back of my building onto a shared courtyard situated between an identical condo complex on the block behind me and owned by the same owners.

"This is the second floor, but this balcony is low," he remarked, looking out the window at the courtyard. "You're next to an empty lot. Someone can easily put a ladder up here and come into your apartment. Be careful with that. Don't leave the door or windows open when you're not home. But otherwise, this shit is fresh to death!"

Aside from the balcony, my condo had two bathrooms and three bedrooms, two of which could easily be converted into one. The walls were an intense white. The floors were white marble. The chef's kitchen was complete with two sets of stainless steel stacked stoves and two sinks. I thought the kitchen was designed for entertaining but later came to learn that, being in the predominantly Jewish Crown Heights neighborhood, the building owner purposely designed the units with two sets of appliances to adhere to the Jewish customs of separating dairy from meat.

The living room's décor was confined to a snug space resembling a white box. Upon entry, an ivory art deco leather couch hugged the left wall. It sat parallel to a large, black and sleek entertainment system. The two walls were joined by imposing floor to ceiling windows; ivory curtains hung, dressing them with scalloped edges, feigning some semblance of discretion.

A huge rattan chair with ivory cushions was positioned in front the glass wall mocking a French designed chaise lounge on the opposite side.

The chaise lounge was a *conversation love seat*, as it had two seats facing each other. I imagined, had there been another inhabitant, the dialogues on that particular sofa would've been intriguing with two sets of eyes ogling the other. Behind it were three ivory bar stools overlooking the kitchen. A black-lacquered upright piano was placed catercorner, seldom played.

The art work, a mix of wood carvings and Jazz scenes, blended in beautifully with the Ebony and Ivory theme, recessed, dimmed lighting, and Sade who streamed hauntingly through sunken speakers. In the middle of it all, laid the prototypical Picasso-esque floor rug, adding a wild splash of blacks, burgundies, browns, beige, and whites, attempting to make everything coalesce into one central piece.

The bedroom, decorated with an ivory leather platform bed, chaise lounge, and wireless speakers, was regularly perfumed with sandalwood incense, so music and woody fragrances were ubiquitous.

As a finished abode, its design was a juxtaposition of pulchritude and sterility. Simply put, it was cold! It was cold as the marble floors upon which I stood when I forgot to wear socks, penetrating the skin and freezing my internal organs. Cold like my heart that had its fill of hurt, magnificently adorned to the human eye, masked in perfection, and absent of homeliness. It epitomized barren beauty fit for an Ice Queen.

Collin was impressed with the come up and pictured himself enjoying a different life with me in this new space. I, however, found his Rasta singing, loc swinging, weed slinging mannerisms too plebian for the sophistication I was cultivating, his presence inapposite in my mausoleum of a home. His wife had since relocated to another state, taking his only son with her. His son wasn't her child, but she'd grown especially close to him and chose to raise him as her own.

We had an opportunity to make a life together, thus we attempted. One fateful night in January he asked a simple question, "Why don't we try to make a baby?"

"You want to?" I asked.

"Yes," he replied.

After he ejaculated inside me, I put a pillow under my butt and bent my knees onto the bed so my body would slope downwards toward my head. I remember my girlfriend Halle telling me this was the easiest way to ensure that the semen would reach the egg. Instinctively, I tried it. Life was conceived.

The next morning I awoke in obscured panic. What the hell did I just do? What did I commit myself to? I asked Collin if he had any second thoughts about our plans and he assured me he was fine. I, on the other hand, wasn't. I was meeting my mother that day for dinner and a movie in the city, but before I did, I made a pit stop at Duane Reade to pick up some Plan B.

We finished watching a movie in our preferred theatre on 14th Street and Broadway in the city and made our way over to an Indian restaurant named Café Spice along University Place. It was a quaint bistro recollective of olden South Asian style. We sat toward the back of the teeming eatery in a private booth under the crimson luster of a traditional Chinese lantern. Red and gold-trimmed drapes secured us from roaming eyes and invasive chatter, but did little to guard our nostrils against the stabile whiff of curry.

Dinner was a palate of dahl, tamarind, tandoori, saag, and biryani alongside Basmati rice, accompanied by gassy indigestion and bile-fueled stomach flurries. My mother loved Indian food. If you knew her well, you'd know to make sure to indulge her in all things that she loved, otherwise you'd suffer a tyranny of tongue-lashings filled with criticisms and complaints.

I loved her; a small but insanely strong woman who managed the vicissitudes of life with a steady, centered sense of self and integrity. She took no shit and spoke her truth at all times. She was fun-loving, affectionate, and laughed so loudly in movies that I'd often admonish her in embarrassment, only to have her scoff back at me in indignation.

Unable to focus on our dinner conversation, I excused myself to the restroom to tear open the Plan B box in an anxious rush. I swallowed the pill trying to wash it down my dry esophagus with my saliva. Returning to the table, I quickly gulped some water hoping the pill would land in the appropriate spot of my body that would facilitate the termination immediately.

Two weeks later, and no menstrual cycle in sight, I sat in my gynecologist's office with a positive test result.

"But I took Plan B," I told the doctor incredulously.

Dr. Michaels was a smart-mouthed Grenadian whose insults were so smooth I often didn't feel their sting until minutes after their delivery.

"Well, apparently, your Plan B reverted to Plan A because that fetus is alive and well," he said, laughing jovially. "Don't look at it as a negative. Life is a blessing, no matter when and how it's derived.

"I have a patient who was forty-five years old and, like you, took Plan B. She gave birth to a lovely baby girl who's now a child prodigy. She says it's the best thing that ever happened to her."

Dr. Michaels was bubbling with love and excitement. Any other time I visited him, he'd speak to me with the monotonous drone of a bored college professor, peering over his glasses, reading my yearly lab results. He'd end every report with, "Don't take too long to get pregnant now. You're getting older and it may be more difficult with age."

On this day, his long-awaited wish was granted. I was devastated.

Collin had gone out of state to visit his wife and son, over this, we were on the outs. We argued over the length of time he was staying. Amidst other harsh words I ended the conversation with, "And you don't have to rush back, because I'm not pregnant. There's nothing over here for you!"

That was a time prior to these new events; a time when I rested all my faith in Plan B. Calling him with this news snuffed my ego.

"So first you tell me you're not pregnant, and now you're telling me that you are?" he asked with snarky sarcasm. "So what happened? You impregnated yourself or what?"

"Well, I took Plan B on the same day we had sex. The box said to take it within seventy-two hours for it to be effective. Since I took it within the window of time, I thought I was good. But the doctor told me yesterday that I'm pregnant, and the fetus is healthy and growing." I was defeated in this battle.

"Okay, I'll be back in Brooklyn next week. We'll talk about it when I get back. Just know I love you, Empress." I was still too confused to respond, so I disconnected the call.

I confided in my girlfriend Lorraine. I told her I was pregnant as a result of the condom breaking. The awareness of me making a conscious decision to have a baby with a married man was awkward. I knew when I eventually told my mother, and I dreaded telling my mother, I couldn't tell her that truth. It was easier to alter a sliver of the story for consistency rather than juggle different versions.

"So the condom broke?" Lorraine asked in disbelief.

"Yeah, girl, you know I'm always complaining about the rough sex. Not that I mind the roughness. It's just, every time he does it rough, the condom breaks. This time I got pregnant." I lied.

"Hmm, so what're you going to do?"

"I don't know. I haven't yet decided. I have to tell my mother. I know she's going to flip when she hears this shit."

"Yep, she will. But you can't live your life aiming to please your mother. Yes, he's a married man, but things like this happen every day. Life is a blessing. Who knows? You were probably supposed to bring this life into the world for a reason."

Again, talks of blessings and destiny. I was still uncertain. Collin was thrilled with the news when he came back. He wanted a baby girl, and he wanted one with me. For a while I went along with it. I thought things would be different between us, that we'd finally have a viably functioning home.

His resoluteness made me feel secure enough to break the news to my mother during one of our movie outings.

"Yeah, I knew you were pregnant," she declared with motherly wisdom. "You ordered popcorn with butter. You never order popcorn or eat that nasty butter. And you're moving slowly. Who's the father?"

"Collin. I didn't plan it. The condom broke!" I lied.

"Collin?" she yelled. "Jacqueline, he's a married man."

"I know, Ma, but he and his wife are separated. She lives in another state."

"And? And that means what exactly? She's still named WIFE!" Disappointment registered on her face with great emphasis on that word. "I can't believe after all this schooling, all these accomplishments, you would lower yourself to get pregnant by a married man. You can't talk about this child proudly in public. It was conceived in sin! Of all the men, all the men outside you could've laid down with, you choose one who's married. I'd have rather you came and told me you were pregnant for Joe on the street corner instead of him, honest to God."

My mother was never a religious woman. She'd send my brother and me to church on a Sunday with enough money for bus fare and collection while she stayed home to cook. On this day, I swore she was a bible-thumping Baptist.

"You have that child and I wash my hands of you. You'll be on your own with that one. Don't call me. I don't approve. And don't tell me no shit about the condom broke either."

If you knew my mother, you'd know that she never made idle threats. What she said, she meant. It would be a cold day in hell before she'd breathe on me or my child. I knew this to be true. I had another conversation with Collin.

"So you're having second thoughts now?" He was upset by my emotional fluctuations. "Empress, you can't live by your mother's rules for your whole life."

"Yes, but she's the only one in my corner. I won't have the support I'll need to raise and take care of the child. This is my first. I don't know what I'm doing. I'll be alone!"

"No you won't. You have me and my mother. We'll help."

He uttered these words so convincingly I could feel him believing everything he said. I wasn't convinced. There's nothing like having your own mother around when you need her most. Until that point, she'd always been my cheerleader, my rock.

The tipping point was our first couple's check-in at the doctor's office. Knowing that Collin was always too busy with his street-side agendas, I prepped and reminded him days in advance. I texted him the address. I called him with the address. I talked him through programming the address in his Jeep's GPS. He was still late. He was so late, he missed the appointment. Even if he'd arrived five minutes into the meeting, Dr. Michaels would have forbidden his entrance. Dr. Michaels had a strict policy on tardiness.

Lorraine had accompanied me on a regular visit before I was pregnant and arrived five minutes late because parking by Long Island City Hospital was an impossible feat. He spent more time reprimanding her than he did reading me my results. Being the expectant father, I knew he'd have laced into Collin in a treacherously cutting type of way.

When Collin arrived, we only had time to eat Chinese food on Montague Street. We sat in that restaurant, and I was fuming. Fuming because I was already feeling alone and abandoned. Fuming because here I was with this beautiful man who drew every woman's attention in the restaurant, and he couldn't even get to an appointment on time. I started to question the intelligence of the fetus. Would she get his intellectual genes or mine? That's when the resentment started to grow. When he dropped me off at my door that night, I confessed that I was strongly considering the abortion.

"You know," he said introspectively, "I thought this baby would bring us closer together, but it feels like it's only ripping us apart."

He asked me to take my time and give it more thought--for us.

Think I did. Lying curled up on my living room couch, waiting for my shrimp roti, I thought about the decisions I'd made. I thought about the potential pain I'd cause his wife, who wasn't physically able to have children of her own. I thought about the shame that would be inherently associated with my child. I felt the sizzle of the S branded on my chest.

I wore this S as a tribute to the shame--my very own scarlet letter. I'd let my mother down. I'd let myself down. I was depressed. I oscillated between coldness, abandonment, shame, and back again in reverse order. During my next doctor's visit, when the lab technician asked if I wanted to see the sonogram, I replied "No! Because I'm not keeping her!" I turned my head to the side and wept.

Dr. Michaels refused to perform the procedure. He was the shepherd of life, not the deliverer of death. He did recommend another doctor who was willing, Dr. Davis. My mother was especially happy with my decision to terminate the pregnancy. We'd made plans to go to Carnival in Trinidad two months prior, and she was excited to have me child-free as her company and sidekick.

Our original flight was scheduled to leave a few days before my surgery, so my mother went ahead. I had to reschedule my flight. Dr. Michaels didn't give me authorization to travel in fear I'd be at risk of suffering post operation difficulties abroad. Dr. Davis, however, assured me all would be well and granted me the authorization I'd need to take a load off, literally, and enjoy myself.

Collin didn't go with me to the hospital on the day of the operation. We were at serious odds. He deemed me a mama's girl. I didn't have the energy to tell him the real reason for my decision. I called my trusty girlfriend Felise.

Felise and I met at Five Towns College where I was enrolled as an Audio Engineering major, and she a Music Business major. After a year of carpooling from Brooklyn to Dix Hills, Long Island in her car, Felise drove us to Manhattan one fateful afternoon and we both enrolled in CUNY. I ended up in City College and she in Baruch.

Felise was the kind of detail-oriented girlfriend who'd have all the particulars identified and dealt with in the middle of any controversy. She always saw to it that no stone was left unturned. She was patient with her girlfriends, not so much with men. If we were *Sex in the City* characters, I'd be Carrie and she'd definitely be Miranda. She was exactly who I needed for support at that moment, my weakest to date.

"Don't worry, lovey, you'll be taken care of and ready to go on your trip. But it's not too late to change your mind if you want to," she said, smiling mischievously.

"Felise!"

"I know, I know, I'm just saying," she kidded somewhat. "I'm just exploring all the options. I'll be here when you wake up."

There she was, ready to take me out to eat afterwards.

The next day I went to see Collin at the shop. I needed a haircut for my trip. "How are you feeling?" he asked.

"I feel much better now that it's over," I answered honestly. "I feel a sense of relief."

"Hmm, you feel better now?" he asked, looking at me underneath his eyelids in his customary way.

When I traced their trajectory, his line of sight wasn't on me per se. His eyes were trained at the ID band that I still wore from the hospital visit. He concentrated on it with laser-sharp focus almost as if he could bore a hole in it with his vision. Annoyance etched into his face. He was disgusted. The grotesque absurdity of me terminating his pregnancy and wining down low in the carnival-festive streets of Trinidad and Tobago was too much for him to handle. It was the ultimate disrespect.

To Trinidad I went, a few days after I'd originally planned. Dr. Michaels was beside himself, but Dr. Davis had already authorized the flight and faxed the airlines the documentation. To ensure that he wouldn't be subjected to another emotional ordeal orchestrated by my impulsive whims, Dr. Michaels put me on birth control.

Coupled with the influx of hormones remaining from the pregnancy, the birth control quickly widened my hips and engorged my breasts. I had the body fit for carnival season, but physically I couldn't keep up. The bleeding was especially heavy, and my movements were limited as a result. Needless to say, my mother had her company but not the kind she was anticipating.

When I returned home, Collin and I were distant. We tried to maintain a barber-client relationship, but it proved to be futile, because we suffered in silence. He'd attempt to vex me by inviting other love interests into the shop to converse over me while I sat in his chair. I'd yawn in boredom.

Later, I'd request half the hospital fees for the termination. It was an imposition made more out of spite than necessity. The termination was covered under my insurance plan. He initially gave me half of his half and refused to pay the latter. As far as he was concerned, he didn't sanction the procedure, so he wasn't going to finance it. In his mind, I decided, in isolation, to rid myself of his primordial seed which he desperately wanted.

Our final verbal altercation was so vicious, we both said things that were incorrigible. He disconnected my call. I called him back to announce that if he ever hung up on me again, it would be the last time we'd ever speak. He obstinately disconnected the phone a second time. That one gesture would forever form a chasm between us too wide and too far to bridge with words.

A year later, I received word through the grapevine that another woman birthed a baby girl for him, and his wife and son moved back to Brooklyn.

Collin's love, existing in the purest form I'd ever encounter, haunted me in the years to come when I, in my deepest solitude, longed for the simplicity of his affections.

2

THAT APRIL, I CELEBRATED MY THIRTY-FOURTH BIRTHDAY BY THROWING A get together in my condo with my girls. I called it the *Sistah's Heartwarming Soiree*. It was essentially a housewarming party, but I'd already furnished the apartment. I wanted to infuse some loving frequencies into its cold demeanor, so I asked Trent, my friend, boss, and chef in his free time, to cater the event with several rounds of small bites. I invited my girls to come with empty hands, open minds, and warm hearts.

I enjoyed bringing women together in fellowship. I found it to have such a strong spiritual energy when executed with love and light. Also, I had many girlfriends going through similar issues, and instead of revealing their personal information to other friends in like circumstances, I thought it better to have us all speak to each other and share our stories in an open, trusting, and risk-free forum over great food and strong drinks.

The idea originated with Felise. She'd often summons a small circle of friends that only included Asha and me over to her house where she'd cook Surinamese Lo Mein and make strawberry mimosas in sugar-rimmed champagne glasses. She termed this exclusive club *The Convening of the High Council*. We loved it. It was our special bonding time.

During these times we'd laugh, share our stories, address lingering issues, and hold each other accountable. Depending on the conversation, we'd sometimes leave with hard feelings, but we knew in our heart of hearts all sentiments expressed came from a sincere, sisterly place.

Considering all that I'd gone through at the start of the year, I wanted to throw a Thanksgiving of sorts to show my appreciation for life, my achievements, and strong friendship ties.

On the menu were elite food selections like langoustine tails in mango salsa, chipotle-blackened salmon, classic bruschetta, lamb puffs, spicy mushroom quesadillas, red velvet cake, and a finger salad because we had to get our ruffage in as well. In the line of alcoholic beverages, we had my mother's Rum Punch, the *ultimate* strawberry lemonade, and white wine. The menu was stacked. Even if my girls had no idea what the expectations were for the night, they'd come for the food alone.

Twelve ladies showed up. I invited Felise, but I never received a response from her. I found that particularly odd because I had called and emailed. I figured she needed time to herself as she'd just gone through a series of deaths, one of which was her grandmother. She'd lost her father a few years before and, not only was she grieving his absence, her son's father had become extremely vindictive and ornery when they separated. I noticed her absence, but I thought nothing peculiar about it--then.

Asha came, though. I was especially pleased to see her since I only knew her through Felise. We instantly had a connection during our High Council convenings, and it was nice to see the relationship extended past that circle into my new home.

The night started out on a slow burn and ended on fire. When the ladies first came in, they were all circumspect, on their best behavior, evaluating each other through inquisitive eyes. I opened the floor up with my story about Collin, the pregnancy, and the subsequent termination. The only way I was going to get these women to be vulnerable with each other was for me to get vulnerable and open with them. I told the whole thing, bearing my soul and shame.

"Girl, stop judging yourself," said Asha. "That happens to so many women. You weren't the first, and you won't be the last."

Lorraine jumped in sharing a story about a guy she was currently dating who was giving her the curve.

"Yeah, that's because you gave him too much too soon. He doesn't respect you," interjected Asha.

The comment took everyone off guard and sucked the air out of the room.

"Be easy, girl," I whispered to Lorraine, rubbing her thigh for comfort. "It's cool, just ignore it. You already know what it is with him. You don't need validation."

I had to talk Lorraine off the ledge. She was about to pounce Bronx-style, and everything in my condo was clean and white. I was already preoccupied with the thought that her dark blue jeans were going to stain my white leather couch.

"Yes," Asha continued, "I recently got married. I met my husband online and he caters to my every whim. He's absolutely fabulous. But I set the standard from the beginning."

I rubbed Lorraine's leg some more, but she was preoccupied with Keisha, my brother Lucas's girlfriend.

"Keish," Lorraine said, shaking her head, "you ruined Lucas!"

"Hell no!" Keisha shot back. "Lucas ruined *me*! Y'all don't even know the half."

The room exploded with laughter. Keisha, being the naturally funny firecracker that she was, had the room enthralled with her tales about the love of her life, Charlie.

"Yes, Charlie used to treat me so good. I used to love me some Charlie." A reminiscent glaze came over her eyes.

"Trent?" I called, "please keep the drinks flowing. We need to loosen this up some."

The drinks were poured and the stories continued with a bit more honesty and brevity.

"There are times when I look at my husband," Asha chimed in, enunciating every word clearly, "and I say to him, you're lucky I married you because you don't deserve me!"

After the third round of drinks the truth was revealed. The other ladies nodded in approval. Finally, she was dropping her facade. The veil in the room had been lifted. Thanks to a variety of truth serums on the menu, we were all free of supercilious pretense.

The night continued in this nature. We spoke of love and marriage with the seasoned ladies coaching the less so. We spoke about treating fibroids naturally and surgically, Tyler Perry's *Why Did I Get Married?* which was showing in theatres at that time, Erykah Badu's naked catwalk in the very public Dealey Plaza in Dallas Texas.

It was a steady flow of banter that was only interrupted by my abrupt need to vacuum the living room floor.

"This doesn't mean the party is over!" I yelled over the vacuum. "I just have to get the crumbs."

"Don't worry, y'all," Lorraine reassured them, "just let her do it. She can't help herself."

We all laughed because we all knew I had Obsessive Compulsive Disorder. By the time the night was over we had covered all bases. The ladies, now a circle of new friends, left looking forward to the next event. The *Sistah's Heartwarming Soiree* was a huge success. It was the beginning of a tradition that I'd host for years to come.

Time elapsed, and I still hadn't heard from Felise. It had been two months, and my phone was ringing off the hook with various girlfriends calling to tell me how much fun they had and how I should throw another soiree soon.

The truth of the matter was, I missed my friend. I called her. I visited her home. I sent her messages on the still budding Facebook, all to no avail. I decided to drive to her home again. Upon ringing her bell, her next door neighbor, the mother of her childhood friend, came out.

"Felise isn't there," she advised.

"Hi, Mom, do you know if she went away? I've been calling her, and she hasn't been answering," I replied.

"*She's fine.* She went out with Bunny." Bunny was her daughter. "They'll be home later."

There was a communication implied in her tone when she said "she's fine" that let me know Felise was avoiding me on purpose. It was an assertion blaring loudly in my face. She was good, without me!

Upon my drive back home, I recalled a quote by Tom Stoppard that I'd committed to memory: *All your life you live so close to truth it becomes a permanent blur in the corner of your eye. And when something nudges it into outline, it's like being ambushed by a grotesque.*

I had known all along Felise was avoiding me, but I didn't know why. Not knowing the *why* bothered me to no end. It gnawed at my brain and heartstrings because it was so unlike her to take the route of silence. A Capricorn, she was normally verbose and outspoken, even when you didn't want her to be. I had lost a friend with no explanation whatsoever.

A few days later at work, I went on to Facebook to discover that she'd unfriended me. I was in a state of paralytic shock. This was no simple falling out. This was real. Even in its nascent stages, the unwritten code of Facebook was *if you were unfriended from the social media circle, you were outlawed.* Almost telepathically, my cell phone rang with an unknown number. It was Asha.

"Did Felise unfriend you on Facebook?"

"Oh my God, girl, you're going to live long. I was just wondering the same about you. Yes, she did. Do you even know why she's doing this?" I asked.

"I don't know," Asha admitted. "I've been calling her, and she won't answer."

I told Asha about my visit to Felise's home and the conversation with Bunny's mother. It seemed Felise had unfriended us immediately after that chance meeting.

"Well," Asha started, "I did have a conversation with her when she was speaking to me and she mentioned that she was upset with you because you didn't attend her grandmother's funeral."

"Really? That's why she's mad at me? She couldn't just have a conversation about it? Everyone who knows me knows I hate funerals. I was there with her every night until the actual service. I helped decorate her living room for the repast. I just can't handle mourning. It's too much for me," I revealed.

"It really bothered her," Asha confirmed.

"Okay, but that doesn't explain why she stopped speaking to you," I said to Asha.

Though, I had an idea why. Asha was in the country illegally. Felise, being the friend she was, added Asha to her insurance coverage as her domestic life partner while she was working for Verizon. Felise was eventually let go because she was taking inordinate amounts of disability time off. To further aggravate the situation, her son's father, who also worked as a customer service representative for Verizon, snitched to management about the falsification of information on her insurance coverage.

None of these issues warranted discarding years of friendship. These were choices we all made and had to live with. We hung up, and later that evening I headed home on the train. Incensed, I had to get the fury out of my heart and onto the notes in my phone. I completed the draft and went over to my mother's house for consolation.

"Ma, you know Felise unfriended me on Facebook?" I yelled. The whole idea of a "Facebook" or "unfriending" was a foreign concept to my mother.

"Unfriend?" she asked, laughing. "Is that even a word?"

"Yes, Ma. It means that you're no longer friends."

"On the computer, though, not in real life?" she asked, still looking for clarification.

"It means you're not friends on the computer *or* in real life."

"Wow. That's strange. What did you do?"

I told my mother what Asha shared with me. She wasn't convinced that the infraction was grave enough for a severance. When I got home that night, I sent the final email, copying Asha on it since we were both being slighted, and blind copying Trent because we were both literary junkies addicted to eloquent wordplay.

Subject: Final Thoughts
From: Jacquii
To: Felise
Cc: Asha
Bcc: Trent
Date: June 22, 2010 at 7:18 p.m.

It was my original intent to drive to your home to have this conversation. However, I rationalized that wasted gas and mixed emotions could never convey my sentiments and hurt as clearly as could my thoughts on paper.

I'm in awe that my alleged wrongdoings have moved you to such unbreakable silence. One thing that you've never been during the time I've known you is at a loss for words.

You may accuse me of being an unworthy friend, but one thing I've always been is transparent. You can hold me up to the light in scrutiny and there I'd be naked, vulnerable, and open to your harsh criticisms and quick judgments, which oftentimes were deeply seated in your out-of-touch reality. That was okay with me because I trusted that you always had my best interest at heart.

If I responded in kind, funny, you'd complain of having a migraine, and although I'm using this example as an analogy, it fits you very well. You see, I've always taken that cause and effect relationship between bright light and your migraines literally. I now know that this is also who you are in character and personality. If I were to hold you up to the light, I'd see the same opaque mask that you've carried and hidden behind all these years. I'd see your energy repelling truth and acceptance. I'd see your defense hurled at me in denial and a distorted sense of *perfection*.

Real friendships are not rooted in facades. Real friendships are beautifully flawed, open for growth and improvement. With all of my faults, imperfections, and selfish tendencies, this is who I am, beautifully flawed.

I'm not writing you to keep score of your rights and my wrongs or vice versa. I'm writing because I sincerely believe that Asha and I (whom I've taken the liberty to speak on behalf of and cc on this correspondence) are at least owed an explanation as to why you've gone to such lengths to negate twenty and fifteen years of friendship respectively. While you ponder on whether we are worthy of an explanation or not, please know that we accept your decision to continue on without us and are at peace with it.

I thank you for the great moments filled with laughter, joy, and sometimes pain. I appreciate your open home, open heart, and warm plate. I'm grateful for your presence in my moments of weakness. And I'll always watch out for your children as they grow.

I sincerely hope that the friends with whom you wish to continue your life's journey have the love, wisdom, patience, and dedication to assist you in becoming a better woman, sister, and mother.

Goodbye!

I hit the Send button!

Subject: Re: Final Thoughts
From: Asha
To: Jacquii
Date: June 22, 2010 at 9:35 p.m.

Wow, Jacquii that's beautifully written, so eloquent. Says everything that needed to be said. Having read it, I'd love to continue our growing friendship. Like we've both admitted, we're beautifully flawed and are accepting of that. Feel free to call me your friend.

Subject: Re: Re: Final Thoughts
From: Jacquii
To: Asha
Date: June 23, 2010 at 10:21 a.m.

Thank you, Asha. I was so overwhelmed yesterday that I had to write her to express my feelings before I walked away. From our conversation, I sensed that you've really grappled with this emotionally as well and had to speak on your behalf. I'll be honored to continue our friendship. I've always related to you. Maybe this is what was supposed to be. Will be in touch soon.

* * *

Subject: Re: Final Thoughts
From: Trent
To: Jacquii
Date: June 23, 2010 at 4:24 p.m.

Damn J, you really need to get that book deal going as this is intriguing and very well written, a page turner, if you will. I too want to know what happens next.

Beyond your ability to wax poetic and provide a clear vision/version of the world as you see it, what is your objective? I'm on the train, and the Blackberry only loaded up until this section: "I'd see your defense hurled ..."

However, if you continued down the path of reading your former friend (with black woman neck-jerkin'), I'd question what you wish to come of this? Last word? Closure? An elegant fuck you? Clearly not wasting gas sets the tone of how important this is to you.

One would consider this note, while beautifully written, a dagger of sorts ... either in the back or straight through the heart, J style. Call me later if you wish to discuss, got to run.

That was the million-dollar query of the night. What did I want to come of all this?

At that juncture, I wanted her heart to break, as did mine.

3

To assuage the pain of yet another loss, I buried myself in the throes of work. Professionally, many changes were afoot. For starters, Trent was no longer my boss. Our little eLearning team of eight was being absorbed by what was now titled the iZone. The long and short of it was, Trent was a black man in charge with too much money and too much power at his disposal. He had to be dethroned, and we suffered as casualties.

The focus of the work shifted from online professional development to online learning. For me it didn't matter much as long as the focus was online. Our new boss, Ernest De Vries, was an English PH.D who had entered the department of education by way of the College Board. He had limited knowledge of the online world and what it required to be successful, but privilege quickly opens doors that wisdom and years of training sometimes can't. He took a liking to me.

We'd ride home on the R train where he'd pick my brain about the innerworkings of online platforms and the way in which teachers interact with them as both student and teacher. I shared many of the skills I'd learned from our meetings and work with the pioneers in the field. I also shared a lot of my project management expertise.

I thought I finally had a seat at the proverbial table. My role in all of this was to head the teacher certification piece of the work as the Director of Online Learning. I had to create a model that demonstrated how teachers were going to be equipped to teach within an online environment, produce a corresponding project plan, identify potential partners from whom we could get accredited teacher certification, and build out a cost model. I was elated. This work was right up my alley.

The work continued, and I'd received no word about the progress of my transition into the director's role. I busied myself with reading. I was reading the last book of the three-part series written by Blair Underwood, Tananarive Due, and Steven Barnes, *From Cape Town with Love*. The book was about Tennyson Hardwick, a gigolo turned sleuth who followed the love of his life to Cape Town, South Africa and happened upon a case concerning a missing child while there.

The series was phenomenal, but this particular installment moved me with its illustrious portrayal of the views from Table Mountain at twilight. I'd find myself resting the book down to visualize myself standing on the mountain with a handsome man in my pursuit. I was sold. I was determined to find my way there in the near future.

As fate would have it, I received a *Budget Travel* magazine subscription in the mail on a trial basis that advertised a special going to none other than Cape Town, South Africa. The trip would be ten days, five in Cape Town and the other five in Tulbagh on a wine vineyard. Hotel, airfare, and some meals were included for $1999. It was July in New York City. While it was scorching at home, it was winter in South Africa. I could care less. The next day at work, I received a call from Keisha.

"Hey, Jacquii, just calling to check up on you. Did you get a chance to speak with Happy Hero*Power?"

Keish was a forward-thinking financial professional who was always twenty steps ahead of the game. She had her immediate plan, interim plan, future plan, and contingency plan mapped out for every given situation at all times with the probable odds tested and mitigation strategies charted.

"Yep. Sure did." I stared out the window of my cubicle, brooding over our conversation. "His initial consultation was brief. He didn't go into too much depth about me, but he was thorough about what he did share. He explained the numerological significance of my name and apartment. He even told me which career paths I should pursue based on my birthdate. He's expensive, though. I don't know if I can afford him, girl."

I paused pensively, reflecting on my conversation with the life coach Happy Hero*Power. Dealing mainly with numerology, something he revealed about my chart lingered with me. He mentioned that I may have negatively altered the course of my life by legally changing my name from Jacqueline to Jacquii. His exact words, 'You made your life harder when you changed it to Jacquii. Jacqueline is the better name,' troubled me.

I was curious to find out how a decision I'd made as a headstrong twenty-two-year-old could adversely affect the rest of my life, but at the hefty price tag of five thousand dollars I was reluctant to make the investment. It wasn't a priority since the deed was already done.

"Jacquii, you still there?" Keisha brought me out of my thoughts.

"Yeah, girl, I'm here."

"Oh, okay. I thought the phone got disconnected for a second. He's very expensive. But Jacquii, he's worth every penny. I benefited a lot from his services while I was at Merrill Lynch. He has a payment plan, so you can pay in parts and space out the sessions."

"Yeah. I hear you. But right now I'm trying to hop on a plane and go somewhere to cool my head for two weeks. There's too much drama on this job. I need to think."

"Where'd you have in mind?"

"I'm looking at this special to Cape Town, South Africa," I answered, explaining the details of the special.

"Hmm. $1999?" Keish asked. "That's two thousand dollars plus any other fees. That's expensive. If you go someplace else like Barbados I'll come with you."

"But this is Africa, Keish. That's a steal for Africa. When will we ever get this opportunity again?"

"I know, but you know I'm not working and I'm dipping into my reserve. Look at the fares for Barbados and let's do a comparison."

Keisha had recently left her job at Merrill Lynch as a Senior Director of Surveillance and was living off her tax deferred annuity, a nice sum accumulated from years of hard work and headache.

"Keish, I'm looking at the all-inclusive prices now for Barbados and it's not that much cheaper."

I emailed her some price comparisons. She promised to call me the next day with an answer. Instead, she called me later that afternoon. "Girl, I thought about what you said. Fuck it, let's go to South Africa!"

I was overjoyed. I immediately contacted the travel agency and set the plans in motion.

While events at home were taking a turn for the adventurous, work was becoming bereft of opportunities. The proverbial table had been swept away. The director of online learning position was never mentioned again. It was August and I was preparing to leave to go to South Africa when I received a call from Martine, my co-worker and friend.

"Hey, girl." Her tone suggested oncoming bad news. "Did Ernest speak to you?"

"No," I answered truthfully.

"I just want to give you the heads up and I didn't want you to be caught off guard when you came back from your trip. He's not giving you the director of online learning position like he promised. He doesn't think you're ready for the role. Instead he's making you an implementation manager in the field."

The taste of rejection was pungently bitter after I'd savored the succulence of sweet success. It soured my palate and bruised my tongue. It was the ultimate betrayal.

"Ernest was going to wait," Martine continued, "but I told him that he couldn't because you were leaving for Africa in a few days. Expect to meet with him tomorrow. I know you're disappointed. I am as well. He didn't give me the executive director position either. I'm the senior director of implementation instead." Martine was my new boss.

"We'll be moving out of Tweed and going to Queens Plaza. I won't touch your stuff until you get back. I know how particular you are about your things."

It was official. I was no longer in the big house. Massa had relegated me to the field.

"Well," I resolved myself, "if we're moving to Queens, I'm not going to Queens Plaza. I'm going to Court Square instead. That space still belongs to us, and we manage the training center. I'll pack my things and have them delivered tomorrow."

I met Ernest the next day in the third-floor conference room. The exaggerated elegance of the Victorian windows, framing the Romanesque design of the room, appeared to dramatize his nervousness. Noticing his maladroit body movements, I immediately took an offensive position.

"Thank you for meeting with me on such short notice," he started with a nervous tick. "Martine tells me you're heading to Africa tomorrow. Which part?"

"Yes, I'm going to Cape Town. I'm looking forward to it," I responded.

"Have you been to Africa before, or is this your first time?"

"First time."

Sensing that I wasn't one for small talk, he quickly changed course to the business at hand.

"Well, I asked to meet with you because there's been a slight change in plans. I know you were originally slated for the director of online learning position; however, taking the delayed launch of the platform into consideration and the stalled negotiations with the union, I decided to make you an implementation manager instead. You have strong instructional expertise that's needed at the school level."

"Interesting," I remarked. "My skills span the classroom into the central office. I have policy and project management experience as well.

Wouldn't you need someone in the director's position to assist with planning in the interim?"

"Yes, we decided to make Wren the director of professional learning, and she'll head that work until the platform is completed."

The impact of the blow was dreadful. Not only was I being demoted in title and responsibility, but he'd promoted Wren. Wren, a meek, mild, and syrupy-sweet Jewish girl who'd moved from an external company as a training coordinator into a central position with no city-wide experience in professional learning programs. Wren, who would kowtow to his groundless demands without argument. Wren, who ofttimes played the helpless damsel in distress when she didn't get her own way. Wren, who was safe.

"You know ..." I said, leaning into him with blatant contempt. "I find it strange that in your organization, under your jurisdiction, you choose to put those who have no instructional experience in directorial positions and those of us who do in the field. It should be the reverse. Your directors have a lot to learn about the innerworkings of the department. How can they create policy for that which they know nothing about?"

Taken aback by my insolence, he squared his eyes in pure evil and said, "If I were you, I'd be more humble."

"Well Ernest," I said, getting up from the table. "You're not me." I left the room, visibly angry and frazzled.

I walked out the building and mentally readied myself for South Africa.

After a 16-hour flight from JFK to Johannesburg, we boarded another plane from Johannesburg to Cape Town for an additional three. Although it wasn't first class, we were traveling in style. We had a middle aisle all to ourselves. We ate endless cheese and drank lots of wine, causing us to be and look extremely bloated when we departed the plane. We felt like superstars who'd finally arrived when we saw our driver holding up the sign with our names on it, Grant and Leveine. We'd made it.

The swanky, five-star, 15 On Orange Hotel would be our living quarters for the first half of our stay. It was sexy! Everything from the plush chairs in the elevator, the corridors, to the floor-to-ceiling windows in our room was designed with sophistication and care.

Cape Town was a scene of ineffable beauty best beheld over a glass of lush, smoky Pinotage. From our room's horizon we soaked up the blood-orange sunset, surveying a string of rotating cable cars as they climbed Table Mountain. A towering bluff, it nestled sweeping views of the cityscape beneath; boats departed the hustling harbor, destined for Robben Island. Eight thousand miles from home, I found peace.

We spent our days eating lunch in cafés on a strip within walking distance of the hotel, reminiscent of Bourbon Street in New Orleans. We went on diamond mining tours. We drove around the city looking at national landmarks and shopped in the local markets for artifacts and trinkets to take home. We brought springbok skins to decorate our sofas. We went on tours of the parks and museums. We luxuriated in the hotel spa. We dined exclusively at the Victoria Wharf Shopping Mall overlooking the docked boats.

We took the sky tram to Table Mountain where we spoke with our tour guides about the living conditions. Many of the *coloreds*, as they were called, complained of the existing injustices still rampant in the country despite the abolition of apartheid. They spoke to us honestly about poor living wages and the capitalism of their land and properties by the Dutch. While there was calm existence among the many races, there was an undercurrent of inequity and malcontent.

At night, Keish, a notorious insomniac, would spend her time in the Business Center sending emails out for interviews or sipping wine and serenading the guests in the hotel lobby while the house pianist played tunes she'd requested. Her vibrant personality was an instant hit with the hotel staff, and soon she'd convince the male workers to bring us bottles of wine without putting them on our tab. I, on the other hand, stayed in our room, in bed, playing The Roots' *Dear God 2.0* on repeat.

In the dim of the room, under the warmth and comfort of a zebra-striped faux-fur duvet, The Roots and Monsters of Folks sang a suffrage to an elusive God as I ruminated over the Ernest ordeal, planning my next course of action. I was drowning my egocentric sorrows in the wafting ambient harmony.

I was brought back to reality when we ventured onto Tulbagh, the Winelands of the Western Cape, countryside. The perimeter of Rijk's Estate was framed by a path of white, brick bungalows with log wood terraces suspended by blanched pillars. The pillars, coiled in thick, dried vine, stood on a brick footpath, leading to an infertile vineyard--the stillness underscored a lifeless zephyr. Our water came from a well at the end of the trail, so slight traces of sulfur gave it a natural ochre tinge.

It was in extreme contrast to Cape Town. Where Cape was lively and exciting, Tulbagh was deathly quiet. Where Cape had fancy shopping malls and cafés, Tulbagh had banal cottage life. There was no television nor entertainment in our cottage besides an iPod player. When we weren't partaking in the vineyard tours included in our package, we'd be in our shared cottage listening to Kem.

It was here that our conversation with the locals would really shed light on the trivialities of our lives in relation to the South Africans. My issues on the job paled in comparison to their problems. The vineyard workers confided that they sometimes worked for weeks and on the fortnight, when they expected to be paid, they'd be given wine instead. Wine. As if wine was currency.

How insane were their employers to inebriate people who'd already been downtrodden for years? It infuriated us that alcohol was still being used by colonizers to keep the oppressed too dimwitted to fairly advocate for themselves. The young ladies who cleaned the hotel cottages told us they were paid so little, they often didn't have the fare to go home to their families in the next town.

One young man, who'd taken a romantic liking to me, worked as a bus boy in the hotel restaurant on some days and went to school on others but was so poor he had to sleep at the hotel. He was white. There was no separation between white and colored in this small town. There was the definitive, economical dichotomization of the haves versus the have nots.

We were sobered by those disclosures; our minds were blown. After five long days in Tulbagh, we returned to Cape Town in preparation for our flight back home. We'd have extended our stay, but Keish had a job interview to gear up for. Her documents were on her computer's hard drive. She wasn't yet privy to the advances of Google Docs. Reluctantly, we packed our bags for our departure.

On our flight from Cape Town to Johannesburg we sat next to a gentleman who worked as a financial analyst in Joburg. He and Keish immediately kicked up a healthy conversation in which she shared some of our findings from the laborers. An Indian woman sitting in the row directly in front overheard their conversation and mistakenly took it upon herself to interpose, "I really hate when people come to our country and criticize our way of life. If you don't like it, don't come here!"

I don't know who told her to tell Keisha this, but Keish saw red and read her for filth.

"What? First of all, bitch, I wasn't talking to you. I was talking to this gentleman. And from what I see, this isn't *your* country. You're *not* African. You need to go back to where *you* came from. I can speak to whomever I like about *whatever* I like. Mind your damn business!" Keish must have argued under her breath for the entire flight until we transferred to our connecting flight to JFK.

"And, Jacquii," she snapped, "don't think I didn't notice that you didn't stand up for me on the plane either. But it's cool. I see you're not the confrontational type."

She didn't realize I was gradually losing my volition to fight.

Life back in Brooklyn had returned to a state of normalcy. My mother, a senior citizen living on a fixed income, was unable to maintain her two-bedroom apartment at sixteen hundred dollars a month rent and was flirting with the idea of moving into a room to save money.

"I can't continue to pay rent for this apartment," she stated. "I don't want to get in your way. I might have to call Carine to see if I could rent a room."

It was the ultimate guilt trip. She knew there was no way I'd allow her to live in a room with a shared bathroom and kitchen when I lived in a three-bedroom, two-bathroom condo alone.

"You can move in with me, Ma. Why would you even think about getting a room when you know I have the space?"

"Well, I was in your space before and I don't want you to think I'm cramping your style." She was referring to my previous one-bedroom apartment in Ditmas Park.

"That was different. I have two extra bedrooms and an extra bathroom. We won't be in each other's way."

In September of 2010, my mother moved in. Dependable aromas of homecooked meals and an extra body flitting around my space made it feel more like a lived-in home. I was appreciative of the company and looked forward to coming home to share time with someone other than my subconscious.

We hung out a lot. We often went on shopping excursions at Woodbury Commons and would spend the day there. On one of those occasions, the building maintenance contacted me complaining of a leak in the room below me. I was on the second floor, and there weren't any apartments beneath me. There was either the children's room or an office space. The building policy required all tenants to leave an extra set of keys with the management office in case of emergencies. One to follow rules, I complied.

On this such day the super was calling to get permission to enter my home. I granted him pardon while I was away since he was exceptionally pleasant and forthcoming with help whenever requested. It would take about three visits to my apartment to identify the source of the leak. I was home for one of the three. It took them months to detect the leak coming from the plumbing of my washing machine in the linen closet.

It was during my habitual nightly call with Lorraine that I decided I needed another vacation.

"Girl, I'm thinking about going away for a few days in December. I've never been to Mexico, but I don't want to go to Cancun."

"Cancun is the happening spot, though. That's where all the clubs and the night life is," she insisted.

"I know, but I want something a little more upscale than that. I'm looking at Cabo San Lucas."

"Well, damn, I want to go on vacation too. I'm not sure that my boss will let me go around Christmas time since we'll be closing out the fiscal year."

Lorraine, whom I'd met fifteen years prior in Barnes and Noble when I was cashier and she my supervisor, now worked in accounting. She sat quietly on the phone for a while brainstorming to herself.

"You know what?" she said after some thought. "Let's just book the trip for five days. I'll wait until we get closer to the date to tell my boss I had a death in the family and have to fly out to Jamaica."

"Sounds like a plan!" I gathered all our information and booked the trip. With intentions of just lying out on the beach for five days, I packed one carry-on bag two months in advance and let it sit in my bedroom as both reminder and incentive.

In December of 2010, we were heading to Cabo on the redeye. I, so excited to be transcending another border, went on Facebook to bid my friends a farewell: *Bikini wax ... check, haircut ... check, pedicure ... check, suitcase packed ... since October. Looks like she's ready for Cabo, y'all. See ya when I get back.*

My phone rang; it was Lucas. "Yo, sis, I just saw your post on Facebook. You goin' out of the country again?"

"Yeah, I'm leaving at midnight," I confirmed.

"Oh, aight. Yo, don't be posting your whereabouts like that on Facebook. You're making international globe trotter moves. People are haters; they don't want to read that shit. People won't be happy for you."

"Okay," I said, perplexed by my naiveté. "I really didn't think anything of it. But I hear what you're saying. I'll keep my moves to myself in the future."

"Aight, be safe. I'll holla at you when you get back."

I left my mother at home sleeping when I called the cab and made off to LaGuardia Airport. I called my normal cab service and went outside to wait so I didn't wake her up. I jumped into the first cab that came, not realizing that this was someone else's cab and my car was still on its way.

The cab company called my house phone to complain when they did finally arrive and I wasn't there, waking her up anyway. She put the chain on the door behind me and went back to sleep. Assured that I was safely on my way to Mexico, she fell into an unusually subterranean slumber.

I arrived at LaGuardia all smiles, but Lorraine was in a bit of a funk. Lorraine was the kind of girlfriend who loved to despise you. You never really knew which Lorraine you'd get on any given day. One minute she'd be singing your praises and confessing her love for you, the other she'd be snapping with snarky, backstabbing remarks that felt calculated and contrived. That morning she was the latter. I didn't know the reason for it, since I just got out the cab and only said hello. I also said my routine prayer before I left my condo asking for a fun, quiet, and peaceful trip without disputes.

Yes, she was *that* kind of friend, one who required a prayer before every encounter. She was mentally and emotionally exhausting. Our relationship was tumultuous. We'd argue in public, she thinking she had the upper-hand because she was physically bigger and louder than I. We'd have silly arguments over the phone, and I'd often slam the receiver down in her ear.

I'd leave her in restaurants, stuck with the bill, and would drive back to Brooklyn when I didn't feel like dealing with her emotional tirades. She'd call crying, asking for absolution because she was a *work in progress*. I'd patiently grant it time after time, wondering when the work would cease and the progress begin. Fleeting instantaneously upon each reconciliation, her growth seemed inconclusive.

That was the nature of our emotional rollercoaster of a sisterhood. I accepted her for who she was and hoped that she did the same. This morning, I ignored her obvious need for attention and proceeded through the check-in process with feigned oblivion. My carry-on couldn't fit in the overhead compartment on the plane because Lorraine rushed to make sure hers did. She ran to get the window seat.

She was a woman of firsts. She'd do things like get visibly peeved if you so much as ordered a drink before she had a chance to look at the menu. On the way back from taking my bag to the stewardess for storage in the front cabin, D. L. Hugley, who was sitting in first class, gave me the once over wink like *How you doin' girl?* I smiled and kept moving on to economy. I cracked the secret code. Lorraine was tight because your girl was looking too damn good for an overnight flight.

The trip was just as I'd planned. On the Grecian-inspired beach of the RIU Palace, we lolled under a spicy sea breeze, laden with the saltiness of a turquoise ocean and coarse white sands; the crashing of 10-foot waves and pull of a fierce undertow lulled us to sleep.

We spent our time between the beach and buffet. We may have shopped once, if that much, but the main focus was rest and relaxation. I savored the turn-down. Lorraine was a bit beside herself because she was used to the turn-up, and the remnants of habanero on her tongue offered the only heat in her night.

It didn't help that the hotel and wait staff would fawn over me every day saying that I was beautiful. I'd sink into myself with every compliment asking for peace, hoping we wouldn't get into any quarrels. Ultimately, she just surrendered and replied, "Isn't she?" and we were fine.

While I laid on the beach or waded in the water, Lorraine would check-in with her boss intermittently with a calling card used on her cell phone. I was unplugged for all five days except for the last. There we sat at the breakfast table on our last and final day. I sipped a mimosa and Lorraine launched into a vehement, built-up rant.

"Nobody knows how much pain I go through--not you or Diana." Diana was her other closest friend. "I keep things to myself because I don't want to feel like a burden, but there's so much that I carry from my job and from my relationships. I don't have it easy. The world doesn't cater to *me*."

I smoothly replied while sipping on my drink, "Likewise."

My quick and trite response both shocked and shut her down. She had no comeback. I transitioned, turning my attention to my phone, listening to the messages that came in. I saw one from my mother that looked urgent. I had four missed calls from her that morning alone. Instead of checking the messages, I called.

"Hey, Ma, I saw you left me a message and called like four times. What's up?"

"Yes, I've been trying to reach you. I'm glad you called me back. Are you on your way back yet?" she asked, slightly concerned but remaining calm.

"No, we're still at the hotel. What's going on?"

"Nothing much. I was just calling to tell you that when you get in, come in from the back entrance. Don't use the front door. Okay? I'll tell you why when you get home."

"Okay." I didn't think much of it. "I'll see you in a few hours."

We arrived home without incident. Lorraine took a cab into New Rochelle and I took my cab back into Brooklyn. I came in through the back entrance as instructed. I came through the shared courtyard into the common lounge area, up the elevator to the second floor. When I got into my apartment, my mother was relieved to see me. She hugged me with tears in her eyes.

"I didn't want to tell you this while you were away because I didn't want to upset your trip, but we were burglarized the night you left."

Apparently, whoever entered the apartment did so about a half hour after I'd left. My mother was sound asleep. She thought she heard the door opening but figured I'd forgotten something and was heading back out. Normally, she'd have woken up to see what it was but on this particular night she was so sound, she didn't stir.

They knew the layout of my apartment. They went into every draw that contained my little bit of jewelry and took all. I had a habit of wearing only silver because Lucas would steal my gold when we were younger and pawn it for miscellaneous items.

They left my car keys but stole my monthly metro card. They took all of my electronics, which I had in excess from working my entire professional career in technology. They stole my Apple computer and hard drive, PlayStation, iPads, iPods--everything of value that would fit into my pillow cases and fitted bed sheet. The only technology I had was the iPhone, iPad, and iPod I took with me to Mexico.

They exited out of the balcony onto the floor of the shared courtyard and out the vacant lot next door, leaving a trail of mud on my beautiful Picasso rug. They never entered my mother's bedroom. She was left unharmed and untouched. I was grateful for that, but whomever the culprits were knew a lot more about me and my patterns to know what was interruptible and what wasn't.

My mother spent the remainder of my time away trying to clean my apartment and restore it to its original state. She spent days cleaning the rug, but there still remained a small stain in the white section that aggravated me for years to come every time I glanced its way.

My world was no longer safe. My haven was no longer a sanctuary. My soul, violated, sang a plangent, mournful dirge of recurrent sacrifice. I was livid. It wasn't about the tangible things. Everyone who knew me well knew I'd gladly give away those things without question or hesitation.

For me, it was about the sense of entitlement to my possessions and lack of regard for my mother's presence. Someone had to be blamed. The police at the precinct, while sympathetic, had little to go on since the cameras in the stairways, coincidentally, weren't working. They revised my police report, and the case was pretty much shut.

I spoke to my brother about his earlier premonition.

"Where were you on the night I left?" I asked.

"I was in Brooklyn. I know you don't think I had something to do with it?"

"Yo, as far as I'm concerned everyone is a suspect until proven innocent. You sure you had nothing to do with this? How did they know not to go into Mommy's room?"

"I don't know, J," Lucas said, trying to convince me. "You sure Mommy didn't have company over and is afraid to tell you?" Searching for answers in all possible places, he'd given me another angle to investigate.

"Mommy?" I asked one night during dinner, "have you ever had someone, maybe a male friend, come over to my apartment while I wasn't home?"

"Jacqueline, what shit you really asking me tonight?" she screamed. "You really think I'd disrespect your place and bring someone here without your knowledge? That really hurt my feelings."

"Ma, it's not about your feelings right now. It's about getting answers," I retorted. "If you're saying you didn't, then I believe you. But I had to ask. Lucas raised it and I said I'd ask."

"So you're listening to Lucas now!" We ended the conversation there.

The burglary bothered me for days. I found myself going into work earlier and staying later just to avoid being home. I felt safer at the office. I even traipsed into Long Island City during a two-foot snowstorm that shut all drivers and city buses down. The trains were running magnificently.

At the office, I'd restore my music library on iTunes by using a third-party application that allowed me to rip the songs off the iPod and into my library. I spent the entire day on the phone with Apple restoring purchases, ripping music, organizing titles, and restoring the album artwork for seven thousand songs and one hundred movies. A connoisseur of music with a highly eclectic taste, I had classics that I'd never be able to find again.

The building management did little to allay my fears or concerns. They just advised me to log my claim with the insurance company under my renter's insurance policy, a mandate for moving in. When I was able to recover most of the stolen items through the insurance settlement, I secured my new belongings in a 200-lb heavy-duty safe I purchased online from Home Depot. It was so heavy my mother had to pay the delivery man forty dollars to get him to take it out the box and put it in my bedroom closet where it fit exactly and unobtrusively, hidden by my clothing.

Convinced it was the buildings' super and his henchmen, I drafted a letter detailing the incident and warned the other renters against the custodial staff as a safety precaution. I put a letter under every single door in both buildings. Though I was a victim, the rest of the tenants didn't have to be. Management was exasperated. They wanted me out of the building and refused to renew my lease. I could care less. There was no way I was staying past my lease anyway. I had six months to find a new place.

On the friendship front, Lorraine was going through her own version of the blues. She was fired from her job upon return from Mexico. Evidently, during her cell phone calls to her boss while away, her boss deciphered that the incoming area code belonged to a region in Mexico and not Jamaica. Angered by the blatant lie, the careless coverup, and inexplicable deceit, Lorraine was terminated, effective immediately.

In true universal fashion, we both were withstanding some hefty lessons in humility.

2011 – SECOND PINNACLE

$$4 + (2+0) + (2+0+1+1)$$
$$4 + 2 + 4 = 10/1$$

One Personal Year

Wheel of fortune, independence, new opportunities, planting seeds, leap of faith. This is the cycle for all things new. It's best for you to strike out on your own in some way, to take the lead wherever required. Under this influence, you may be headstrong, direct, and straightforward in dealing with others, probably because you respond more to will and logic than feelings and emotions.[2] If not tempered, this can lead to your own demise.

---

[2] (Strayhorn, 1997)

"Standing bare before you,
Unconcealed in your view.
Scared of rejection or deep connection,
With you, I'm whole and new.
You make my truths feel frail,
Beaten by storms of hail.
But in due time my words gave you life,
And my heart is free to set sail."

4

LOSS WAS RAPIDLY BECOMING MY FORMIDABLE COMPANION. IT insistently trailed me like a dark cloud. Despite my bleak circumstances, I brushed myself off and kept pushing forward. The world was still turning, and no one was interested in hearing about my grief.

It was April 2011, and I was on the ground fervently looking for a new place. I was strongly considering uprooting myself and relocating to Harlem USA. I, a woman of Caribbean descent who moved to the beat of a Caribbean pulse my entire life, found it hard to connect with the grit of the very American and hastily gentrified Harlem community.

My thirty-fifth birthday was coming, and I needed a new toy that would fill the gaping void in my heart. I received a flyer in the mail from my Infiniti dealer in Lynbrook Long Island and decided to look into the G37 hard-top convertible. I told my mother to get ready for an impromptu road trip. Prior to arriving, I called the dealership to get in contact with the young lady who sold me my G35. She was no longer on staff. I asked to speak with her sales manager Siete (pronounced See-et-ay), since he and I ended up finalizing the first deal. He was working with a client, so I left a message.

We arrived at the dealership. I waited to meet with a sales associate, perusing the cars on the floor with my mother. My sales associate came over hurriedly to assure me that he was finishing up and would take me soon. He was green, just the way I liked them. While on the floor, many of the sales managers congregated to whisper about me. I was looking through the crowd to see if I saw Siete. I saw a gentleman who resembled him slightly and mistakenly thought it was him.

"That's the one you were talking about?" asked my mother with disdain. "He isn't that nice looking," she declared.

"I think that's him, but I'm not sure. It's been three years since we've last seen each other," I responded.

Just as I finished my statement, the actual Siete came through the crowd with his wide salesman smile.

"I remember you. You're Jacquii," he exclaimed. "You called me yesterday and left a message.

"Yeah, how did you know that was me?" I asked, amazed by his perceptiveness.

"I remembered your voice. When I heard the message, I immediately knew it was you." Again, I was impressed. "What are you looking to do today?" he asked, getting right to the bottom line.

"Well, as you probably remember, you put me in a G35 three years ago. Even though I'm financing that car, I'd like to jump into the G37 convertible. My current monthly on the finance is three hundred dollars, I usually pay $350-$400 to accelerate the payments, and I don't want to pay too much more than that for this new car. Think you can do that for me? It's my birthday month," I said, wheeling, dealing, and flirting.

"Nice," he confirmed. "You're gonna love that car. Any idea of the color?"

"Yes, I was thinking about the gunmetal silver exterior, black leather interior."

"We have that one in stock. Who's your salesman? Nick?" He moved quickly. "Nick!" he called my green salesman over. "Run Jacquii's numbers for a trade-in and give her whatever she's asking for."

Nick looked at him, stunned for a minute, and took us into his cubicle to do as told.

"Jacqueline," my mother said in a cautionary tone as we walked over, "I thought you said we were just looking?"

"I did, but you know what I mean when I say I'm looking."

"Oh my goodness, you're so impulsive when you're ready. Fine, it's your money. As long as you can make all your bills."

"I've already budgeted it on an Excel spreadsheet. I checked the insurance premium quote online for the trade-in and I won't be paying much more. I'm good."

I gave Nick all of my paperwork. We waited for him to crunch numbers. I excused myself to the showroom floor again. Siete walked over.

"I like your hair," he said, admiring my tight Caesar with the swimming waves.

"Why, thank you," I said, blushing.

I had since found a new barber, Carlos, who was new as my barber but not as my friend. I knew him from a shop that Collin worked in years before.

"So which one of these cars do you drive?" I asked, making small talk.

"Well, since I'm a sales manager, I change cars often," he bragged, "but right now I'm driving a G37 sedan. It's just me, so I don't need the excess space of something larger."

There it was, the answer to the question I'd been wanting to ask all along.

"Really, it's just you? No wife, no children, no dog, no cat--just you?"

He smiled and said, "Yeah, just me."

"Wow, that's me too. I mean, it's just me." With that, we fell instantly in love.

This specifically was an interesting turn of events, because three years prior, our meeting went entirely different. I came into the shop in December of 2008 after totaling my car in a freak accident on the Belt Parkway. On the night of the accident I was going to a book club meeting in Long Island. I fell into a huge pothole on the Van Wyck Expressway but continued to drive.

During the ride back home, I got on the Belt safely around 10:00 p.m. Just then, something in the car started to rattle. On a busy Saturday night, on a highway known for speed racing, my car began shaking erratically. It spun out of control, hit the median, and threw me back into the right lane of the highway. There were no cars coming on either side of me, a miracle on the Belt. I sat patiently and alone waiting for the EMT truck to arrive, and when they did, I was so tranquil.

It was the calmest I ever remember being under the circumstances. The EMT technicians, two young women, couldn't believe how poised and together I was. They were more concerned with getting me out of my fur shearling and suede ankle boots than they were with taking my vitals. Geico settled the claim quickly and I received twelve thousand dollars from that accident, which landed me at the Infiniti dealership in Lynbrook with my girlfriend and then colleague, Halle.

Halle was the big sister I wish I had. We came together as assistant directors of technology for the Bronx districts under a spiteful, vindictive woman who was Halle's friend in the department many years before. They both left the department of education to pursue careers in the private educational technology sector and reunited under Trent's leadership. Trent rehired our boss, whose name, although fictitious, isn't worth mentioning, as the director of the Bronx. She in turn brought Halle on as one of her assistants. I was the other.

Halle and I immediately connected on a spiritual level, and we consoled each other through two torturous years in this post. It was a hard and trying time for us both. Halle, with the patience and reserve of a saint, would ofttimes tell me, "Be patient, little sis. Things won't be like this always."

She was my savior, and I hers. We'd begin to foster a relationship that would span many years to come. I was grateful for her entrance into my life at that precise time.

It was the Christmas season, and we were anxious to finish our work early, without error, so we could leave the Bronx and head into Long Island. Halle, who lived in Queens, drove into work daily. She'd go with me to all the dealerships and drive me back to the A train at Grant Street so I could head back into Brooklyn. We'd already visited two Infiniti dealerships until that point and we weren't impressed with either.

Halle, excited about my high credit score, used this opportunity to haggle the salesmen with her bad cop routine. I'd sit quietly reserved as the quasi-good cop. At the Lynbrook dealership, we were appointed to a young lady named Abena, who unexpectedly lived two blocks away from me in my then Ditmas Park apartment.

She was still learning the ropes but was personable and funny. She'd leave her cubicle every so often and return with new offers whenever Halle countered with her bad cop negotiation tactics. On her last trip away from her desk, she returned with her sales manager, Siete. He was handsome, slim in a lanky kind of way. His suit was a tad too big and his arm was in a sling.

He put his hand out to greet us and turned on the salesman charm. "Hello, I'm Siete."

We each shook his hand. "What happened to your arm?" Halle asked.

"I slipped in the snow in front of my home," he answered.

"Oh, sorry to hear that. Were you shoveling snow?" Halle continued to dig deeper.

"Shoveling snow?" I blurted, disrupting their exchange. "You didn't feel how soft his hand was? This man hasn't done a day of manual labor in his life. Please!" I was turning the arrogance up high, remembering my days in Verizon as a cable splicing technician.

He looked at me and smiled. Quickly switching back to closing the deal, Siete gave us his final offer.

"Look, we really want to get the car off the lot. I'm throwing in the navigation package, the black leather interior, the Bose speaker system, and the technology package for $34,500."

I was fine with the deal, but Halle, who was now on a negotiating trip, wasn't.

"$34,500?" she yelled. "Nah, that's not good enough. You can do better than that. We're giving you a twelve thousand dollar down-payment, and it's a 2008. It's not even the new 2009 G37."

"There's only so much discount I can give you before the sale starts cutting into my profit. I have to make money on this deal too. This offer is a win/win for both of us." He held fast to his position.

"So there's no way you can take off the five hundred dollars?" I asked, siding with Halle.

He leaned over the table with a straight face and said, "No!"

"Well, it seems like we've reached an impasse," I said, pushing my seat back to get up. He didn't stop us.

"Reached an impasse," he whispered, snickering quietly to himself. "I used that term with a client earlier today. But I'm not going to hold you ladies up. That's my offer. You have the dealership's number if you change your mind. All we'll need is five hundred dollars down to hold the car."

As we were leaving, Halle turned to me and said, "He's a cutie. You know he likes you, right?"

"I know," I said, "but did you notice how small his feet were?" We laughed and walked out the door.

We continued dealership hopping where we ended in New Jersey. The salesman was an older gentleman who didn't have the same hunger or level of interest that Abena and Siete did. Halle and I sat in his office completely disengaged and disinterested. When the salesman left his desk to get us a printout of the projected quote, a cost four thousand dollars higher than what we had on the table, we got up and left.

We drove back to Long Island, my cell phone ringing off the hook with a New Jersey exchange. I dialed the Lynbrook dealership. "Hello, Siete? Does that offer still stand? Good, we're on our way."

Three years later, we stood in the same salesroom floor sizing each other up with love in our eyes. He had since put on a lot of weight distributed in the right places as solid, sculpted muscle. I knew he was working out because he went to the same gym in Queens as Halle. She'd give me occasional updates. Three years of weightlifting had done his body a lot of good. He exuded well-groomed and purposeful virility. After a year and four months of celibacy, I was feeling quite frisky. I was no longer concerned with his shoe size.

Four long hours later, we were on the road in my new Infiniti convertible. The car was significantly lower to the ground than the sedan, but it hugged the curves of the highway like a new pair of spandex leggings hugging the curvatures of a woman's buttocks. It was a dynamo of a machine. To drive it was to indulge in the luxuriant grandeurs of open air and freedom.

It drew attention from everyone who gazed upon it because it was smartly designed, with Bose speakers built into the headrests of the front seats. In that instant, I felt unconquerable. I was basking in the afterglow of conquest. While we were on the highway, my phone rang through the Bluetooth speakers of the car. Familiar with the dashboard controls from the previous sedan, I answered.

"Hello, is this Jacquii?" It was Nick.

"Yes, this is she," I confirmed.

"Hi, Jacquii, this is Nick from the Infiniti dealership. I hope you're enjoying the new ride. I'm calling because Siete asked me to give you his number in case you need to contact him about the car."

"Okay, great. You can tell me the number over the phone. My mother will write it down," I said, nudging my mother to take out her notepad.

My mother hesitatingly wrote the number down, and I disconnected the call. "Are you really going to call him?" she asked.

"Yes, I think I just might."

"Okay," she said with incredulity. My mother knew it usually took a lot for me to show interest in a man. The immediate reception was different for us both.

I did call, the night after. He didn't answer immediately. I left a voice message, which wasn't customary for me. He called me back within the hour. "Good evening, this is Siete. I saw that I missed your call," he spoke with gentlemanly grace. "How are you?"

"Me?" I replied. "I'm handsome. Thanks for asking!" His laughter was uproarious, coming from the gut.

"I can't believe you Googled me. You saw my training video on YouTube?" he asked, stunned by my sleuthing.

"I sure did. I have to say you have quite the stage presence," I said, laughing as well. "You give off a news anchor vibe."

"Thank you. I used to take acting lessons. I was an extra on the *Dave Chapelle Show* before he left for Africa. You should check out the other videos I've done. Those are more down to earth. What else did you find out, Ms. Google?"

"That's it for now, Mr. Jackson. I was trying to find your age and birthdate but didn't have much time."

He told me his full name and birthdate. We were both in our prime at the age of thirty-five.

"Really? I thought you were at least forty. You look more mature than you are."

"You know what, that's it. I'm offended. I have to go."

"No, don't be. I wasn't being slick. I was just saying," I said, trying to soften the blow of my honesty.

"Okay, but I really do have to go. I have a meeting with my contracted writer. I'll explain later. But before I go, have you ever been to a basketball game?"

"No, I haven't. I'm not really a sports fan. I follow it when my mother watches it, but I'd love to go for the experience."

"Okay, great. I'll look into getting us Nets tickets." We hung up.

I called Lorraine. "Hey, girl, I called him," I said excitedly.

"Who's *him*?" Lorraine asked, completely absorbed in something on television.

"I called the guy from the dealership I told you about yesterday. He sounds so nice over the phone, Raine. He's very polite." I gave a full rundown of the conversation and sent Lorraine the link to his YouTube video.

"He looks much older than thirty-five. You sure he's not lying about his age?" she asked.

"I told him the same thing. He said he was thirty-five. I'm not sure why he'd lie."

"Jacq, I have to ask you this. Don't get offended. You sure this guy isn't trying to get at you because of your credit score and income or what he thinks you have?" Lorraine was up to her nay-saying antics as usual.

"No, I don't," I shot back defensively. "We met three years ago. He knew how much I was making and what my credit score was then. If he was interested in the money, he'd have approached me then."

"Okay," she said, unconvinced. "As your girl, I have to look out. Just keep your eyes open."

I changed topics, wanting to avoid the oncoming argument. "It would be good to get some finally. I haven't had sex since the pregnancy girl. That was a whole year and four months ago."

"Yeah, just make sure that you use condoms that won't break with this one. You don't want to have another abortion," she quipped, still upset by my giving the baby up. It seemed every one of my girlfriends wanted the child more than I did.

"Well, I won't have to worry about that because we won't be planning to have a child anytime soon, and I'm on birth control," I answered snarkily.

"Planning to have a child? You told me the condom broke. So you and Collin planned to have that baby and you still aborted it?" My secret was revealed.

"I told you the condom broke because that's what I told my mother. I didn't want to mix the story up so I kept it consistent. I thought I told you this already."

"No, bitch, you didn't tell me anything like that. This is the first I'm hearing. I can't believe you didn't tell me." She was clearly bothered by my mistruth.

"I don't see what the big deal is. It's my business to tell in the first place. The only person it's affecting is me."

"Hmm, I don't appreciate that at all. You hurt my feelings," she said defeatedly.

We continued the conversation, but she, unbeknownst to me, was seething.

My romance with Siete started with a two-week courtship that consisted of many late-night phone calls after he'd get home from work. He worked long days at the dealership, getting in by ten on most nights. He confided that he'd negotiated a low car note on the convertible because if he ended up being my man, as he hoped he would, he didn't want to be stuck with a monthly payment that was too high to afford. I couldn't stop laughing at the practicality of his street smarts.

"I knew you liked me from the first car deal in 2008," I offered, "but I looked at your feet and saw how small they were." It was his time to laugh at my smart mouth.

"Oh, don't you worry about that," he retorted with laughter. "Don't worry about that at all. My shit is good money. It's certified black-on-black crime!" He had a sharp sense of humor. I loved a man who could make me laugh. We related over beats, rhymes and life. He represented Queens and I was raised in Brooklyn.

We discovered that Nas and A Tribe Called Quest were our favorite rappers. We traded verses of obscure Nas songs like *Last Real Nigga Alive* off the *God's Son* album. He was awe-struck and visibly moved that I not only knew the song but memorized the lyrics. He told me about the second part to the song that was laid over a Chuck Mangione sample. I was amazed that he even knew who Chuck Mangione was. I'd listen to his music as a child, raiding my father's record collection on a Sunday afternoon after he'd leave the house.

"Where have you been all my life?" he asked me during one of our nocturnal dialogues.

"I guess I've been here preparing myself for you," I answered sweetly.

"You're my queen, Jacquii, and I put you on a pedestal."

He'd echoed the words my mother would frequently repeat to me as a young girl. She'd affirm my royal standing in the world with that exact phrase, except she was queen and I was her princess. I wondered how he knew that, if he knew it at all. The feeling of a deep familiarity rushed over us. He was the doorway to me, and I to him. We were reflections of each other, mirroring intrinsic nuances that others tried but couldn't. It was official. We were all in.

He explained his meeting with the writer he mentioned during our very first conversation.

"I'm writing a book about my life. In it, I talk about my upbringing, my bout with crime and the drug game, the time I spent doing a bid on Rikers Island, and how I managed to turn my life around."

It was the quintessential urban legend of which many young African-American males were made. "We're only at the second chapter, but the woman who's writing it for me is acting up and becoming inconsistent with our meetings," he continued. "I know you're talented--very talented and creative. Hopefully, as the story progresses, you can help me take the project over and continue writing."

My senses were on high alert. "How did you know that?" I asked, feeling a wave of suspicion. "I never told you I was creative or that I was a writer. How did *you* ... know ... *that*?"

"I just know," he brushed it off quickly, "but what I was saying is that I'm sure, being how intelligent and bright you are, you'll be able to help me--if you're interested."

"Yeah, let me know how it goes," I said, still meditating on his seemingly psychic abilities. "I'll help in any way I can."

We switched the discussion to his crime boss antics. He told me of street fights and drug-related shoot-outs. He was an animated storyteller who enjoyed hearing his own stories. Completely enthralled in the sequence of events, I asked, "Have you ever killed someone?"

The energy over the phone quickly shifted. I touched a nerve. "It's getting late," he said, observing the time. "Damn it's 3:00 a.m. I have to go to work in a few hours. Get some rest, honey. I'll call you later."

He hung up, leaving me in a wave of confusion. I had no idea what happened or why that question would cause him to shut down so quickly. Maybe he thought I was 5-0. He knew I worked for the department of education and wasn't connected to the police. Perplexed, I consumed the next three days in veiled mystery. He hadn't called like he said he would.

"Rosaline, I have no idea what I said."

I was meeting my girlfriend from grad school for our habitual monthly dinner. Rosaline and I met at Teacher's College, Columbia University as graduate students juggling the demands of school and life. She'd just left her job at Price Cooper Waterhouse in search of a new direction, and I was still working full-time at Verizon.

Rosaline was the girlfriend who exuded calm-centeredness. She was heavily involved in the church and was cloaked with genuine light and spiritual sanctity. Though she was saved, she wasn't uninformed about the realities of the secular world. She'd experienced her share of life's unexpected turns as a twice-married woman with a son from her first marriage and a daughter from her current. She couldn't always relate to the wild adventures my life delimited, but as my friend and sister, she tried her best not to judge.

"All I asked him was if he killed someone," I said.

Laughing, she replied, "All you asked? You do realize that's a heavy question to ask within a week of knowing someone, especially a man?" I thought about what she said. "And what will you do if you find out that he has indeed killed someone?"

"I don't think I'll leave. That was his past. He's a different person now. I've grown up with many men who grew up in the streets. For me to judge him would mean I'd be judging my brother," I defended my stance, "and he's writing a book to inspire other young men in similar conditions."

"Wow," she said, processing it all. "That's deep. Well, give him some time to come around. He will. It's still early. What's his book about?" I gave her the synopsis he had given me.

"I'm not impressed," she said. "That story has already been told countless times. What's going to make his different?" That I couldn't answer.

Come around he did. The next day, a full five days later, he called.

"Hey," he said quietly.

"Hey," I answered, overjoyed to hear the sound of his voice. "Are you okay?"

"I am now," he said. "Yeah, I'm fine now." I didn't pry and he didn't offer more. We continued the conversation as normal. All was right with world again.

A week later we were going out on our first date. After two weeks of phone conversations, he'd finally taken a Sunday off for us to be together. He wanted me to drive since he was always driving to and from work. He drove to my condo, where I met him out front.

He was dressed totally different than he did at work. There was no tailored suit or Ferragamo loafers. On this day, he adorned a black Champion hoodie, blue Levi jeans, and classic Timbs. I was a bit put off by the look considering how dapper he dressed at the dealership but was too distracted to pay it much mind. I greeted him in a panic.

"Babe, I can't get the car to start. I'm trying to move it, but the gears won't shift."

"Okay, where do you have it parked? I'll look at it."

"It's in the garage," I said, leading him to the underground parking garage in the building.

"Okay, press the ignition button, press the brakes, and pull the gear back gently." He led me through starting a car, something I'd done for several years with four cars of my own to date. The car started, but the seatbelt wouldn't budge.

"Now I can't pull the seatbelt." I was visibly frazzled again.

"Yo, calm the fuck down!" he yelled. "You need to relax. Now pull it gently." It protracted with ease, but I looked at him, squinting my eyes, slightly aghast. I wasn't one for the verbal disrespect. Sensing my condemnatory look, he continued with levity, "Don't look at me like I'm sunny! You're bugging, honey. You need to calm down."

I did manage to calm down in time. We dropped the top and I drove to the city, Negril Village, the brunch destination. I played him Frank Ocean's *Songs for Women* and he, in turn, played me Dwele's *I Think I Love You*. We arrived without incident except for my almost wrong turn down a one-way street into oncoming traffic.

"Babe, watch out! You can't go down that street." He was a good co-pilot. I was making mistakes I never made before. For some reason, he made me extremely nervous. I was usually in control on dates. With him, I lost my sense of cool.

Brunch was mediocre. I made up for the choice of restaurants by walking through the Village, where we stopped to watch the basketball game at West 4th Street Courts. He'd never witnessed the rowdy cheering of spectators who clasped the cage's fence, watching the most aggressive *streetball* the city had known. It was like a new world had opened up for him.

"You don't get into the city much, do you?" I asked.

"Nah, I stay locally in Queens or in Long Island at the dealership. I don't have a reason to be out in the city like that."

How could he not have a reason to be in the city? I loved the very heartbeat of New York City, it was the mecca of the world. We continued to walk, but I, trying to be extra cute, wore 6-inch platform pumps and my ankle kept bending inwards with every other step. When we got to the corner I stumbled a little onto oncoming traffic. He pulled me back before I fell. Startled by his aggression, I pulled my arm away.

"I'm fine. I got it. I cross the street every day without you," I said, asserting myself as an independent woman.

"I know you do," he said calmly, "but I've been waiting my whole life to find someone I can provide for and protect. Now that I found you, just let me do it." He was smooth. I softened my stance and started to let my guard down a little.

We marveled at the sex and smoke shops--really, he did. I was familiar with both. We stopped to buy sneakers so I could walk around comfortably. I ended up with eighty-dollar ballet flats. He couldn't fathom paying so much for flats. As long as it was my money, I'd pay the price for whatever brought me the most comfort.

We ended our excursion in the Village at Barnes and Noble browsing the books. I told him of my tales working as a cashier. He was surprised I ever worked in retail. I told him it was some time ago, which it was. I had come a long way from there.

I explained that I loved to read and chose that particular franchise on purpose to be closer to words. He admitted that he loved to read as well. We bonded over books. I spotted my old supervisor in the aisles. She moved from the Lincoln Center branch, where we worked together, to the West 8th Street branch. I had to speak to her.

"Hi, is your name Melanie?" I asked.

"Yes, it is. Do I know you?" She looked at me with faint recognition.

"Yes, I'm Jacquii. We used to work at Lincoln Center together when it first opened. You were my supervisor."

"Good to see you again, Jacquii," she said. "You've grown into a stunningly beautiful woman."

"Thank you," I answered, and we parted ways.

Siete, overhearing our conversation, turned to me and said, "You know you really are."

"Really are what?" I asked

"Stunningly beautiful!" He was winning me over with every word.

Still dissatisfied with my choice of restaurants, I drove back into Fort Greene, Brooklyn where we got a drink at Night of the Cookers. He was in bliss. I'd found his ideal spot.

"We should've come here from the beginning," he said, loudly sitting at the bar. "We got good soul food, drinks, and the basketball game is on."

He watched the game screaming at the screen boisterously, obliviously drawing attention to us. I used the Shazam app on my phone to get the names of the bar songs that were playing. Overwhelmed by the rightness of the day, he turned to look at me in silence.

I took his hand. "Your eyes are so sad. I want to be the one who takes that sadness away." It was the sweetest, quirkiest first date I'd ever had.

I drove him to his car. He looked at me. "I enjoyed myself. I want to kiss you goodbye, but you're still a bit uptight." He caught me off-guard with his candor.

"I'm uptight, aren't I?" I confessed. "I know. Something about you makes me nervous. I've never felt like this before."

"I won't hurt you." He pulled me in for a simple kiss--no tongue, just simple and sweet.

When I got inside, I called Lorraine with the update. "Raine, I just got back from my date with Siete, girl."

"How was it?"

"It was good. He came here in a hoodie, jeans, and Timberlands. And he's loud. Girl, is he loud. I was right. He's had a hard life. He's a hustler. He straddles both worlds, street dude in Timbs at home and a savvy businessman in Ferragamo by day.

"Damn, that's the man I've always dreamed of. How'd you end up with that guy? You normally like the white-collar ones."

"I thought he was white-collar when I met him. Trust me, I wasn't looking for the thugs."

"Well, one thing you need to know is thugs are sensitive. You can't be mouthing off telling them everything that comes to your mind. They can't handle it. You know your mouth is reckless."

I laughed. She was right. "I'll keep that in mind."

It was Monday, a few days before my actual thirty-fifth birthday. Siete and I were in great standing. Things were moving at a steady pace. I was at work in Long Island City when I received a text message from Lorraine:

Suzie, can you believe that bitch had the nerve to lie about the condom breaking? Why is she always lying on the dick, though? She accidentally sent me a text that was meant for her sister.

I sat for a while. I could feel blood rushing to my face. I was enraged, but I maintained my composure and simply wrote back, *I believe you sent this text to me in error.*

The realization of her gaffe caused her to freeze. It took her about an hour to write back.

No, Jacq, that message was for you. I was writing to tell you about Suzette. I got the names mixed up.

Now she was lying. I reached my wit's end. To know that I confided my private information only to have it vilified in a public forum was the straw that broke the camel's back. I refused to be scandalized by my own truth. I didn't respond to that text, nor the forthcoming one, nor the one after that.

On my birthday, Lorraine sent me a bouquet of red roses. I asked my mother to make sure they were from her, and when she confirmed, I told her to discard them in the hallway's incinerator. Unsure of the energy associated with them, I didn't want the flowers anywhere in my home out of fear they'd upset its spiritual balance.

Now, two friends down, I found myself confiding in Siete. I told him the full story from beginning to end and asked that he not pass judgment on my past indiscretions. If we were to be together, he should know what he was getting into and be okay with it. He was quick on the comebacks and ready to pick up my fire rage.

"Give me her number. I'm good at pulling pranks," he said, trying to inveigle me in his mischief.

"No!" I barked. "Pranks? What is this? High school? We're grown-ass women. I don't need you to pull any pranks on my behalf. I just need someone to vent to. This isn't about revenge."

"Well, damn. I was just trying to help you get her back," he said, defeated by my hostility.

"My ending the friendship is get-back enough. She'll regret it when I'm gone." That response silenced him.

A few days after, I received one last text from Lorraine.

I see that you're not going to respond to my phone calls or texts. Like the saying goes, people come into your life for a reason, a season, or a lifetime. I guess our season is over.

She was trying to move me to tears. I was beyond tears. I was tired, weary, and in some ways relieved--that was the real truth. She wasn't going to get a heartfelt email or text from me. There would be no outpouring of emotions over this split. I was done.

I'd never get a chance to tell her that her earlier warnings were correct.

5

IT WAS MAYTIME IN THE CITY. WITH THE COUNTDOWN ON THE LEASE, I'D been hitting the pavement heavy in Harlem looking for the best place. I was closing on a two-year lease for a two-bedroom apartment on 118th Street and Fredrick Douglass Boulevard when I decided to pull out of the apartment, and Harlem, altogether. It was simply too far from my mother and too hard for Siete to get to on a regular basis.

The realtor, who spent many months going from place to place with me at all times in the evening, was pissed. When I sent her the message to tell her I was no longer interested in the apartment, she contemptuously refused to acknowledge me in the same manner I'd repudiated Lorraine. Siete, utterly smitten with my apartment, wanted to know why I was even moving at all. I told him of the home invasion.

"Don't worry, honey," he reassured me. "I'll never let anybody hurt you ever again."

We were a month into our relationship, and Siete was planning his version of an upscale romantic outing for us to consummate our union. He reserved a room in the LaGuardia Marriott. It was a nice gesture, but I would've preferred the lived-in atmosphere of his apartment. He chose the hotel instead because his place, although inhabited for several years, was barely furnished and didn't have the same look or feel as my own. He didn't want me to lie on his bare box spring and mattress that sat on his floor without a frame.

I arrived at the hotel before he did. An avid sports fan, he'd meet me after the big Pacquiao and Mosley fight. I had dinner on his tab and retreated to the room to lie in wait. He arrived closer to midnight, and as promised, there was a crime scene. His sexual prowess was as advertised, his feet trickily deceptive. We spent the entire morning in the heat of passion. When we finally did pause to bask in the afterglow, we surrendered in sweet prostration.

We saw each other regularly during the month of May. Excited to have him in Brooklyn with me on a Sunday, I took him to my old neighborhood. We visited my friend Karen's *Sacred Vibes Apothecary* on the corner of my old block.

I cherished Karen's charming shop because it had magical herbs that could cure every ailment. She sold incense, healing stones, tinctures, teas, salves--everything natural to treat the body, mind and spirit. Siete read the jars of herbal concoctions adorning the shelved walls. I introduced him to Karen. Reading intensely, he ignored the introduction. Karen was offended.

I was embarrassed, "Don't worry, girl, he heard me. He's just being rude right now."

"No, I was just reading about the herbs," he said, still not acknowledging Karen in his normal way.

I ushered him out the store before he did anything else offensive. When we got out, he turned to me. "Stop going into those natural stores, honey. You're always into some weird herbal stuff." I brushed him off as we got into the car toward our usual Night of the Cookers.

While at brunch, Lucas called to borrow money. "Yo, sis, I'm kinda down right now. You have eighty dollars you can lend me?"

I was annoyed, but he was my brother. I excused myself to the ATM across the street. Siete, discontent with my enabling, took a formal stance against it.

"Isn't your brother older than you? Why do you have to give him money?"

"Yes, babe, he is. I know what you're saying is right, but he's my brother. It'll be the last time."

I knew it wouldn't be. Siete abdicated to my pleading, and we drove back into Flatbush to meet up with my brother. When I pulled up, Siete gave Lucas the once over. I don't know who he was expecting to see, but he was clearly surprised by how neatly groomed and handsome my brother was. My brother was one who took care of himself and his possessions no matter how much or how little he had.

He was a street sniper who hankered for the danger and rush of the life. He was always on alert and always saw you coming before you would ever see him. He was smart but chose to employ his intelligence in the criminal world. He jumped from place to place on a regular basis, and it would be difficult for anyone to keep up with his whereabouts. He and Keisha had broken up. He was living in a room in the heart of Flatbush.

My brother came to the car to greet me and get the money. With a fresh haircut and waves spinning, he was wearing a Polo shirt, True Religion jeans, and Gucci sneakers. He needed eighty dollars, but he didn't look like he did.

"Thanks, sis. Yo, what up, my man?" he said, acknowledging Siete. Once again, Siete fidgeted with the knob to the radio and didn't look up to say hello. He nodded briefly. Lucas and I spoke for a bit, he kissed me on my cheek, and I drove off.

"He looks just like you. You guys can be twins," he said, finally acknowledging him.

"What part of *he's my brother* didn't you understand?" I said jokingly. My brother and I always received that reaction when people saw us together. That was our clichéd response.

"What does your brother do?" he asked.

"He chills," I said matter-of-factly. "He doesn't have a job right now. He was working in silk screen printing for a while, but they laid him off."

"That's his Sunday afternoon get up? My man was sitting on the step all handsome, looking dapper in a Polo button-down shirt, and Gucci sneakers!" he said, laughing.

"He's always crisp. It doesn't matter where he's going or what he's doing," I answered. He sat in the passenger's seat quietly, thinking. To alter his sudden pensive mood, I put on Anthony David's *4Evermore*.

"I'm dedicating this song to you," I said. Anthony David and Algebra crooned in the background over a hard hip-hop backbeat. He nodded to the syncopated rhythm. I found a winner.

"This is dope," he confirmed. "You really dedicating this to me?"

"Forevermore!" I said. He took those words to heart.

Visits from Siete would cease for a month afterwards. I was becoming irritated with his schedule. One night, on our typical phone call, he offered to buy me a dog.

"Honey, do you like dogs? I saw one today that would be perfect for you."

"A dog?" I answered, looking at the phone suspiciously. "Don't get me any goddamn dog. That's shots, veterinarian appointments, clothes, food, etiquette classes. I don't have time for that."

"Damn, I was just asking. I thought you'd like it."

I was privy to his reasoning and three steps ahead of him. "No, you said to yourself, *let me get this bitch a dog so she can stop sending me these irate text messages every Friday night when I'm not there.*"

He busted out laughing. His plan was thwarted. "Don't try to get into my head, buddy."

"I'm already in your cerebellum, partna [sic]. It's too late."

Every single night after that conversation he'd text me a riddle of some sort to crack.

There's one in every corner and two in every room, what am I?

After a half hour, I wrote back: *An O.*

Each forthcoming riddle would be along these lines, and I'd solve every single one. He claimed his mother sent them to him and he, in turn, would send them to me.

Finally, I got aggravated with him and his riddles. I understood what he was trying to do. He was sizing my intelligence up. He wanted to see how smart I was. It struck a chord with me because I had friends who, intimidated by my intelligence, would throw random crossword puzzle clues or questions to miscellaneous factoids at me to see if I knew the answer. I had a logical mind. Anything pertaining to sequencing and order of events was a cakewalk. I began to shut down. I started Googling the answers and telling him I did so he'd get mad at my cheating and stop. It worked.

My mother moved out shortly thereafter. Realizing that Siete would be a fixture in my life for an unknown period of time, she wanted to give us space. His visits were infrequent, as he was always in the dealership. He never invited me over to his home because he was *hardly ever there*. Bored, and often left alone with my idle thoughts, I called the California Psychic network and told my complimentary psychic his name.

She paused for a minute over the phone. "Hmm, he's a strange one. He's not a womanizer. He has a strange personality. I don't know that you'll be able to deal with his personality. Ugh!" she said as if she was shaking his personality off like a cockroach.

There wasn't much detail. The reading was subpar by normal reading standards. She was nothing like my Haitian spiritual advisor whom I'd seen for years. The problem was my regular was in Haiti for an extended amount of time. Afraid of what I'd hear, I never followed up again in the years to come. I guess knowing wasn't worth the risk of destroying the fortress of illusions we'd both built.

I began to suspect the presence of another woman and asked that he give me a FaceTime tour of his home. He submitted, taking me through every barren room, corridor, and closet. He lived in a near state of destitute minimalism. There was no sign of a woman's touch. His plan was to move into the bigger, nicer Opal Luxury Apartment complex, for which he was on the waiting list.

I, on the other hand, found a one-bedroom apartment directly across the street from my previous Ditmas Park residence. It was a subleased coop owned by a Bollywood DJ. She wanted to relocate to Jackson Heights, Queens with her wife and needed someone reliable to take care of her first owned property. I inspected the place with my mother. We found it to be simple enough for one.

No longer wanting to draw any extra attention to myself or possessions, I downscaled a lot. My cost of living had become quite comfortable with a seven hundred dollar decrease. Siete offered to assist with the moving fees. As we got closer to the move-in date in July, he was nowhere in sight and hardly answered texts. I, willing to engage him in our first tête-à-tête, wrote a lengthy soliloquy of a text message disparaging his character as a boyfriend and calling him out on his lack of involvement in my time of need.

So I just have to get this off my chest to avoid taking on additional stress right now. You really need to decide if you want to be here or by yourself. I'm too good of a woman to be put on the back burner continuously.

I struggle, find myself at cross roads, feel stagnated, neglect the ones I love just like you do. But you rarely ask how I'm managing or if I need consolation. I'm trying my best to be patient because we are both older, and finding someone you love is hard these days. But I want to be happy more than I want to learn patience.

I intend to be happy. I want you to decide if you plan to be happy with me. So while you're out doing much today, I want you to reflect on that. I don't want to hear any more of your words, Siete. You have too many of those, and your actions are few when it comes to us. It's all on you now.

He wrote back. *That was an eyeful. I am empathetic.*

Still simmering over the text, he wrote again.

Greetings, Jacquii. It's clear that you don't believe I'm ready to be in the relationship you deserve to be in at this stage in your life. So I will take some

*time to mature, build my career, and become the man you want. I will race the
process as best I can, and I pray you aren't taken when I become ready. Please
send me your bank info so I can be more than words. Sincerely yours, Siete.*

I was devastated. I pleaded, *Siete, I love you. You're the man I want. I
just want you here with me. I don't want to do this alone. Building your career
is important but doesn't determine our happiness. I think you're putting
pressure on yourself for things that you think will make me happy. I don't know
what else to say.*

Just like that. We were done.

I moved the next day with the same movers I used to move into the
condo. The company sent the same exact guys, two years later. They were
surprised to see me and even more surprised to see that I was moving back
to the same block they moved me from into a smaller, less sexy apartment. I
told them about the violation and they understood, once they had to move
the 200-lb safe. While they were loading the truck, I told my mother about
the breakup.

"Jacquii," she said, scolding me, "you don't give men ultimatums. They
don't respond well to that. It's only been three months. You can't pressure
a man into moving quickly. Sometimes you're just too hot-headed for your
own good."

I listened, too heartbroken to reply. I turned to Facebook for reprieve.
*I'm embarking on new beginnings on familiar ground. Today has already been
life-altering in six short hours. Sometimes we plan journeys with others in mind
when it was always meant for us to travel alone ... Happy Friday, FB fam.*

Throughout the move, I'd text Siete to give him the account
information. No reply and no money sent. I spent the next two days
unpacking and situating everything in its rightful place. I assembled my
book shelf and bar table; I hung up all the pictures; I assembled the TV stand
and sound system. I did everything I could physically do by myself. I just
needed Trent to assist me with putting the molding around the wires of my

sound system. I was officially occupying my new dwelling, another apartment 2E.

Feeling accomplished, I posted again on Facebook.

Finished packing, furniture set up, pictures are hung, floors are swept and mopped. Yesterday I was feeling sad about downgrading from a three-bedroom back to a one, but today I'm absolutely satisfied. Tomorrow I'll reward myself with a lazy day in bed and red velvet cake.

I sent Siete a text message.

I'm moved in. I spent the day getting everything in order. I finished unpacking and setting the place up. Everything is in its proper place now. The only thing that's missing in our home is you. He didn't respond.

The next day I stayed in bed, as I'd promised myself. The text tone on my iPhone sounded, "Hey, Beautiful! You've got a text message." Siete texted me back with the first half of the chorus to Anthony Hamilton's *Since I Seen't You.* I wrote him back with the second half. We sang a digitized duet. We spoke finally about our argument and smoothed things over. He came over to the new place a few days after. We were back on.

The relationship continued as it had in the past. I busied myself by hanging out with Trent, who was waiting to close on a beachfront two-family house in Averne, Far Rockaway. We'd often go shopping for light fixtures and amenities for his new home. Sometimes, Erica, his friend of many years, would come with us.

Trent, home-free, lived between places and stayed at various friends' homes for two-week stints. In exchange for his room and board, he'd make any home repairs or add extra MacGyver-like comforts. He was staying with Erica at the time. They came over to my place for my step ladder.

I just received a card in the mail from Siete telling me how much he loved me. It was a weak *just because* expression of his love, but he put his address on the envelope. I filed it in my phone for future use. He called to see if I received the card while Trent and Erica were there. When he realized I had company that included the male kind, he hung up on me indignantly. Trent and Erica were platonic friends, who, when told about the incident, asked why he didn't come over to hang. I couldn't answer that. He was clearly home.

It was a love affair shrouded in secrecy--not because I wasn't able to speak of it with others but because there was a limit to what he'd allow me to know about him. He loved me stealthily, claiming he never learned how.

The sad truth of the matter was, I loved every part of him, bone and fiber, down to the nerve endings in his toenails. He represented the potentiality of exclusivity, expertly tailored for me. He symbolized a false reality that he himself painted. I was all in, like a simple brushstroke swallowed up by his ostentatious machinations.

There were days that I'd be in cerebral and emotive anguish, haunted by his absenteeism. What was he doing? Was he really at work? Did he really live alone? Why can't I leave him? I envied the fortitude of the past women in his life who had entered, quickly discovered his scheme, and gone.

The only way I can make sense of what I was enduring to my rational mind is to liken it to a longing for my favorite food. It was as if I stumbled fortuitously upon the perfect shrimp roti after driving miles and miles of road. The dhalpourie was soft but sturdy enough to contain the peas. The balance between potato and chick peas was just right. The shrimp, cooked well but not rubbery, was curried and seasoned just the way I liked it, spicy and savory. The archetypal ensemble, finished with a twist of curry mango and tamarind sauce.

It titillated and confused the senses. Eyes tasted spices; ears heard textures; and the mouth perceived vivid hues. I was euphoric and alive in a way I'd never been. I needed this shrimp roti at my disposal evermore.

I'd continue to make the trip to and from only to find the roti shop closed on Mondays. I accepted that because it was standard to have a day off. Everything and everyone needs its space to be. Though, the shop would dole the roti out in parcels over days and hungers. I'd receive chick peas on one day, potato on the next, shrimp when they felt like cooking it--never a full composition like the first bite.

Ultimately, the shrimp roti would stop being served altogether! I was in an addictive and obsessive frenzy searching for the initial piquant sensation. My dopamine and serotonin levels were spiked. To adapt, I dulled my senses, convincing myself I could survive an insipid existence.

Needing to get away to clear my head, I decided to book a trip to St. Lucia. I asked Siete to come with me. He stalled for a month, finally admitting that he never put the vacation time in and had to work. I booked the trip anyway. I'd go it alone.

It was September and Trent was still home-free. I offered him my place and convertible for the two weeks I'd be away with an agreement that he wouldn't bring any of his sexual partners into my home. Knowing how clean and detailed my place was, he was elated. We had a deal. In return, he'd put up the wire molding and fulfill the list of honey-dos I'd left for him.

Siete wasn't amenable to Trent staying with me when I first passed the idea by him. He said, as a Leo, he'd be the only king to reign over my queendom. I respected his position, but this was my place and Trent was my true, tried and trusted friend for years. He was in my life before Siete and would be in it long after. I didn't tell Siete about my final decision to let Trent stay. I kept the classifieds to myself.

For two weeks I slept on the beach, ziplined, and parasailed. Trent blogged about his nomadic life and completed his home improvement projects. Siete, being uncharacteristically insubordinate, fell out with his boss and long-time mentor who released him from work, with pay, for a week. He ended up getting the time off after all.

I'd FaceTime him between excursions. He'd be lying in bed most times watching ESPN, his favorite channel. Upon my return, Siete picked me up from the airport and we drove to my home around midnight. I came in and was greeted by a beautiful bouquet of flowers on the bar table. Trent had outdone himself with the home makeover.

Noticing my surprise by the floral arrangement Siete asked, "You didn't know these were there? Who sent them to you?"

"My mother comes in and out of my place. She left these for me." I fibbed to avoid a disagreement.

"Hmm, your mother gave you those," he said more as a statement than a question. "I stopped by your apartment while I was home last week." My ears perked up. "I didn't believe Trent wasn't here, so I stopped by to see if he'd answer the door, but he didn't."

In my mind I said a thankful prayer for the ever-busy Trent who evaded a run-in with rage.

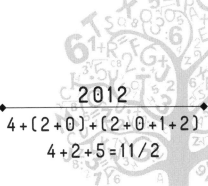

$$4 + (2 + 0) + (2 + 0 + 1 + 2)$$
$$4 + 2 + 5 = 11 / 2$$

Two Personal Year

Tests, patience, companionship, harmony, abstract impressions, revelations, spiritual awakening. Changes are likely to be slow rather than rapid, but ideas and hunches come with lightning speed. Your sense of idealism and human understanding will take on a deeper meaning. You'll be compassionate and forgiving about the flaws, faults, and frailties of others.[3]
This cycle also foreshadows a danger of hidden agendas and betrayal from others.

[3] (Strayhorn, 1997)

"I watch the mirror tell a story,
Of biceps and broad shoulders.
Like John Henry overthrowing boulders,
With his bare hands.
Mirror! Mirror! You misunderstand,
Can't you reflect the burden I wear under this dress,
Man?"

6

WE BROUGHT THE NEW YEAR IN TOGETHER, IN MY APARTMENT, WITH Chinese food and no preparation whatsoever.

I asked Siete earlier that day if he was coming over, and he initially told me no. When I threatened to start the new year without him, he quickly changed his tune, told me he'd call me back, and readjusted his preceding plans. I offered to cook the traditional collard greens with black-eyed peas and rice, but he told me he'd take care of the food. I was relieved.

He showed up to my place closer to 11:00 p.m. with Chinese food in hand because that was the only cuisine he could find open on Old Year's Night. He had a bizarre New Year's Eve ritual that involved him spending the countdown in the shower. I'd surmise he was cleansing himself of his yearly indiscretions, atoning for his sins. When he finished showering, we listened to Jay-Z and Kanye's *Watch the Throne* album, *New Day* specifically on repeat. It was a ghetto-sanctioned welcoming of a new day indeed.

I endeavored to bring some culture into our relationship by introducing Siete to Broadway. I gave him the option of going to see either Stick Fly with Mekhi Phifer and Alicia Keys or the Mountaintop with Angela Bassett and Samuel Jackson. He chose the Mountaintop. I was fine with the choice because I'd see both regardless.

A few days before we'd see the show, his phone lost his contacts during an Apple update. He sent me a text while I was at work.

Good morning, your number is in my phone but my contacts were erased. Can you please tell me who this is?

I was mortified. Earlier that morning, I sent him a text telling him I loved and missed him. For him not to know who sent the text meant he was receiving texts of a similar nature from other women.

Who would be sending you I love you *texts?* I wrote back.

Stop playing, he wrote. *Who's this?*

It's Jacquii, and we now have a problem. I answered and shut the phone off.

We didn't speak that night. I was beginning to think he wouldn't meet me for the show the next day, but two hours before, he showed up to my Long Island City office as planned, wearing jeans and Timbs, which we had *not* planned.

"I thought you were going to wear a suit?" I asked.

"I was, but I wanted to be comfortable on my day off," he said coyly.

"So, you want to tell me about the text message from yesterday?"

"There's nothing to tell. You were overreacting. There's no one else, no other woman. Nobody wants me but you."

There would be days when I wished I didn't want him either.

We went off to the Mountaintop. Thinking we were going to see a movie, he didn't understand why the theatre was so cold or why everyone was sitting so closely together. I had to explain that this was a Broadway show where the actors would be on stage performing, live. It was his first time experiencing anything like it. He marveled at Angela Basset's flawless monologue at the end. She held frontcourt with her delivery, and he, an aspiring motivational speaker, ate every minute of it up.

One evening after work, I met Trent at the wine bar around the corner from my apartment. He still wasn't in his home, but he met a love interest who worked as a mixologist at the Purple Yam during his stay at my place. We drank wine while he waited for her to finish her shift.

"J, I'm telling you. I've been saying this for years," he said after I cried to him about my current work and love situation, "you'll never find a job or romantic partner to fulfill your every need. You need to pursue your passion, something that you really love and is only for you and no one else. I promise you, when you find it, I'll be there to support you 100%."

The wine bar had a Jazz band playing in the background. The lead singer wasn't particularly great, but she wasn't bad. She made every song she sang sound the same, prettily forced with too much vibrato. I knew I could do better. Sitting there with an empty plate, an empty relationship, and no professional satisfaction, I knew what my next move was. I was going to find myself a professional vocal coach and put my Bachelor of Fine Arts in Music to good use.

I started out getting lessons with a Russian opera singer, Katya Kortny. Katya was a great spirit and teacher. She had a language barrier, so she couldn't always articulate her directions well. I knew the basics and I had a great voice, but there were a lot of technical things that needed tightening up, like my breath control and support of the notes.

I met with her privately each week and took weekly workshops as well. Needing an outlet, I threw myself into singing. I struggled a lot with songs in my lower range because I still didn't understand the support, but I loved it and was determined to get it by hook or crook.

During this time, I met a young man named Lucius. Lucius was from Alabama and on his path to stardom. He was an amazing singer with lots of power and range. He sounded a lot like Rahsaan Patterson. We hit it off immediately. Moved by my voice and classic style of singing, Lucius asked me to be in his newly formed band as one of his backup singers. With my absentee boyfriend and open schedule, I agreed.

"Baby, you won't' believe this. I'm in a band," I said excitedly to Siete on our way to Night of the Cookers.

"A band. Oh really?" he asked sarcastically. "How'd this happen?"

"Well, my friend Lucius at my vocal workshop--" He cut me off midsentence.

"Wait a minute, his name is Lucius. Stop. Stop. You're kidding me, right? Your boy's name is Luscious."

"No, his name is Lucius." I was used to his silly sense of humor. "Anyway, he formed a group and asked me to be a background singer."

"That's nice, honey. As long as you're happy doing it." He continued making jokes about Lucius's name for the rest of the car ride.

Practice with Lucius was intense and moved at a rapid pace. He had a vision of exactly what he expected to hear and see. He had since hired another background singer. She was really good, with many years of experience. She was also helpful to me with some of my struggles. Lucius expected that we make up the background vocals and corresponding dance moves prior to our rehearsals with the band. This was all new to me.

In addition, I didn't too much care for his song choices, and he always gave me the lower harmonies to sing, which were my Achilles heel. Enamored of my beauty and look, he had a bad habit of calling out the other background singer for mistakes that were sometimes my own. She'd grow to resent him and the entire setup.

She started missing practices, leaving me to fumble through them on my own. After two such meetings, I was no longer being called for rehearsals. I received a text from Lucius telling me that he had changed directions and to keep on singing.

I still took my private lessons with Katya. Completely smitten with my voice, she allowed me to get away with technical faux pas. I found songs from the standard Jazz canon which suited my personality and built a small repertoire. We had our end of term recital in May. I invited Siete to attend.

"A recital?" he mocked. "How old are we? Eleven?" He didn't take the time off from work.

Trent, as promised, did attend. He sat through two sets of mediocre to horrible singing. Convinced this was the overall quality of singers for the night, he fell asleep. Katya put me at the end of the second set and gave me three songs. I was nervous sitting through the entire show and my throat hurt, but I gave everyone on stage encouraging smiles because I knew how nerve-wracking the ordeal was.

I said a silent prayer that I'd stand and deliver. When it was my time to go on, I started out with *Misty*. I was off to a good start. My nerves disappeared and I was in my own world with the pianist. I sang to the audience, but I'd occasionally sing to the pianist. He'd play with me as if we were conversing. I followed up with *Harlem Nocturne*, which was my favorite, and the audience was thoroughly impressed by my ability to sing a song so complex and wide-ranging.

I finished with *Cry Me a River*. Because my own relationship was so disappointing, I sang the song with all the power and might I could muster. The audience was sold. I was the star of the night. I received congratulatory hugs and was told I'd be a superstar. I was elated. I just wanted to sing.

Trent was thankful he didn't have to give me bad reviews. "Whew J, I'm saying. After the first seven acts, I was beginning to think the entire night would be a bust. I was sitting here thinking about what I'd say to let you down easily. But you turned it out. I'm so proud of you. You found your passion."

He was absolutely right.

A few weeks later, I found myself in the office of the Ear, Nose, and Throat doctor for the pain in my throat that still hadn't subsided. He diagnosed it as Gastroesophageal Reflux disease, also known as GERD. I was floored. I'd never been sick with any ailments outside of a cold or flu. I had to readjust my eating habits, which meant less spicy or acidic foods. I took the medication that the doctor prescribed. A month later, even though the coughing stopped, the pain was still slightly present.

When I told Siete about it, he dismissed it with his habitual childishness. "Eww, you got the cooties. Is it contagious?"

He had a propensity toward extreme vanity and immaturity at times. I went up the block to see Karen at the apothecary. Karen had a warm, comforting smile, and she always greeted everyone with sincere kindness in her eyes. I used to frequent her shop often before I moved to Crown Heights and we'd talk about life and love for hours. As a natural healer and doctor of sorts, she had become my neighborhood confidante.

"What's going on, Jacquii? I haven't seen you in a while," she said, happy to see me.

"Girl, I've been busy with the job, and I recently picked up singing. I had a show a few weeks ago. I'm really enjoying it."

"Singing? You have to invite me out to your next show."

"I will. But I've been experiencing some pain in my throat. I went to the Ear, Nose, and Throat doctor and he says its GERD. I've been taking the medication he prescribed, but my throat still hurts. It feels like I have a lump right here," I said, pointing to the spot.

"Is there something you have to tell someone that you haven't?" she asked with knowing eyes. My mind immediately went to Siete, who had a habit of being incognegro or shutting conversations down whenever he was in the wrong and I was confrontational.

"Your throat chakra is blocked," she continued. "You need to clear it by wearing blue stones over your throat area and speaking your truth."

That small revelation moved mountains for me. It made all the sense in the world. Like years of things unsaid piled up in a hard-boiled abscess, still too young to pop but ripening slowly. I wanted so desperately to push a pin in it and extract the words as a single, long thread, pulling and pulling until it was emptied and flat, the root excavated.

I began researching the chakras in my spare time and learned that there were seven in general. The first was the root (red) located at the base of the spine; the second was the sacral (orange) located at the bottom of the stomach closer to the pelvis; the third was the solar plexus (yellow) located under the heart; the fourth was the heart (green); the fifth was the throat (sky blue); the sixth was the third eye (indigo) in the middle of the forehead; and the last was the crown (purple) located at the top of the head. Still too new a concept to fully grasp, I put it aside.

7

IT WAS THE BEGINNING OF JUNE, AND I THREW ANOTHER SISTERS' CIRCLE. WE were long overdue, and I really needed the warmth and healing of my girls. This gathering was entitled *Brown Bombshells on the Beach: A Girlfriend's Gala*. Trent hosted the communion in his new beachfront home in Arverne, Far Rockaway. June was a hard month to schedule, so we had a small crowd of ten.

We nestled comfortably on the carpet while the hired wait staff served us small bites and signature drinks. We were moving on up in the world with our menu and service. This year's selection included grapefruit brûlée with pistachio brittle, shrimp and grits, chicken and waffles, garlic confit, codfish fritters, watermelon salad, blackened salmon, bruschetta, crab puffs, red velvet strawberry shortcake, and a finger salad for ruffage, as usual. On the drink menu we had rum punch and the signature Mai Tai.

Maintaining conventions, I kicked the conversation off by telling the ladies about my recent relationship turmoil. My open admission opened the floor for us to deliberate over the enigma that was Siete.

"So you've never been to his house?" asked Sidney suspiciously. Sidney was my girlfriend on the job. We were both on Trent's team, when he had a team, but continued to work together in the iZone.

"No, I haven't," I admitted. "He's always working and is never home."

"What does he do for a living?" Belle asked.

"Well, he's a sales manager and trainer for a car dealership. But his passion is motivational speaking. He has a gift for public speaking." I beamed, touting his laurels.

"Yeah, but you need to go to his house. Where does he live?" Sidney, a Delta who believed in sisterhood to the end, wasn't about to let this line of conversation slide. I read her the address that I filed in my phone.

"Oh, I know exactly where that is. He's in the small buildings. My ex used to live in the apartment complex around the corner. You've never done a drive-by in the middle of the night?"

"No, girl, I'm trying to leave my old ways behind and respect his space."

"Whatever. Call me if you need someone to go with you. I'll drive from Long Island in a heartbeat. And start researching his background online. Something doesn't sound right about him. How did you even manage to put up with him for so long?" Sidney was the older sister providing counsel.

"Ladies, you have to cut her some slack now," Keisha chimed in. "She met him at a vulnerable point in her life."

Keisha referred to our meeting as a moment of vulnerability, but I called it kismet.

The discussion took a turn to the professional side. We spoke about Brynn's transition into principalship in Newark school district. She was in the market for a new chief innovation officer and wanted me to be her right hand. I, becoming disenfranchised with education on the whole, told her I'd send my resume and think about it. Belle and I spoke about our plans to go to the Dominican Republic later in the month. We were looking forward to seven days of all-inclusive luxury on the beach. Keisha stole the night with her tales of her nephew Baby Mace, who threatened his teacher by telling her he'd cut her to the white meat after she attempted to correct him in class.

"And where would he possibly learn that language?" asked Mallory facetiously.

"Girl, I have no idea," Keisha denied her involvement.

As we all laughed, I was in my head hatching a plan. Sidney had planted a seed.

* * *

The next day I drove my convertible to Queens using the address Siete put on the card he'd sent me a year earlier. I don't know what I was expecting to find. I knew he wasn't home because it was Sunday and he worked on Sundays. I thought a woman would answer his door. He and I weren't on good terms at that moment and were taking a break.

Our breaks would usually last around three days tops. I'd send him a text saying I was done. He normally wouldn't respond until the witching hour. I'd awake to a barrage of text messages that comprised hundreds of heart emojis and *I Love Yous* in repetitive succession.

I'd write back, *What makes you like this? Why can't you just act right?*

He'd send me the link to Lil Wayne's *How to Love.*

On that Sunday, at his apartment building, I stood debating my next course of action. I rang his bell. I must have rung it four or five times. Someone buzzed me in. I wasn't sure if the person was in the apartment or if it was one of his neighbors who tired of hearing the annoying trill of his bell. In any case, I was in. With no elevator, I walked up to the second floor and knocked on his door for a good fifteen minutes, listening to hear rustling movements inside.

I left the building after twenty minutes and no response. I walked the perimeter of the building to get a feel of the neighborhood. He lived in a predominantly Jewish and Muslim neighborhood. It was quiet and uneventful, with little around it except apartment buildings and houses. Weary of looking conspicuous on his residential streets, I got back into my car and drove home.

The spying, however, didn't stop there. At work the next day I did exactly as Sidney advised and entered his name in an online search database. I found information on his entire family. I knew their names, birth dates, previous places of residence, legal infractions. I even discovered that Siete had a middle name. Whenever I'd ask if he had one, he'd always tell me no.

In due course, being the pompous individual he was, he conceded and told me it was *The Great*. On this Monday in the middle of June I was staring at my computer screen with his full birth name, and I was saddened. If he was lying to me about his middle name, what else was he concealing? I filed that information away for future use. This wasn't going to be a three-day break.

Belle and I flew to Punta Cana and stayed at the luxurious Iberostar Grand. We had an assigned butler who catered to our every whim. It didn't hurt that he had a crush on me as well. At nights, he'd teach me how to dance to Merengue and Bachata in our room. He'd help me pick out clothes and dress me. It was too adorable. Belle had jokes for the entire trip.

I met Belle at work when Halle and I worked as assistant directors in the Bronx. Belle was impressed with the idea of an all-black, all-female administration and quickly befriended us. She was also friends with our tyrant of a boss. Belle was the unassuming friend. She saw a lot and was wise beyond her years, but she had a bubbly, seemingly naïve personality that would lead one to believe she was clueless. She was, however, sharp as a tack. She missed nothing. She noticed everything.

With a background in sociology and previous experience as a social worker, Belle read people accurately and succinctly. She was the life of the party, especially when there were men around, and dressed her behind off in stunning designer labels at all times. She was great for a girl's getaway.

Our trip was one of lazy beach days and reflective discourse. We spoke about our hopes, dreams, aspirations, childhoods, relationships with our parents. It was one of the most spiritually connected trips I'd ever taken with another woman. We enjoyed each other's company, and there was no competition nor ill-intent.

At some point I noticed I was getting welts all over my skin. I'd be fine in the day, but at night I felt like a wave of mosquitoes were attacking me. I'd awake itching and scratching frantically. I was so paranoid, I'd have our butler spray the room with mosquito repellant during the day while we were on the beach. That wouldn't work. I began turning the air conditioner all the way up at nights, freezing poor Belle to death. She was such a good spirit that she allowed me to go through my mania.

Finally realizing that these weren't mosquitos and I'd eaten bad fish, I visited the doctor's office at the resort to get an allergy shot. I was having a severe allergic reaction that only flared up at night. With my health on the decline, I reached out to Siete, returning his texts. We were making amends slowly, but it would take time for us to be back where we were.

When we returned to the states, my allergic reactions worsened. I was now allergic to fish of all types. A pescatarian for years, I didn't know how to adjust. I wanted to maintain my figure because Siete, a gym rat, had a predilection for women who leaned toward the thick and curvy. I was more gracile with wide hips, fit for my size, and an ample behind. I couldn't afford to lose either.

In addition, I had a bronchial infection caused by going to the beach in the day and sleeping in frigid cold at night. Faced with intense allergic flareups and coughing fits of green mucus, I drove myself to the emergency room. I received nothing other than Benadryl and was told to let the infection take its course. Siete wouldn't come to tend to me. Instead, he ordered food from the neighborhood restaurants and had it delivered to my home. When I asked him to be with me, he'd write back saying he'd try. After my second visit to the emergency room alone, I'd had enough.

I sent him an irate voice message over the phone app, Voxer, "So, I just got back from the emergency room. You said you'd be here to make sure that I'm well. In true Siete fashion, you're not. You could've at least called when I was driving back home, medicated. I'm so tired of being in this relationship by myself. You're a self-centered, selfish, and immature little boy. If those characteristics aren't on the list of things you don't like about yourself, I suggest you add them. Oh, and the next time you decide you want to try something on my behalf, TRY MOTHERFUCKIN' HARDER!"

He didn't respond that night. He was furious.

He responded the next day with a simple text message of three words: *What have you?* That was his typical response whenever I'd hit the fan.

I wrote back. *You tell me Siete Terrence Jackson.*

I dropped the big joker on the table with his first, middle, and last name. This caught his attention. He didn't bother to text back. He called me immediately.

"What do you want from me?"

"For starters, I want honesty. Why did you lie about your middle name?"

"How did you even find that?" he asked the question he really wanted to lead with.

"Don't worry about my methods. I have skills. Why did you lie?"

"Your methods," he said sarcastically. "I don't like the name so I don't use it. It doesn't fit who I am."

"Who are you, Siete?"

"I'm The Great!" He was back to his old self. He had managed to lighten the dialogue through digression. He quickly changed topics and the dispute dwindled. The next morning I awoke to a text with Nas's *Stay* from the newly released *Life is Good* album.

August was a month of changes. While I was pleased with Katya as a vocal coach, I needed someone who understood Jazz music and the art of improvisation. I needed a sistah. I'd recently found Fay Victor online through a Google search.

Fay was affiliated with the New York Jazz Workshop and gave private lessons in her Bed Stuy home. Having studied Jazz her entire adult life and mastered the art of both regular and free vocal improvisation, she wasn't easily impressed by me. She had performed with and seen most, if not all.

I was happy to find someone who understood my needs as a student and would call out my mistakes. Fay had a natural ability to identify vocal impediments during our lessons. She was a teacher, voice doctor and healer. Her instincts were always on point. She challenged me in ways that made me want to quit sometimes.

She showed me how to sing from the gut, supporting each note with the abdominal muscles, expanded ribs, and diaphragm. I didn't like the sounds coming out of my mouth. They were too jagged, unrefined, and primitive. Fay asked me to trust the process and assured me the sound would smoothen out in time. She was correct.

During one of our weekly lessons, I was practicing the Crusaders' *Street Life* but was holding back my voice.

"You have to feel the song in your body," Fay instructed. "You're intellectualizing a physical activity. This is often the case with people who are intelligent and use their minds to steer through life. But you can't think through this. The thinking has you too much up here and not enough in here." She pointed from her head, to her heart, and gradually down to the stomach. "Try it again and try your best to live the lyrics."

This was a lesson that would take me years to understand.

In addition to changing my coach, I was in the mood and market to change my car. I liked the convertible--at first--but it was quickly becoming a burden. It was a hard-top convertible so the roof would retract into the trunk area, leaving me with a tiny trunk space. The doors were heavy because they had to support the weight of the roof.

Whenever it rained, the roof sounded like a flock of cooing pigeons. I'd complain to Siete about it, but he'd just tell me to turn the radio up louder to drown out the noise. To seal the deal on its riddance, it was a front wheel drive that didn't handle well in the snow. I needed to get out of it immediately and into something new before winter hit.

I decided to jump into the Mercedes Benz GLK 350. It was a small compact SUV that drove like a car but had the weight and height of a jeep. I could buy the 4matic model and not have to worry about the snow. Siete was always speaking of having our son, so I figured the car would be an investment in our family's future. He wasn't a fan.

"Mercedes Benz?" he asked annoyed. "Why would you go to Mercedes when you can get an FX 35 or 50 with me?"

"I don't like the shape of the FX. The hood looks like that big flying dog in the movie, *The Neverending Story*. And besides, I've already bought two cars with you. Why must every car I buy be an Infiniti?"

"You know what? I get it. You're moving up in life and you want a car that represents prestige; Mercedes Benz signifies status. But I can put you in a fully loaded FX of your choice tomorrow, delivered to your door. You won't have to continue any payments on your current lease. I'll complete all the paperwork here and have my guy drive the car over to your home with thirty-five hundred dollars down and the same monthly payments. All you'll have to do is sign the contract when my guy comes."

It was the greatest deal ever. I didn't accept it.

"Baby, I know you want the sale, and I thank you for the offer. But I've already ordered and put money down on my custom GLK. The car is coming in December." I was determined to stand my ground.

"So what? You can get out of that. How much is your down payment and monthly?"

"Seven thousand dollars down, six hundred dollars monthly!"

"What? Are you kidding me? On a lease for that punk-ass truck? Honey, that makes no sense," he pleaded. "It's a crime for you to pay so much for a car. That's wasted money on a lease. I can't, in good faith, as your man and sales manager of a dealership, allow you to go into that."

Ever the salesman, he made all valid points; however, I wanted what *I* wanted. Truthfully, I was tired of him eating off me. If he was putting his money up to get me the FX, I would've obliged. All he was doing was brokering the deal. I was over it.

"No, baby. I'm staying with the GLK. I'm paying the next six months on the current lease off too."

"Fine, I don't want to talk about this anymore. I have to get back to work," he resigned in defeat.

He'd reveal years later that my decision to move to Mercedes was the beginning of the end of our relationship. I'd pay gravely for that decision.

It was October, and my office was New Orleans bound. We were invited to present at the iNACOL Symposium. After our presentation, Martine stayed at the casino to meet with my nemesis, Ernest. Ivy, Martine's deputy, and I went to a VIP dinner thrown by one of our partnering vendors. We were ready for free drinks and free food NOLA style.

The company hired a psychic reader for the first three hours of the event. Ivy and I got in line. The reader was a misleading woman. She had a ditzy air about her that made you second guess her abilities. When she got into my reading, I quickly realized that was just an air.

She put the cards on table. "Who's this man I'm seeing in your life?" she asked with slight contempt.

"I don't know." I was usually timid at the beginning of every reading. "It may be my boyfriend Siete."

"He's a man around your age. Ugh, he's an asshole." I was blindsided by her language. "He's a real asshole. He's not a good person. Not at all. He's going to do something that'll make you lose a lot of money."

She continued with the reading and focused on the job. She predicted that people would be unhappy working under Martine. She said there'd be changes, I'd leave to do something else. My mind was still on what she said about Siete. I needed a second opinion.

Ivy and I had established a deep friendship while working with Martine. She proved to be a trooper who was down for whatever. Familiar with New Orleans terrain, I convinced her to get a reading with me by the spiritual advisor I normally visited when I was in town. It was a commercial shop on Bourbon Street named Marie Laveau's House of Voodoo.

I liked going to this reader because he always read me fully. He spoke about health, wealth, love, and life. He'd proven to be accurate in the past. I wanted to see if he corroborated the first reader's story.

He told me that Siete had a quirky personality, was often preoccupied with work, and loved to watch sports on his off days. He mentioned we'd have to work hard on getting a rhythm and schedule that worked for us both. In the end, we'd come to a good compromise, settle down, and have a son. That was the story I was sticking with. I never told Siete about any of the readings I received when I returned home.

Back in New York City a few days later, Hurricane Sandy hit, sending the city into complete disorder, shock and confusion. As a city, we weren't ready for the infrastructural damage caused by excessive flooding and loss of power. Manhattan was without electricity for weeks. Houses along the coast were flooded, destroyed, or just plain washed away.

Trucks had no way of getting into the mainland to fill the stations with gas. Vehicles were lined up for miles and miles at gas stations, full of people waiting to fill their cars. It was pure chaos and commotion. I stayed home because I, living in the mainland, experienced no disruptions at all. The cable still worked well and the electricity was on. My car was parked safely and securely in the garage under me, and I had no place to go.

Siete was busy working at the dealership. With the flooding, cars were flying off the lots like hotcakes, but they weren't really making much of a profit because people were putting very little down and forgoing any extra luxuries. Folks just needed transportation to get to and from. In addition to Sandy, we were hit with a nor'easter that brought significant early season snow to the East Coast. It seemed mother nature was paying New York City back for several uninterrupted years of complacency.

My car came in a month earlier than scheduled. Not one to stand in lines for anything that wasn't a necessity, I used the little bit of gas I had in my tank and prayed my car would make it to the Mercedes Benz dealership in Rockville Centre without going empty or swerving out of control on the slippery asphalt. After a taxing two-hour drive, I arrived and switched cars.

Safely on the road in my new truck with a full tank of gas, I called Siete to ask that he have one of his guys drive my old lease from the Mercedes dealership back to Infiniti. Siete asked for my sales representative's number and told me he'd call me back. He called the representative at Mercedes Benz, berated him for the poor quality of service, guilted him into bringing the car to Infiniti himself, which he believed he should have done from the onset, then subjected him to a long, torturous wait on the sales floor before he sent someone out to get the keys.

When Siete did finally greet the Mercedes representative, who was a soft-spoken and meek younger man, he made sure to inform him with haughty certitude that *he* was my man and expected no less for his lady.

November was a hard month. Tamia called to tell me that her father, Francis, had suffered a stroke and was hospitalized. Francis was an uncle to me. He was an intellect like myself, and we'd spend hours debating love, life, philosophy, and the mysticisms of the world throughout my childhood and adult life.

He introduced me to obscure mystical texts such as the *Lesser and Greater Key of Solomon*. I bought both books but was daunted by the complexity of the spells. Other times, we'd sit in tranquility trading music selections of the past and present.

He was the father every daughter wished they had. Born on July 26th, he was a Leo who didn't give a shit about societal norms or expectations. He delivered his truths rough, rugged, and raw, tilting ugly on its axis. He was an omni-dimensional magician. I'd tell him my problems and he'd accurately reveal the ways of the world.

I took the entire day off from work and spent it in the hospital with Francis. His speech was slightly slurred, but he was able to hold an intelligible conversation. I spoke to him about my love life and admitted he'd been right about all the things we argued over when I was younger and inexperienced. He laughed at my humility.

As the one who pointed out my arrogance early on in life, he was happy to see me grow. While I was there, Siete called. He wanted me to come see him that night. I was finally going to his home. I didn't want to drive over because I was going to work in Long Island City the next day. We debated over which mode of public transportation I could take from his house into work the next morning.

"Who was that?" Francis asked me.

"That's my boyfriend Siete. You won't believe he's a Leo like yourself."

He replied, laughing, "A Leo. I'm surprised you ended up with a Leo. You're too strong of a personality for that. How old is he?"

I confided we were the same age. Without hesitation, he offered worldly wisdom.

"The two of you aren't going to last. You're too close in age. You're way more mature than he is. I don't have to meet him to know that. There were things my wife wanted me to do that I didn't have the foresight to see at the time. I regret not listening to her now. You don't want to fall into that trap. You'll get resentful. By Muslim teachings, a man is more compatible with a woman half his age plus seven."

I did the math in my head. "So you're telling me I need to be with a fifty-eight-year-old man? Nah, you're bugging, Francis."

"Better to be an old man's darling than a young man's slave. Never forget that." He dozed off. I waited until he was fully asleep, kissed his cheek, and left.

I never ended up going to Siete's house that evening. After I left the hospital I was physically and mentally fatigued. We argued over my change in plans. I didn't care. He'd get over it. He'd let me down enough in the past. Now he understood how it felt. We'd go a week without speaking until he called me one night in a depressive mood.

"Baby," he started, "I have a problem that I know you can help me with because you're a smart and bright girl."

"Okay, babe, what is it?" I asked, up for the challenge.

"The IRS just sent me notification that I owe twenty thousand dollars in back taxes. Apparently, my accountant was filing my claims incorrectly and I owe them."

I wasn't one to come off money that quickly, especially not for the IRS.

"Honey, that's not as big a deal as it sounds. I owed the IRS when I was in college because I filed exempt for the entire year. All you have to do is call them and work out a monthly payment plan. You can pay them as little as twenty-five dollars a month, with interest, of course. As long as you make the payments each month, they'll leave you alone. They'll just garnish any refunds you get from future filings. And that, my dear, is all there is to it. Problem solved." We laughed at my silliness and hung up.

He needed more time to think.

December came and took Francis away with November's exit. It was a sad time for the entire old block. The good thing about his death was that it brought all of us, from near and far, together to mourn. The only person who didn't make it was Lucas. He had since moved upstate to Kingston and chose to stay there.

Tamia was in shambles. She'd lost the parent she was closest to. We all attended the funeral. I hated funerals and everyone knew it, but there was no way I was going to miss Francis's send off. We sat in the first two rows. While the pastor gave his blessings and read the eulogy, I took my phone out and began to type. Tamia's former sister-in-law sat next to me.

She turned to me with the side-eye. "Big funeral going on, and you're texting somebody?"

"I'm not texting," I responded. "I'm writing my speech. I have to say something on his behalf."

I stood at the podium, took out my phone, adjusted the mic to ensure that everyone standing in the back could hear me clearly, and spoke from the heart.

"Francis truly embodied the many dimensions of a man. He was a man of many complexities and contradictions, and I believe this is what made him so beautifully flawed. He was a man who boasted about his manly conquests while he spent his life in pursuit of an unrequited love.

"He was the prototypical father who treated all of his children fairly and loved unconditionally. He was a man who touched and influenced many with an intellectual and worldly guidance that we so needed and yearned for.

"In my quiet moments I'll miss my friend. We dreamed, reminisced, debated, and argued, but in the end, we laughed, and I'm at peace that he knows I love him so.

"When I remember Francis, I'll remember Chubby, the life of the party with the loud laugh who admitted his faults and lived in humble honesty. I'll hold fast to the dreamer, the lover of music, the chef, the electrical engineer, and the intellect.

"I love, respect, and miss you. Please know that your life lessons haven't gone unheeded. I release you now with one request; please let my father know I love him too. It's long overdue."

Tamia, wholly comprehending the power behind my words and the strained dynamic between my father and me, cried with enormous agony. The reality of her father's final departure was too much for her to endure. Years later, Francis would visit me twice in my dreams to say hello.

It was Saturday, December 15th. I returned to Brooklyn from a shopping excursion at Woodbury with my mother, heading straight to my private vocal lesson. I was making steady progress with my singing. This afternoon's class took an interesting turn. After our usual technical drills, Fay gave me five minutes to write my own lyrics to a Blues progression. Once I wrote the lyrics, I had to sing them.

I wrote a quick, poetic verse that flowed over the chords describing my shopping trip to the mall and my hurry to get home to cook for my man and his friend, who were coming over the next day to watch the game. It was the truth. I did have to get home to prepare for Siete and his best friend, Quan, who decided to watch their Sunday games at my apartment.

Fay was awe-struck by my writing abilities. "Jacquii, that was great. Usually my students freeze at an assignment like that. Not only did you write lyrics, but you actually told a story that the listener could follow."

"Thank you," I said, shocked that my little song made such a great impression. "I used to write lyrics to calypsos that my best friend Anthony would arrange. Writing comes naturally to me."

"Well, since you're not a fan of the vocal standards, you should find instrumental standards that you like and write your own lyrics to them. It'll help you connect to the music more."

That was one of the best ideas I'd ever heard. It would take years for me to gain the assurance to actually do it.

Sunday at my apartment was busier than ordinary. I taught my regular graduate class at Touro College from 8:00 a.m. to 12:00 p.m. but had to rush home to get there by 1:00 p.m. The football game started at 1:00 p.m. and Siete was finally bringing his friend around. This was a pivotal point in our relationship because I was getting a glimpse into his world and one of the main people in it.

We originally planned it to be a couple's hangout, but Quan's girlfriend had to work. I set the table with various flavored wings I'd bought the night before from Wing Wagon on Flatbush Avenue. I took the potato salad out of the containers and put it in Tupperware to create the illusion that I made the food from scratch.

112

It wasn't that I couldn't cook; I cooked for Siete a few times before. I swore, after Collin I'd never cook for another man unless he exhibited an ardor that inspired me to. Let's just say after two years of being with Siete, I was lacking inspiration. Nonetheless, the table was set with food, snacks, and top shelf Vodka of various flavors. The fridge was stocked with sundry organic juices in case they wanted to mix their drinks. Everything was in its place when they arrived exactly at 1:00 p.m.

Siete walked in beaming with pride at the set table.

"See, Sun?" he boasted. "I told you she'd already have everything laid out when we arrived. She's so efficient."

My organizational skills were the topic of conversation on their drive over. It was customary for me to put Siete's food out on the table and leave two wash cloths and a towel in the bathroom when he'd come in from work at night. I guess he was so rapt with my attention to detail, he had to notify his friend.

I greeted Quan pleasantly. At last, I was face-to-face with the lone friend I'd heard so much about. He eyed me quizzically as if he didn't know what to make of me. Probably, I wasn't what he was expecting. He hesitated when I put my hand out to take his coat. Checking his pockets to make sure he didn't leave anything of value in them, he decided to surrender his outer garment to me so I could hang it up in the closet.

"We don't usually give our coats up. The guns might go off."

He didn't know I grew up with shooters. Real shooters didn't talk about their guns; they just busted them. I didn't acknowledge the comment. It was dumb.

While they feasted on the chicken, I left them to go into the kitchen. I didn't put the glasses or the bucket of ice on the table, and I had to finish my preferred shrimp roti. I came back out ten minutes later to see them looking out the living room window.

"Why are you guys looking out the window?" I asked. Something about it didn't sit right with me.

"Yo, you can have the ill party back there," Siete said. "There's a roof right out your window. It's big as hell. You know how many people you can hold back there?"

It was more a statement than a question. I often entertained the idea myself but being in a stiff coop building, doubted the board or neighbors would be agreeable. I brushed it off.

The night was awkward, to say the least. Quan would verbally spar with me whenever I said anything. He seemed to want to best me in front of Siete. It was the weirdest reception I ever received from a man. Usually men would try to get my attention or tease their boy about taking me for themselves. This one was intentionally vying for Siete's approval.

They had a strange dynamic. Siete was most certainly the alpha and aggressor in their relationship. Quan, younger than Siete, fluctuated between a display of adulation, cynicism, and fear toward him. I was close to cursing him out and telling them both to leave but kept it classy because he was Siete's best friend.

We spoke about my technology collection, my automated sound system that Trent set up and programmed while he stayed in my apartment, my music collection, Bluetooth headphones, and the Invisalign treatment used to close my front gap.

Quan, consumed by my gadgets, looked at my classic 120GB iPod connected to the sound system. "Ooh, an iPod!" he exclaimed with excitement.

Out of the peripheral of my right eye, I saw Siete, who was sitting to our right on the couch, shake his head no. I paid it no mind. All the while, I was typing on my 13" MacBook Air, which was what I did from the time I awoke until I went to sleep.

Siete would often tease me about greeting the computer before I did him each morning. I couldn't help it. I was a technophile. I'd go back and forth from the bedroom retrieving things from my safe to show them.

At some point they got tired of the wings. Quan saw me eating my roti earlier and asked if I had anymore. Siete wasn't a fan of roti because it had too much flour, but I offered to go to the shop to buy more. I didn't mind the drive in my new Mercedes truck. I left them in the apartment while I went out.

Half hour later, I returned with no roti in hand. The shop closed just as I'd arrived. They were stuck with the chicken wings. I left them in the living room to watch football, and I retreated to my bedroom to watch the *Housewives of Atlanta*. Siete came into the bedroom to hug me.

"Thank you for opening your home to me and my friend. You've been a great hostess. I love you."

I was moved. I kissed him and followed him back out to see what they were watching. The game ended, and they were now watching a documentary on ESPN called *30 for 30: Broke*. It was a documentary that highlighted how millionaire athletes lost all their money after an average of five years.

"Why are you watching this?" I asked. "I'm going back into the bedroom to watch my housewives."

"Oh, you *want* to watch *this* show," said Quan, encouraging me. Siete just sat and laughed.

We ended the night on better terms than we started. They left around 11:00 p.m. I'd cleaned up while they were there, so I gave them the remainder of the food in takeaway containers. I was tired. I retreated to bed. Siete called me while on the way home to get the name of my dentist and the model information for the Bluetooth headphones I'd shown them. Feeling like I made an imprint and was deemed valuable, I gladly provided the information.

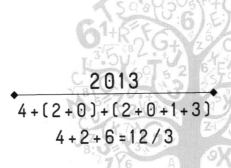

$$2013$$
$$4 + (2 + 0) + (2 + 0 + 1 + 3)$$
$$4 + 2 + 6 = 12 / 3$$

Three Personal Year

Surrender, sacrifice, suspension in time, creation, imagination. This is the cycle of caution and circumspection where you must avoid becoming the sacrificial lamb who is used for other's amusement or personal gain. Doing something creative, such as writing, painting, or making music will add to your personal self-satisfaction.[4]

---

[4] (Strayhorn, 1997)

"Listen to the spirits of the night,
Buried in glasses and caskets of sadness.
People drinking hopelessness away.
Burdened by the heaviness of life,
Searching for answers and ends to this madness.
Screaming from the depths of the red clay."

8

THE DAY FOR LOVERS WAS FRET WITH CRYPTIC TEXT MESSAGES AND analyses of the mind--Siete's mind. It seemed the dark aura of the historical Valentine's executions swathed our partnership with deathly, low-spiritedness. There'd be no angels with bows nor celebration of hearts for me.

On Valentine's Day, Siete sent me a text.

I'm reflecting on my life and I don't like the direction it's taking. I need a do-over--a mulligan, if you will.

Alarmed by his morose tone, I wrote back, *Baby, what are you trying to tell me? I can't help you if you don't let me in. Relationships aren't easy. For us to grow, we have to go through the good, the bad, and a whole lot of ugly.*

Don't worry, honey, he answered. *I'll work it out. Just give me some time.*

It was February 15th, and I was driving back to Ozone Park where I worked one day a week. I preferred the quiet of Long Island City, but Martine liked my company. I gave her Fridays.

I got a call from Tamia.

"Girl, what you doin' later? Come hang out with me, Tyra, and Samiyah. One of my friends at work is having a raffle dinner. I'll buy your ticket."

The last time we'd all seen each other was at Francis's funeral. We hadn't really hung out in a while, and we always had a ball when we did. I agreed. We were supposed to meet on Water Street in Manhattan at 6:00

p.m. I, always early, got there around 5:30 p.m. Tamia, habitually late for everything, was still at home getting ready. I stood out in the cold for an hour.

Fed up, hungry, and cold, I called her. "Yo, where are you? I'm about to hop in my car and go home. This shit is ridiculous now."

"No! Don't leave. We're coming. We'll be there in ten minutes."

They arrived close to 7:00 p.m. I was too peeved to be happy. The night started out pleasant enough. It wasn't really a dinner. We had finger foods and sat while items were either sold or raffled. We had more fun cracking jokes and being silly with each other. Having known each other our whole lives, we had an arsenal of inside jokes that crossed decades.

The joke was currently on Samiyah, who didn't win anything at all in the raffle. The rest of us got trinkets for our homes. I, in particular, got a pretty fire glass decorative plate made with burnt orange and gold hues. It matched Samiyah's home décor.

"Give me the plate, nuh?" Samiyah asked, trying to get me to hand over my prize.

"Nope. Not doing it," I replied. "Burn your own glass." We laughed at the silliness.

Around 7:45 p.m. I received a text message from Siete.

I have lived on the lip of insanity,
wanting to know reasons,
knocking on a door.
It opens.
I've been knocking from the inside.

What does this mean, honey? Keeping his strange mood from the day before in mind, I thought he was sending me a clue. *Are you going insane?*

Read what it says, honey. Read deeper.

I was frustrated. This wasn't the time for one of his riddles. I wrote back.

Look, I'm out with the girls right now. I don't have time for this. I'll call you later.

Okay, baby, I love you!

I love you more! I countered. He didn't respond.

I found that strange. Normally when I'd write or say that, he'd say "I doubt that highly" or something to indicate that he definitely loved me more. Not on this night.

We left around 8:00 p.m. Tamia asked me to lead the way into Brooklyn since I was most familiar with driving in Manhattan. Samiyah and Tyra drove with Tamia. I had my truck to myself. I prepared myself for the road. I straightened the rearview mirror, pushed out the side view mirrors, adjusted my seat to my programmed setting, plugged my iPhone into the console so it could play over the speakers, set the phone to my favorite road vibes playlist, and programmed the address into the navigation system.

Samiyah sat in the front seat of Tamia's car with the window rolled down. She was impatiently beside herself.

"What the hell? Who are you right now? Kevin Hart's frigging friend Nate? Shit man! Let's go!"

We all cracked up laughing at the *Seriously Funny* reference. We all loved Kevin Hart.

"Nah, I have to get my shit right for the road. It's a long drive. Don't rush me. *You wanna go night-night, nigga? Everybody go night-night!*" I defended myself with another Kevin Hart joke.

Tamia was in tears. She hadn't laughed that much or hard in months.

"I can't even. I love my friends. Y'all are the funniest ever."

We pulled off. We decided mid-route to go to a bar named Fish Eye in East Flatbush. On the way to Fish Eye, around 8:30 p.m. my phone rang. It was the front door intercom of my apartment building.

"Delivery!" It was a delivery man with a Spanish accent.

The intercom was programmed to dial a specific phone number for each household. I had my intercom routed to my cell. It gave me the flexibility to buzz people in no matter where I was from the convenience of my iPhone. Obviously, I wasn't home and didn't order anything.

"What? Delivery?" I asked, perturbed by the obvious blunder. "I'm not home. You have the wrong apartment." I hung up.

We laughed some more at Fish Eye's over food and drinks. We drank so much, we didn't leave until 1:00 a.m. Samiyah was fine because she lived around the corner. Tamia, Tyra, and I had to travel. Starting our Saturday morning off right, we went home.

I felt a bone-chilling consciousness upon entering the front door of my apartment; the stench of the crisp night air assailed my sensibilities. I navigated in shadowy darkness with my coat and shoes still on trying to intuit what, exactly, was wrong. I noticed my Picasso rug was flipped upwards in the bottom right corner but still held in place by the rubber pad underneath.

Looking around, still observing for inconsistencies, I noticed the living room window to the farthest left was open. My window locks were faulty. I often called the super to have them fixed, but I never left the windows open. The window wasn't slightly ajar; it was wide open and the outside screen removed.

Panicking as my body went into a familiar rigid state, I knew my home had been burglarized—again. With the lights still off, I couldn't see what was missing. Everything except the rug seemed to be in its place. My body started to convulse with the realization of what it could be. I ran into my bedroom and put on the light. Flinging the closet doors open with desperate wishful thinking, my brain slowly processed that my 200-lb safe was gone!

It came out as a low guttural howl from the subjacent depths of my belly, a loud ancestral cry of karmic debts prepaid with compound interest. I screamed until my voice broke like shards of glass. I summoned the super, who was fully dressed at 2:00 a.m. He came running through my door to my aid. I told him what happened. He was one of the few people to be in my apartment.

Resigned that there wasn't anything much he could do, he left and went back to his place. My cell phone sounded with a text message. It was Tamia telling me she'd just dropped Tyra off and was safely inside. We had a habit of checking in after every hangout. I called her back instead.

Crying so softly, I could only whisper, "Tam?"

"Hey, you inside?"

"Yeah." I could hardly think long enough to formulate full sentences.

"J, what's wrong? You aight?"

"No! Tam, they robbed me. My apartment was burglarized again."

"What? Again? I'm going to get Tyra. We're coming over there now." She hung up. I called my mother and told her the same. She too was on her way.

I called the police and reported the burglary. They told me they dispatched my case to their officers on the beat. All I could do now was wait. I called Siete. No answer. I called him again. No answer. I texted his phone. No answer. I must've called him ten times. His phone went straight to voicemail.

"Siete, why are you not answering your phone? I've been calling you all morning. I was robbed. Call me back as soon as you get this."

Tamia, Tyra, and my mother all arrived within minutes of each other. I told them I'd called the police. We waited, theorizing about what could've happened. I was too shell-shocked to be of intellectual value. The illogicality of being hit twice, a little more than two years a part, both apartments numbered 2E, was too much for me to fathom. If I didn't believe it before, now I undeniably believed I must have been a horrible person in my past life.

"I'm being paid back. That's it. I'm paying for all of my sins. I'm a horrible person."

"Don't say that, J," Tamia tried to console me. "You're not a bad person at all. Bad things just happen to good people. That's all. But it's a good thing we made you stay in the city. Suppose you left us and came home? They would've entered while you were sleeping. You wouldn't have had your hearing aids in. Can you imagine them being over you in your sleep?" I didn't want to imagine it.

I played the events from the previous night over and over in my head like a broken record, repeating the same melancholy and dull chorus. Dejected and enervated, I beat myself up, mentally boxing with my inner voice. Why didn't I arm the ADT system? You had it installed for that very reason. Why was I so trusting? You thought you were spared, free from harm in your old neighborhood. Who rang my bell at 8:30 p.m. last night? It couldn't have been a delivery man. Why did I say I wasn't home? Damn, you talk too blasted much. Why isn't Siete answering his phone? You're in this by yourself. You're all alone. Where are the fucking police when you need them? This is still Brooklyn we're talking about.

My mother asked me to run down what was in the safe. "So give me a list of the things you remember."

"I had my MacBook, all my technology—iPads, iPods, laptops, Bluetooth headphones, Tiffany's jewelry, but just silver—no gold; all my identification, social security card, birth certificate, US and Trinidad passports, credit cards, high school diploma." I couldn't remember everything. My brain was still too cloudy.

"And my financial investment documents," my mother continued. "The money I put in the safe for you, was it in there too?"

"No, I took that out and put it in the bank yesterday morning."

"Whew, at least you did that." She was pleased about something.

"They also took my remote control that automates my sound system. I wonder why they left this classic iPod, though."

I was grateful they did leave it because it was now a collector's item. Learning from the last burglary, all my music and data files were stored in the cloud. I disabled the Dropbox connection on my MacBook Air from my iPhone.

We waited. I busied myself by arming the CompuTrace Lo Jack installed on my laptop. If the thieves put the laptop on, we'd get a location. Thus far, the location kept registering upstate in Rochester. I also activated *Find My iPhone* on my iPods and iPads.

"Tam?" I was tired of surmising and tracking, "when you leave, take the plate to Samiyah for me please."

"Wow, with everything going on, you're still thinking about other people."

I looked at the fire glass plate propped up on the bar table like a lumbering foreign object.

"It doesn't fit in here. She might as well have it."

We waited until 6:00 a.m. First the ballistics team came to take fingerprints. They asked for details. We told them what we knew. Siete finally called.

"Baby, what happened? Your message said you were robbed. Who robbed you?" he asked with urgency and concern that were four hours too late.

"Siete! Where were you?" I cried a fresh stream of tears, hoping they'd deluge the ache in my soul. I cried from abandonment. "I've been calling you for four hours. You call me back now?"

"Sorry, honey," he said apologetically. "You know I have a habit of taking my phone off when I've had a long day at work. Last night I came in, took a shot of Nyquil, turned my phone off, and went straight to sleep."

"My apartment was burglarized." I told him what I'd discovered earlier that morning.

"What? Again? Who the fuck has it out for you like this?" He readjusted his tone, trying to be the calm savior. "Okay, let me call into work and tell them I'm not coming in. I'll come over as soon as I finish taking a shower."

The ballistics team was finishing up. They found no fingerprints.

When Siete arrived, he greeted my mother at the door, kissing her on the cheek.

"Hey, Mom, good to see you. I wish the visit was under different circumstances."

He walked in with the authoritative gait of a man who came to dictate his order. He glanced at the couch where Tamia and Tyra sat. Registering their presence without words, he mean-mugged them and made his way into the kitchen, directing me to follow.

"Let me talk to you for a minute privately. Who did you have in your place besides me?" he asked as soon as we got in the room.

Confused by his line of interrogation, I stuttered. Why was *I* being questioned? I was the victim.

"I didn't have anybody in here. Only you, my mother, and sometimes the super. This is the first time my girls are even in this apartment."

"Jacq, if there's something you're hiding, now would be the time to say something. Who else did you have in here?" he was adamant.

"I already told you who!" He was pushing a nerve. "That's it. I don't have time to lie about anything. It's my shit that's missing. No one else's."

"I'm just making sure." We walked out the kitchen and into the living room. Still not acknowledging Tamia and Tyra, he sat on the living room floor against the wall that led to my bedroom. While we ran down the possible events, he was busy typing on his phone.

"Anything show up on the computer's tracker, J?" Tamia was on it.

"No, it still says Rochester. They haven't started the computer yet," I answered, looking at my phone.

"Your laptop was in the safe too?" Siete looked up from his phone to inquire. "I thought you take your laptop to work with you?"

He recently bought me a Michael Kors tote bag for Christmas so I could transport my laptop to work. I didn't need the bag because I had a 27" iMac and a MacBook Pro at work. I asked for an updated iPhone, not a bag. I wasn't a fan of Michael Kors and made sure to let him know that.

"No, I leave it at home. I don't need it at work. You knew I kept it in the safe," I answered.

"It has a tracker on it then?" he asked. I confirmed. He nodded and went back to his phone.

Tamia and Tyra were still channeling Cagney and Lacey.

"So they came in from the outside roof into your apartment. But how did they get inside the gate? Does that gate open?"

"Yeah, but only the super has the key," I responded.

Tamia and Tyra weren't satisfied. They got off the couch, went through the window, and out onto the roof. When Tyra got up, Siete was at attention. Tyra, although short, had a shape that was too exaggerated to be true. She was small on top, with a small, tight waistline, but her hips and butt were three times the size of her waist. He followed them outside to investigate the crime scene, or Tyra, further.

Like my previous apartment, this one was on the second floor and had no apartments below. It was situated over the garage space. The windows of my living room and bedroom faced the back of the building, overlooking the length and width of the front of the garage. It was a roof deck big enough to hold a hundred people easily. It was enclosed by gates that were high enough. If I was facing north, I could see stairs leading to the roof on both the east and north sides. There were two points of access, one from the adjacent block, the other directly around the corner. I could jump out the windows of my living room or bedroom comfortably onto the roof of the garage in the same manner in which Tamia, Tyra, and now Siete, did.

They walked the path from the gates to my windows. Tamia stopped to speak with an older woman in the house on the block behind, who said she heard the wheels of something moving on the roof around 7:00 p.m. or 7:30 p.m. The time didn't mesh with the delivery guy. My girls discussed possible scenarios as they smoked cigarettes. The super saw them on the roof and came up the north entrance. How was it possible that no one saw anything between the hours of 7:00 p.m. and 8:00 p.m. on a Friday night? Tamia questioned the super.

"Did anyone report any noise to you?"

"I was walking around the corner and the lady in the house next door said she saw a truck looking like a cable van parked in the yard in front of the garage. She said she saw a young man pushing something big and black on a dolly. But they pushed it from the back of the building around the corner."

That was the safe. They pushed it to the block facing the east entrance.

"Wait, you're telling me they pushed the safe away on a dolly between 7:00 p.m. and 8:00 p.m. at night, and no one called the police?" This was the noise of the wheels the older lady heard.

"Do you have a camera on the building?"

"Yes, I have camera in basement." The super was Russian.

"Was it on last night? Can we see the tapes?" The super granted Tamia's request. We were finally going to get some answers.

We waited patiently while the super rewound the digital tape, anxious about what we might or might not see. The timing of the tape was off. The tape was an hour ahead of the actual time, so it read 8:00 p.m. instead of 7:00 p.m. He stopped when Tamia saw a motion on the tape.

"Stop right there. I see someone."

"Okay, let me rewind a bit so we can see full picture." The super cooperated.

The video was one out of a paranormal activity scene. The picture was black for five minutes. Abruptly, out of the darkness emerged a light figure wearing a dark hoodie. We all freaked out at the sight and jumped back, holding our breaths. The person was about my height, slim, male, and light-skinned.

He walked up the north stairs, moved his body along the gates on the west side, and scaled the fence with the ease and agility of a seasoned construction worker. He walked closely against the building, making sure to keep his head down and out of the camera's direct view. He looked straight ahead, making sure he didn't turn left or right.

This was no amateur. He tried to open the left most bedroom window first. It didn't give. He walked over to the living room and tried the left most window there. Whoever gave him instructions knew the left most window of the living room had the faulty lock. He pushed the window knob open with a slim Jim. Removing the screen, he entered the apartment. After that, there was no movement at all.

We waited twenty minutes. He came back out the window onto the roof. Again we held our breaths. He walked diagonally now toward the north gate and opened it. Another male, darker skinned and chubby, came following him with a dolly. There was a third person, a light-skinned girl. Her thighs, although muscular and toned, were shapely like a woman's.

"Oh shit, that's a girl!" I was shocked to see a female.

She followed the two men, skipping behind like she was elated to be on a heist. They all entered the apartment, and ten minutes later, the men pushed the safe out the window while the girl held the dolly in place. They ran, rolling it away through the north gate, down the stairs, in front of the garage entrance and around the east corner. The picture went black again.

To know you've been violated is one thing. To see evidence of the violation is another. The imagery of the invasion would stay in our minds for weeks to come. It was the scariest thing we'd seen because it was real footage, not a *Blair Witch Project*. Though, it had the same feel and cinematic effect.

We were all visibly shaken. We went back upstairs to my apartment where my mother waited. Tamia made sure to tell the super to hammer wood beams in the bedroom and living room windowsills to prevent future entry. The detectives still hadn't arrived.

Tamia told my mother what we'd seen. Tamia was the friend who was your ride or die. She was the friend you wanted around when you were about to get into something and needed backup or when you knew you couldn't be around at all but needed a trusty spy.

She had a photographic memory and the ability to relay a story so vividly, you would imagine yourself in the actual scene. A natural-born actor, she'd act the story out as well, flawlessly. I often told her she missed her calling in Hollywood.

"What I can't understand, though," Tamia was thinking aloud, "is why when the guy first went into the apartment, it took him twenty minutes to come out. What was he doing for so long?"

"I know what he was doing," Siete volunteered. "He went into the bedroom and in the closet. He tried to push the safe out himself. He realized the shit was too heavy, so he pushed, stopped, pushed, stopped. You see the skid marks on the wood here. Then he stopped to catch his breath. He called his boy and the female over with the dolly because he couldn't do it alone."

His theory made sense. We nodded in agreement. The detectives came at 10:00 a.m. They questioned us again about the events of the night before. We told them all we knew and what we'd gathered from the neighbors.

"But how can you prove someone actually came into the apartment?" one detective asked me.

"Because we just saw it on the building's tape."

"Wait, there's video footage?" he asked. We confirmed.

"Sweet. Take us to see it." I took the detectives back down to the super's room. Tamia, Tyra, and Siete all left. Siete told me to call him when I was done. I had no idea when that would be.

The detectives made a copy of the video and took it with them. One detective turned to me and asked the million-dollar question. "You have an alarm system. Why didn't it go off when the burglar was in the apartment?"

I answered bashfully, "I didn't arm it. I didn't think I had to in this neighborhood."

"I bet you won't ever make that mistake again." He didn't know how right he was.

KNOCKING FROM THE INSIDE

After the super came to put the wood beams in every window, my mother and I went to the bank and changed my account information and bank cards. I canceled all my credit cards and got new ones reissued. I'd have to get new ID and passports. I was overwhelmed with the many steps I needed to take to get my life back in order. When the night was over, I called Siete.

"Baby, I'm coming over to your house. I don't feel safe in mine."

"Did the super put the barricades in the windows?" he asked.

I answered in the affirmative.

"I have to work all weekend. I don't want to leave you in my apartment by yourself. There's nothing around here either."

"I don't need anything around the building. I'll just stay inside and sleep until you get in."

"Honey, I know you don't want to hear this, but the burglars are not coming back there. They won't risk getting caught. You're safer in your own home than you are anywhere else." He paused. "I thought you said you were going to your mother's house anyway?" He was determined to dissuade me from coming to Queens.

"I was going there, but she wants to know why I'm not going by you. Fine, I'll go there instead." I packed my carry-on suitcase with a week's worth of stuff and pulled my baggage up the block to my mother's.

Although reluctant at first, I was happy to be in my mother's apartment once I was settled in. I slept on the blowup bed in the living room, but I felt comfortable. It was the first time I was able to rest in a full day. When I laid my head on the pillow, my dreams were lucid with clairvoyant visions. My dreams pointed me to the day in December when Siete and Quan were in my apartment looking out the window. I woke up startled by the revelation. It was Quan. He set the entire thing up.

The next morning I couldn't contain myself. Siete texted me to see how I was doing. I responded.

I know who did it. It was your boy. He set me up to be burglarized. I saw it all in my dream. He took an hour to respond.

What? Quan would never do that. He's like my brother. He loves you the same way I love you. I doubted that highly after our first meeting. There was no love there at all.

Honey, I wrote back, *I know how you feel. If it were you and you told me Tamia did something like that to you, I'd doubt it too. But I know what I'm talking about. My dreams don't lie.* I was in a state of calm.

Nah, I'm not buying it. He'd defend his friend until the end.

I asked Tamia and Tyra to meet me back at my place after I cleaned and mopped everything up. I wiped the black fingerprint powder off my white closets, swept and mopped the floors, fixed the rug and put it back in order, and smoked my apartment out with charcoal, frankincense, and myrrh, a ritual I failed to perform on the first Friday of that month, as I normally did every month.

Tamia and Tyra arrived just as I finished cleaning and smoking.

As soon as they entered, we said in unison, "I know who did it. It was his friend." Tamia ended with, "It was your man."

"What?" I didn't want to hear that at all.

"J, we spoke to the entire family about it." Her brothers and cousins were still in town two months after the funeral. "They all said it was Siete."

I told them about the dream and my text message exchange with Siete earlier that day.

"Shit," she said. "They told me to tell you not to mention anything to him. Don't tell him anything else. You don't want to make him aware of our movements."

I called Lucas to see what his take was. "Word, sis? Your place was burglarized again? Yo, dude you're with, where's he from?"

"Queens."

"Yo, I didn't know homey was from Queens. Had I known, I would've warned you. Queens dudes are grimy. Brooklyn dudes get into identity theft and credit card scams, that's their hustle. But Queens dudes--masterminds of home invasion. They'll get with you just to set you up. And I was in Brooklyn this weekend too, but the po-lice snatched me up for peeing in the subway. They held me for a day. I'm just getting out now." I was finished. Everyone had the answers after the fact.

Thereafter, whenever Siete texted, I kept it close. I was short on my responses. I spent the next few days away from work trying to get my legal documentation back. The first stop was the Bureau of Records on Worth Street. While I was in line waiting to get my birth certificate, I received a text from Siete.

Hey, Mom. I've been busy studying for this interview with Mercedes Benz. I'll call you later. Tell Grandma I love her.

I didn't answer. Mercedes Benz? Why was he interviewing with them? He gave me so much grief for changing brands? Realizing his error, he sent a correction text.

Hey, Beautiful. I'm sorry for the text. That was for my mother. Is everything okay? I told him it was and that I'd call him later.

That evening I called. "Hey?"

"Hey." He was low-keyed. "I've been studying for this interview for the past few days. I'm sorry I haven't been around. I'm still shook up by that video we saw. That shit was crazy."

"Yep, I get it. So you're going to Mercedes Benz now?"

"I'm interviewing with them. I need a change."

"Listen, I'll need that MacBook Air I gave you back. With the burglary, my job wants to inventory all the items left. So I'll need that." It wasn't true. Martine didn't ask me for anything. Now that he was a prime suspect, I wanted my laptop.

"Okay, let me get my information off it. I'll bring it to you on Sunday." We hung up.

Tired of my mother complaining about me eating her food and using her items incorrectly, I packed my stuff and went back to my apartment the next day. I was still scared to be alone, but I was happy to be in my own place again. It was Tuesday, and I'd spend the day fighting with the insurance company who wanted receipts for all items stolen.

I was taking a huge loss with this insurance claim. They rewarded me much less than Liberty Mutual, who'd recently stopped insuring New York City residents. I had to tap into my investments to buy the essentials back. I was also moving yet again. I needed a place of my own that wasn't subleased or on the second floor.

Sunday came and I was in my bedroom watching TV when I got a call from my friend Brian. Brian was a childhood friend who grew up two blocks away from us. We were all like brothers and sisters. I knew he was calling because Tamia told him what happened. I answered.

"So why haven't you called to tell me what happened?"

"Brian, I don't know. I've been overwhelmed and tired. I've just been keeping to myself."

"Well, come out to brunch with me."

I agreed. We met up at Peaches in Bed Stuy. I confirmed what Tamia already shared with him. I also told him about my plans to retrieve my laptop from Siete later on that night.

"He's coming back to your apartment tonight with the laptop?" he asked. I confirmed.

"Well, I'm coming over to your place too. Don't tell him I'll be there. Let's see how he reacts when he sees me."

Brian was a bouncer in his spare time. He used weapons often. He was also a masseuse. When he wasn't restraining people with pain, he was relieving them of it. We ordered pizza, sat at the living room bar table, and waited.

When Siete entered the apartment around 8:00 p.m., he was stunned to see Brian sitting at the table. He paused for a quick minute, nodded in Brian's direction, and looked at me with hatred in his eyes.

"Can I see you in the bedroom for a minute?"

I, scared by both his demeanor and the thought of danger, followed him docilely. Brian walked to the other side of the living room to get his nunchucks. He already had his brass knuckles on. Siete handed me the laptop. His eyes looked wild. He wanted so badly to hit me but didn't. I regained my composure when I saw Brian out of my peripheral.

"Where's the power cord? You brought the laptop and not the power cord?" I put bass in my voice.

"It's right here," he said softly, removing it from his pocket.

I grabbed the power cord and was done conversing. I gave him a look letting him know it was time to leave. He walked back into the living room, gave Brian a pound.

"Take it easy, champ." He fumbled with the lock that he'd turned on several occasions in the past and walked away.

"That lame isn't a gangster!" Brian said coolly amped. "First of all, he was nervous when he saw me. There's no way, I'm coming into my lady's house, see a man at the table eating pizza, and walk out first. I would've waited him out. He was going to know that *I* was king of this castle."

I listened with fascination as he continued with his reasoning.

"He was mad because we ruined his plans. His plan was to come over here, woo you with some bullshit talk, fuck you, and strike again. Whatever he didn't get in the safe, he was going to get from you directly!

"And you were scared when he called you into the bedroom," he continued. "He's not a street dude. That's all propaganda and lies. I'll tell him that to his face."

We called Tamia. She came over with Leticia. It was a childhood reunion thirty years later. Brian and I conveyed the story. Leticia, also street smart, asked to see the computer. I logged in and went to the browser I'd shown Siete how to use, Chrome. He didn't know how to erase his browsing history so we followed his digital trail.

A month of browsing verified that he'd been on gambling sites. He frequented the poker sites. He was a gambler. He visited the New York

State's Comptroller's site for unclaimed funds several times. He was in dire need of money. We checked his call log. He made a FaceTime call to a 914 number during the time of the burglary. We called the number from a blocked phone. A woman answered.

"Who's calling this number from a blocked phone?" she asked. We, in turn, asked who she was. "No, you tell me who's calling this number from a blocked phone." We hung up.

"Jacquii, you ever been to this dude's house?" Brian asked.

"No, he was always at work." I knew my response was flimsy.

"No, he has another woman. You're not the main chick. You were the side chick. And she's probably a hood rat too." Tamia was laying it on heavy, but I listened quietly.

I mentioned to Leticia that my credit card was used at a Brooklyn CVS close to Borough Park. It was a ninety-eight dollar charge that was made on the night of the burglary. She told me to give her the transaction number. She'd contact the CVS headquarters and get me a contact that would trace the credit card transaction to the exact location, the exact cashier at the exact time.

The next day, she sent me a text message with the number. As promised, Leticia delivered. I called the contact, and she was very helpful. She provided all the information Leticia said she would. I called the detective assigned to the case and asked him to visit the branch to pull the tapes.

"You sure you don't want to do my job?" he asked. If it meant solving my own crime, I sure did.

Playing the waiting game became my pastime. The detective hadn't contacted me. Back at work, I stared at my computer screen, lifeless. After putting the pieces together, I was rendered soulless and comatose. I sat in reticent capitulation.

Martine, feeling helpless, would offer me apples or oranges. I'd smile a faint one and return to my trance. I was zoned out for days. After a week, the detective sent me screenshots of the man who used my card at CVS. He purchased cigarettes, Gillette shavers, and a fifty-dollar gift card. I sent the screenshots to Tamia and Leticia.

"Jacquii, you have a picture of Siete's friend?" Tamia thought she recognized the face.

I sent her a picture of Siete and Quan. Leticia cropped the picture of Quan next to the picture of the man in CVS. The man in CVS had a black shirt wrapped around his head, but the faces looked similar. I sent the juxtaposed picture to the detective. He swore the man in CVS was white. I told him to look again. He assured me he followed him on the tape throughout the store, and he was a white man.

With little else to go on, we'd hit a dead end.

I went to see my Haitian reader in a morbid back room of a commercial storefront that sold dusty ornaments in cluttered displays and shelves. I needed answers that one could only obtain spiritually. She saw the burglary and the loss I'd suffered. She saw Siete and said he was confused. I asked her to ask the spirits if he planned the burglary or had anything to do with it. She smoked her cigar, shuffled her cards, shook her maracas over the deck, and summoned the spirits. Placing the deck back on the table, she advised me to cut the shuffled deck into three piles and place them back into one. If I pulled the 7♠, the answer was yes.

The blood in my face drained, and my stomach back-flipped when the 7♠ came away in my hand.

The 7♠, being equivalent to the seven of swords in Tarot reading, is the card of betrayal and deception. It's indicative of the hardships associated with attempting to abscond a wrongdoing through covert tactics. The card warned that when one does something secretly, hoping to be concealed and safe, something goes awry to expose that secret.

The card only served to affirm my dream and the heeding from my family. Of all Siete's riddles, this was by far the easiest to crack.

9

MUSIC WAS MY REFUGE. IT WAS MY SPIRITUAL OINTMENT DURING THAT time of affliction and distress. Rachelle Ferrell's extraordinary vocal range counseled my heart through the slow progression of compassion with every iteration of the words *I Forgive You*. I sang along with her for days and days on end. It was the only way I knew how to cope. In a blue mood, we harmonized a solemn refrain of absolution.

I continued my vocal lessons with Fay. Sensing my drastic change in disposition, she asked me to share what I was going through if I felt comfortable enough to do so. I told her everything as I knew it.

"Wow, that's a powerful story," she said, looking at me with genuine remorse. "I'm so sorry you had to go through that. Put it in the song. Take all those emotions and put them into the song. Don't hold anything back."

I was working on *September Song* at the time. As told, I put all the feelings of hurt and disappointment I could muster into a melody about the autumn months with few precious days quickly dwindling away.

My birthday season brought the family out again. I commemorated my year to come with dinners and gatherings planned on every weekend. April was the month of me. I met with my childhood friend Nivea.

Nivea and I met when we were twelve years old. Our mothers respectively put us in a Steelpan camp of sorts. She had a fiery energy with a bright smile that lit up every room when she walked in. She had the presence of a Celia Cruz even at that age. She was happy, loud, boisterous, the life of the party and a genuinely good spirit.

She sat next to me in our music theory class. To combat her boredom, she asked if she could take my notes. When I quietly said yes, she snatched my pen and pad away with such zeal my mother called me over to ask me who she was and why I was allowing her to bully me.

"No, Ma, she asked me first," I pleaded on her behalf. "That's just how she is." We understood each other from day one.

Twenty years later, we were the same little girls. We didn't see each other often, even though we lived within walking distance. We had that solid kind of friendship that allowed us to go without speaking for the majority of the year, but being a month apart, we made sure to see each other on our birthdays. It was our annual ceremony of life. Filling each other in on the yearly happenings, I told Nivea the full story of Siete.

"So that's it?" She wanted to get a proper ending. "He just walked out the apartment that day and you haven't heard from him since?"

"Yeah, I don't want to speak to him. I'm so hurt. I still can't believe he set me up like that, but I want to get this shit off my chest so badly."

"Write him a letter," she said with certainty. "You don't have to send it to him. The exercise of writing alone will help you purge your feelings." I listened to her.

That evening I got back in and wrote what came to my heart. I disposed of everything he was a part of. Whatever I couldn't donate to charity, I threw away. I needed to rid myself of the maleficent energy.

On my actual birthday, I awoke to a text from Siete.

Good morning, Queen. I want to wish you a happy birthday. I know you don't want to hear from me right now, but I just want to let you know that I'll miss and love you forever. I ignored it.

The 37th Street crew assembled again in celebration of my day. Tamia, Samiyah, and I went to Peaches for brunch and followed the afternoon up with evening tattoos. Tattooed on our wrists, we each got two hearts tied together with chains and stamped with the initials PL. The PL signified our childhood appellation, Porch Limers.

Our summers were spent hanging out on Tamia's front porch from sunup to sundown every single day. Our neighbor from three blocks down began calling us the "Porch Limers". Liming, a Trini slang, meant to hang out.

On the way back from the Village, my cell phone rang with an email. It was from Siete again. He, believing that I didn't receive his earlier text, sent the same message to my email. I finally responded with the letter I kept pre-drafted in my notes.

Subject: Re: Happy Birthday

From: Jacquii

To: Siete

Date: April 20, 2013 at 11:30 p.m.

I debated whether or not I should write to you. Considering all that you've put me through, I didn't deem you worthy of my words. I have been replaying that night over and over in my head from the poem you sent to the actual burglary.

I can't believe you would do that to me--me, of all people. All I ever wanted to do was love you. You've been living on the lip of insanity, wanting to know the reasons because you're doing the same things and expecting different results. The difference with you is your knocks will remain unanswered. No doors will open for you, from the inside or out.

You're using your talents and God-given gifts for evil and not good. There's no way you'll ever reach your full potential by keeping the company of those gutter rats you call friends.

I understand now why you like games so much. For you it's all about winning. Our entire relationship was just a game. Well today I say: Congratulations, Champ! You've won! I surrender. You came, and you conquered. Does that make you feel better?

I hope the next time you're graced with the company of royalty, if you're ever granted a next time, you'll recognize it and know how to act in its presence. Please stop contacting me.

When I first wrote the letter I, as always, sent it to Trent for his gut reaction. He wasn't a fan of this particular rebuttal.

"It sounds like you're admitting defeat; *You won?* What's that about?"

"No, he'll understand what I mean. It's more sarcastic than it is conceding." I was trying my best to sell my literary intent. "He won't read it as a win at all."

The subconscious truth was I was at my lowest. I was reduced to a decadent condition of weakness. Siete never responded. I was sure he read it, but he didn't say a word. His silence drove me into a deeper fixation. I found myself reading and re-reading the letter I'd sent. Each time I read it, I relived the betrayal, hurt, and pain. Instead of healing my wounds, I was gouging them. What could I do if he wasn't stirred by my defects whereas I loved his?

I needed someplace out of reach where I could banish it. Someplace out of sight and out of mind. As long as I held tight to the missive, it would forever haunt me. I decided to delete all traces of the letter from my computer, iPhone, and being. I'd be remiss if I didn't mention that the message herein is an assimilation of the real one, but I know he still has the original.

Deleting the letter didn't address the craze, though. I spent my spare time researching personality traits and disorders. I had to understand what made Siete function the way he did. I found three that spoke to his personality traits and had similar attributes; narcissism, sociopathy, and psychopathy.

After comparing these personalities, everything I'd experienced crystallized in my mind. While I definitely couldn't speak to the intricate balance of nurture versus nature, all of what I knew about Siete and his childhood pointed to the fact that he was a psychopath. If I was off by a little, he was most definitely a malignant sociopath. He was a chameleon who viewed the world as nothing more than a playground on which he could manipulate the players and pieces to achieve his goals, good or bad.

May 2013, I began opening myself up more and more to the possibilities of love. I spent a great deal of time in Carlos's barbershop. One reason being his notorious lateness and the other because he created a happy and familial vibe. Carlos, a barber by day and DJ by night, was a genuinely good spirit. He loved laughter, food, drinks, and happiness.

Not one for confrontation, he did his best to ensure that everyone was content at all times. His soul brought people together in a way that the music alone couldn't. When Carlos was around, we all knew we'd be in for a good time. Friday nights had the most action. The shop would be full of clients, music, home cooked meals, and drinks. It was an afterwork hang that helped ease my mind of its troubles.

"Don't worry yourself, Jacquii," Carlos, always the optimist downplayed the burglary. "That's a small thing. Life is good."

I took up with one of the barbers, Grayson. He was a younger, handsome man who erred on the side of pretty. He grew out an unkempt beard to make himself seem less so. He was tall, skinny, and had the voice of Barry White with a thick Southern drawl. He spent the majority of his life in Georgia and was two years new to Brooklyn after completing six years of a ten-year bid for armed robbery at age eighteen. His early release was predicated on his ability to prove a legal mishandling of his case on the prosecution's part.

Despite his past, he was a gentleman with the ladies and a father-figure to the children. He was often quiet, observing everything through the corners of his eyes. The most disciplined in the shop, he cut his clients nonstop, only stopping once or twice for a bathroom or weed break. He had a crush on me, and I was finally free and available to notice it. I liked his discrete style.

I figured he'd be able to keep our clandestine affair a secret, and we thought we were doing a good job at it. He had an immature quality about him that brought out the jealousy and possessiveness in me. He'd bring other girls who were just *friends* to the shop to hang while he worked. They'd be unnaturally close, eating from each other and cozying up in the corner. One to keep my cool, I'd in turn, flirt with the male clients in the shop whom I knew liked me, leave with them, and call Grayson when I got home to see if he was okay. It was a senseless tit-for-tat that would take us over the deep edge.

It was during the Friday night festivities at Carlos's shop that I met my gay BFF, Andrew. Andrew was a smooth dark-skinned man with bright, big eyes. His eyes, which often made many uncomfortable, possessed the ability to see beyond. He was a spiritual Baptist teacher who only wore the top designer labels. He had a sharp, cutting wit that was lethal to the faint of heart.

He held nothing back. Whatever came to his mind came to bear. He detested the *queens* and was sure to let them know this every chance he could. His denouncement of his own kind confused most heterosexuals but made him a favorite of the *straight*, curious male species. We bonded over his MacBook Air that he recently purchased but didn't know how to use. I immediately fell in love with his sense of humor and candor.

One night on our ride back home, I revealed my relationship with Grayson to Andrew.

"Honey, you're just slow to the race. Everyone in the shop already knew that. The only two people who didn't were you and Grayson." I couldn't stop laughing at his delivery.

"Is it really that obvious?"

"I knew about that for months now. You can't hide something like that from black people, Jacquii."

He was right. Black people just had an innate aptitude of sensing two of their own in love. It must've been a spiritual aura that exuded a pheromonal scent which screamed, *Alert! These two people have the same sexy funk! They're smashing!*

"But let me just tell you. You see how quiet he is? Still waters run deep, honey. Don't get it twisted. When you put that one down, put him down *EA-SY!* He's a lu- to the na- to the tic. You hear me? I'm not asking you. I'm telling you!"

"What do you mean, Andrew?"

"Oh, you fuckin' women. I swear all of you are so flipping slow. He's crazy! And it's genetics. His mother is a madwoman. I know her well from the church."

"But what does crazy mean? Crazy how?" I was determined to understand what level of crazy I was supposedly dealing with.

"You go ahead with him and find out. He has demons of a different kind. And you know how to push a man's buttons. Don't worry, they'll find your ass in Georgia somewhere strung up in a basement. Keep trying to see how crazy he is."

I laughed so hard. Andrew had a way of telling me things that, although were meant to warn, were so funny I'd take them lightly.

Grayson and I continued, not concealing as much. We hung out openly at the shop and started to display ourselves as a couple. This made a lot of the hairdressers on the other side of the store envious. My name was constantly jumping up in *steel band*, which was the Trini way of saying confusion and gossip.

On the home front, I was still in apartment 2E. Although I felt much safer, it began to attract a swarm of flies through my kitchen window. Somehow, several flies would come in and I'd trap them in the closed window until they died. My apartment was never dirty, and I didn't keep food out at all. I'd later learn that the flies were a spiritual omen warning me of potential danger lurking in the midst.

In addition to the gossip and lies being told about me, the flies signified me spending too much time with something or someone of a destructive influence. The flies bothered me for weeks afterwards, but I continued on with Grayson, who was helping me move from apartment 2E back across the street to the building where I first lived as an independent woman.

I found a nice, spacious two-bedroom, two-bathroom apartment with a balcony in the building where everybody knew my name. I knew I'd be safe there. Lucas and Grayson bonded during the move, and Grayson was surprised my brother was older and so thuggish.

Happy to be in a new apartment, I spent the majority of my days putting things in order and buying new electronics. I gave my old 55" flat-screen to Carlos to put in the shop. It was old to me but was new to everyone who saw it. I gave away chairs and TV stands to make way for the new. It would take longer to decorate this apartment, but Trent and I shopped often, gradually making aesthetic changes.

The shift with Grayson came in early August. I met him at work in Long Island for lunch one evening. We were having a conversation about one of the girls he'd developed a close friendship with in the shop. He warned her about her current love interest telling her that, with this fellow, she should've just *wet her feet*.

I turned the conversation back to us and asked if I was his friend and came to him for advice about he, himself, what he'd say. He said he'd tell me to *wet my feet* as well. That burned in my brain. My inner-voice often pestered me to put a succinct and happy end to my dealings with Grayson. I just had a deep-seated perception that if I didn't, our relationship would have a volatile finale.

What sent our fling into a downward trajectory was Carlos's annual boat ride party. We didn't come to the event together. I came with Tamia, Samiyah, and Andrew, and Grayson came with the female hairdressers from the shop. He spent most of his time on the boat ride with them.

He was flanked by one of the beauticians' friend whom he'd flirted with in the past. It appeared that I came on their scene and interrupted their brief courtship. Noticing my apparent disapproval, he danced with me for five songs and quickly returned to the other side of the boat.

I spent the rest of the ride with another man I was rumored to be in a relationship with, even though we were just friends. This sent Grayson into an uncontrollable rage that he took out on an innocent bystander because he was too egotistical to avow my careless actions affected him deeply. The entire day was cataclysmic and would only get worse.

Later, at Negril Village, Andrew and I went over the events of the boat ride.

"You and Grayson really need to admit that you two like each other more than you're saying. I don't understand why you're keeping your feelings so close."

In true gay fashion, he vacillated between consolation and scandal. "But, girl, I have some tea. And it's about you, honey. If you tell anyone you got this from me, I'll deny it. One of Grayson's clients came in the shop the other day and said you were a homewrecker. They said you ruined Collin's marriage and you mashed up his shop. Grayson didn't say anything, but you can tell he was listening."

"Oh really? Who's the client?" I was seeing red.

"I'm not telling you because you'll start a whole big drama and I'm not able right now."

"No, just tell me who it is. I won't say anything. I just want to know for my own edification."

"Mm-hmm, edification, my ass. You want to start a bacchanal."

I let it go. I knew without doubt I had to end the relationship with Grayson. This was getting to be too childish, and I felt myself regressing into a morass of adolescence. I called Grayson that night, but he didn't answer. This only put my imagination in a surmising place. He's probably laid up with that girl from the boat.

I said a prayer to my ancestors asking for guidance. "Ancestors, I pray to you this evening to guide me in this relationship with Grayson. If we're to be together, please bless our union, but if we're not, I ask that you please bring a swift ending and that I come out of it all unscathed."

Closure was coming.

We spoke the next day at lunch. "Hey, Gray, I called you last night after the boat ride."

"Yeah, I saw I missed your call," he offered innocently. "After the boat ride, I came home, smoked a blunt, and knocked out."

I didn't believe him. "Oh, okay. Listen, I've been thinking. *Let's chill.* There's rumors circulating in the shop that I'm a homewrecker and I destroyed my ex's marriage. I don't want my name in anybody else's mouth, so let's just take a break. I'd still like us to be cool, though."

"Who called you a homewrecker?" Remembering Andrew's oath of silence, I maintained mine.

"I'm not saying. But it's true and came from a trusted source."

"Aight. If that's what you want. I'm cool." He seemed to be fine with my decision. I breathed a sigh of relief. "Yo, let me call you back, love." He hung up.

I thought he went to eat. About a half hour later, he called back.

"I called Carlos and told him the next time I see him at the shop, it's on."

"Wait." My ears couldn't believe what Grayson was saying. "You just threatened your boss and told him you're gonna fight him when you see him?"

"Yeah, I did. I know he had something to do with that homewrecker conversation. He's a hater. Every time I have someone, he got something to say to break it up. I told him I'm gonna break the windows to the shop. So when he see that, he's gonna have to fight me. And I called Bryce and told him the same thing. People want to talk, then let's talk. But I'm kicking ass first."

I froze. The shit went from zero to one thousand in a matter of minutes. I had no idea how I was going to clean this one up.

"Gray, I need you to calm down. Then I need you to call Carlos and apologize. You're taking this way too far. No one even had to know what we spoke about. How did it get to this?"

"Nah, if he want to talk to me, he knows my number. I'm going back to work." He hung up.

An hour or so later, my phone rang. It was Andrew.

"Jacquii! You told Grayson anything?" he asked with an exasperated tone.

"Yeah, I just finished talking to him. I told him let's chill."

"Chill? You told him *let's chill*? Bitch, I told your ass to let him down easy. This mad-ass gone and called Carlos and Bryce and threatened to beat both of them the next time he sees them. He's talking about getting a gun and breaking all the windows in the shop. Carlos is calling me panicking, talking about 'he doesn't know what to do.' Bryce is calling my phone saying, 'he's scared Grayson will cut him with a straight razor while they're working' and 'how he didn't sign up for this.' You sure all you told this man was *let's chill*?"

"Yes, Andrew. All I said was *let's chill*. Those were my exact words. I told him I didn't want my name in anyone's mouth and people in the shop were calling me a homewrecker."

"Well I can't believe this man would do all this over a *let's chill*. This could only mean one thing. Your vaginal walls are diamond-coated, honey!"

It would take several phone calls from several different people to talk Grayson off the ledge. When he did finally calm down enough to realize the folly of his ways, he, embarrassed by his actions, decided to quit the shop. Andrew was right all along; Grayson was a walking paradox of a man.

Once again, I was a wrecker of sorts. Just this time it wasn't a home, but a barbershop, which felt like home to many, including me. All his clients were covertly furious with me, and the beauticians no longer had their daily dose of eye candy. I couldn't catch a break. I was an outcast. I lost ten pounds in a matter of two days. The compounded stress took a physical toll on my body. With a naturally slender body of a dancer, I was losing my feminine curves. At Andrew's bidding, I continued to cut my hair by Carlos's shop.

"Who cares if people talk about you? The only time people stop talking is when you're dead. And sometimes that doesn't even stop them."

He was right. My actions wouldn't be controlled by Grayson's lunacy, and Carlos was too much of a good barber to start from scratch.

I waited a week before I contacted Grayson again. I felt badly that he quit his job at the barbershop. I visited him at his day job in the city. He worked as a dog groomer in the day and made house calls at night so as not to leave his clients stranded with no barber. Carlos was out of town on a gig, so I asked if he could come to my house to shape me up. He agreed.

"So, you don't think what happened was a little too extreme?" I asked, trying to psychoanalyze his paroxysms of rage.

"When I get mad, I just go off." He wasn't lying about that. "With my disorder, I usually have to breathe and count before I react, but that day I just blew. That's why I smoke weed. It keeps me calm."

I appreciated his honesty. His use of the word *disorder* didn't slip by me either. He was diagnosed with some sort of mental illness and was given tools to cope. I could only guess he was referring to Borderline Personality Disorder.

"So, you don't think you should talk to someone frequently about it?" I continued but didn't want to pry too deeply. "Someone like--a therapist?"

"Nah!" He was suddenly defiant. With the chilliness of a killer he said, "I'm good!"

With that, I was finally persuaded I was trying to have a rational conversation with crazy. He finished the cut and decided it was still too early for us to be platonic friends. I was still a trigger for him. He kissed me on my forehead and that was our goodbye. I spiraled out of control.

* * *

Early the next morning, I met Pamela. She drove us to JFK airport where we departed to Montego Bay for five days in the sun.

Pamela was my right hand in the office during the summer months. She was my sister from another mister. The same age as I, she was a self-proclaimed *fiery Leo* who took no shit and quickly removed herself from any unhealthy situations.

She was the kind of woman who annulled her marriage within a year when her then husband didn't meet her expectations. She chose to become closer to herself. She was comfortable in her own skin and loved the company of her cat.

Pam was also my accountability buddy. She called me her *Green Post-It* because my expectations were always unrealistically high, and I required everyone around me to perform on the same intellectual level as I.

"Jacquii, this is you," she demonstrated one day at work by standing on an office chair and putting a green post-it on the ceiling. "You're up there. Not everyone can reach that level. Sometimes you have to be okay with the idea that some of us, if not most, can only meet you half way."

Stubborn, it would take me a while to truly grasp what she meant and accept it.

On the beach, the day after my Grayson saga, she was in her glee. Her *green post-it* was having a normal, humanly-flawed breakdown.

"It's okay, my green post-it, you'll survive. This too shall pass."

"Whatever, Pammy Pam. I'm just going to lie on this beach for three days and eat jerk chicken."

Lie I did, for three full days from dawn to dusk, on the beaches of RUI Palace with no sunscreen. Sam was equipped with her collection. She'd occasionally refresh the coat and turn ever so often to distribute the tan. As a Jewish woman who spent her summer vacations at Coney Island beach, she was a pro. I didn't think black people tanned. Was I ever so wrong.

When we returned home, Andrew was the first person to see me besides my mother.

"Well, you look entirely horrible. So this is what you went to Jamaica to do? Lie in the sun for three days and get crispy black. Eww, look at your skin, it's blistering and bubbling. God is too wise to make a mistake, honey. Darker skin does *not* suit you." Once Andrew got started, he didn't stop. "Why would you do that to yourself? What happened? Grayson's madness rubbed off on you?"

I was annoyed with his banter, but I had to laugh. There was only one Andrew.

He was correct. I was burned. I was so badly burned, Halle had to bring me cases of water from Costco. She made me put Shea Butter on my skin every day to soothe the burns. Between the shea butter and water, my skin peeled every single day. It was as if I was shedding my old skin and making way for the new--a rebirth. It would take two whole years for the tan to fade completely. I never laid in the direct sun ever again.

I over-indulged myself with work. This seemed to be the pattern whenever my personal life was too over-stimulating. Once again, I was asked to present at the iNACOL Symposium. On October 27th, Sidney and I flew out to Orlando for three days where we stayed at the Disney World Resort.

The trip to Orlando brought a sense of peacefulness and serenity that I hadn't had in a long time. I was extremely relaxed and at ease. It was usually in this frame of mind that I had my clairvoyant visions. The night before we left, I had an interesting dream that I had to share with Sidney.

"Sid, last night I dreamt about Siete."

"Well, thank God it was just a dream!"

Of my sister circle, Sidney was the one who was affected most by the burglary. When I sat in Starbucks and detailed the total nightmare to both she and Halle, she cried. While she knew he was withholding information and advised me to do my inspecting, she didn't suspect him of theft. Witnessing my hurt upset her deeply.

"I know how you feel, but the dream felt so real, Sid. He and I were a couple. We were in the police precinct talking to the detective about solving the burglary. He wanted to catch the real guys who did it. Apparently, he was innocent in the dream. Then it switched to me being in the barbershop in Carlos's chair. Siete drove by the shop to drop off our son, kissed him goodbye, kissed me, and said he'd see me later. Grayson was back in the shop cutting as well. He was standing in the station next to me cutting his own client."

Sidney looked at me for a minute, processed the dream, and said, "Please don't reach out to him. Leave that in your dreams." She ended the conversation there.

Thanksgiving came. One not to celebrate the holidays, I'd planned to spend the day with my mother at her house. I was thankful and decided to share my thanks on Facebook.

This morning I awoke to welcome a new day of thanks and gratitude. Greeting the attributes that I dislike most about myself...

I sent thanks to Hughloy, the pimple that comes up on my forehead every time I ovulate. I thanked my tan, that's a direct result of three straight days in the sun and that which refuses to leave. I thanked my body that fluctuates between slim and slimmer, depending on life events. I thanked the grey hairs which seem to sprout out between the brown hair follicles every day.

I'm thankful because these flaws keep me grounded. They make me realize that behind every pound, pimple, blemish, and grey hair there's a story. Something profound that makes me uniquely Jacquii. So I say all this to say that I'm most thankful because I'm not just beautiful, but I'm beautifully flawed. Happy TG Day, my beautifully flawed FB fam.

Pam read the post and commented immediately.

You finally got it! I'm jealous of the tan you still have as mine has faded, but thankful you're my Green Post-It friend. Happy Gobble Day! I had to love her light-heartedness.

That night I retreated to my home, sat on my living room couch, and watched *The Purge*. Enthralled with the movie's tension between the absurd and the highly possible, I almost didn't hear or see the phone ring. It was Siete. I hesitated for the first three rings. I answered on the fourth.

"I know you're dialing the wrong number." My attitude was on ten.

"No," he said calmly.

Not satisfied, I repeated, "I *know* you're dialing the wrong number right now."

"No. I'm not."

"Why are you calling me, Siete?"

"First of all, hello. How are you?"

"I'm fine. Why are you calling me?"

"I was in Brooklyn. My friend out in Coney Island invited me over for Thanksgiving dinner. And being out here I remembered you, of course. But I also remembered the dinner you made for me last Christmas. And it bothered me that we weren't on speaking terms, so I decided to reach out. I tried calling you before. I was surprised you answered this time."

"I wasn't going to," I admitted. "I don't know, Siete. I really don't know what to say." Tears, accumulated within a nine-month long dam, flowed limpid. "I just don't want to believe that the entire two years we were together was all a lie."

"It wasn't," he answered contritely. He sounded as if he was crying over the phone. "I neglected you. As your man, I wasn't there for you. And because of my absenteeism, you accused me of something I'd never do. I didn't keep you safe. I admit I was a bad boyfriend. That I'll admit to, but I won't admit to violating your space."

"So who did, Siete?"

"I don't know. It could've been the super. Or there's a possibility that the people who committed the first burglary followed you to your new place. But it wasn't me or Quan. He's not even built for that kind of stuff."

We stayed on the phone for a half hour talking about the highs and lows of our experience together. With the knowledge that we weren't going to solve anything over one phone call, I ended the discussion.

I awoke to a text message.

Good morning, can we talk?

I knew his patterns well enough to know where this would lead, but I wrote anyway.

Siete, I really don't want to maintain contact. In fact, I don't even want to write this message to you because it'll only open the floodgates. At this point, I don't think we have anything else to talk about.

He came back with a speech that felt staged.

I know how you must feel. I apologize for the way our relationship ended. Our relationship was dysfunctional at best, and it was all my fault. I didn't respect it enough to realize its value. The only reason we remained together as long as we did was because of you. You were determined to keep us alive with your love and hope. I know I shouldn't be asking you this. In fact, I'm pretty sure you'll say no, but do you think we can meet to talk about this over dinner? I understand if the answer is no.

I concurred and told him to meet me at Peaches that Sunday evening for an early dinner. When I arrived, I sat outside in my truck and sent Tamia a text message.

Hey, Tam, I'm over here at Peaches meeting Siete. Yeah, you read right. Siete as in Siete Jackson. We are meeting up to talk. Check on me in a few hours. If I don't respond or go missing, here is his full name, his phone number, his address, and his place of business.

She wrote back, *I'm on it. I have it filed. I'm not judging you. I understand you need closure. I'll check in on you every hour.*

I walked in thinking I arrived before he did when he came out the bathroom and behind me. My heart did a little jig of happiness. I wanted to hug him, but still unsure and ill at ease, he extended his hand for a business-like handshake. We sat, ordered food, and drinks.

"I've been here before. I like the food here." Being from Queens, he relished the Brooklyn-based food locations that resonated with his stomach. "Thanks for meeting me. You look nice."

I thanked him. I'd taken extra care in putting myself together. Having lost a significant amount of weight since we'd last been together, I didn't want that to be the main focus of our reunion. I distracted him with my beauty. He spoke about his promotion to director of finance in the dealership. I spoke about my brief affair with Grayson. He wanted to know if we were still together. I told him no.

"I'm sitting across from you," he said between bites, "and it's like I'm talking to a mini female version of myself. Your movements are like mine. You're using similar jargon. Stop copying my style, buddy."

"What can I say?" I was amused. "You made an impression on the kid."

"You know," he reflected, "I can't listen to A Tribe Called Quest anymore because of you."

"That's on you. I listen to everything still. Nothing will come between me and the Tribe." We laughed a familiar laugh. It felt good. It felt like home. After we'd exhausted all threads of communication, we called it a night. He paid the bill and walked me to my car.

I, putting my hand on his cheek, professed, "I miss you!"

"I miss you too."

We drove our separate ways. I called Tamia to let her know I was safe and to fill her in on the specifics.

When he got in, he sent me a text with a sad emoji.

Why the sad face? I asked.

He wrote back, *Because you're there, and I'm here. Alone.*

Parking is too crazy in your neighborhood. Was I really considering driving out to Queens?

I know. I wouldn't ask you to at this late hour anyway. He followed this text up with another one of a card with the King of Hearts on one side and the Queen of Hearts on the other. The King had a tear in his eye.

Why is the King crying? I asked.

Because he knows this will be the last time he'll ever see his Queen.

I thought for a minute before I wrote back.

It doesn't have to be. I was mindfully hatching a plan to get closer to the veracity of the night in question.

Fully cognizant, I enthusiastically ventured into the lion's den--again.

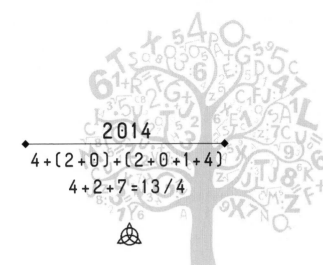

$$2014$$
$$4+(2+0)+(2+0+1+4)$$
$$4+2+7=13/4$$

Four Personal Year

Death, rebirth, foundation, organization, structure, work. This is a cycle of rebirth. The old you, and everything that no longer serves you, have been put to death. It may not feel good to lose that which has given you the most comfort and security; but it was just familiar. The familiarity of your past is now over, as it can't follow you where you're going. The weeping of the night is now over.[5]

---

[5] (DannyTarot, 2020)

"We are a broken melody, song incomplete,
And here still I lie with you and kiss you softly.
Two kindred hearts in search of a love so divine,
But can't give love completely.
I envy your ability to sleep when
You are the cause of all my hurtful memories.
You are my blue in green."

◈

1 0

A MONTH IN WE WERE OFF TO A MUCH BETTER START THAN THE FIRST time. The second time was definitely the charm. The pleasures of being engulfed in the arms of a lover already versed in the curve and the line, the depth of the stroke, the press of the lips, and the taste of the tongue felt like generational time travel over many past lives. Our souls danced, a soul spasm outside our bodies, in amorous astral projection. Teleported home, we were born again.

I spent more time at Siete's place. He was excited to host because he'd just purchased a new sleigh bed. His home had more of a lived-in ambiance. I recently opened my home up to Erica, who was between apartments.

Erica was originally Trent's friend, but we took a slow liking to each other. She and I both grew up in Flatbush and had similar upbringings even though she was of Dominican descent and I of Trinidadian. She and I were Midwood and Murrow High School girls respectively. It didn't make sense to have an extra bedroom and bathroom and not share with someone, reliably in need. I had a new roommate, if only temporarily, and Siete needed his privacy. I made the trip to Queens multiple times a week.

We kept our reunification secret--not because he wanted to. I didn't know how to tell my people. I was especially concerned about telling my mother. I wasn't sure how she'd react. For this reason, we attended family gatherings singularly. We'd call or FaceTime each other while there wishing the other was as well. It would take some readjusting, but we were willing to do whatever it took to make this reinstatement right.

Siete was expressly attentive. He'd matured a great deal in the nine months we were apart. He called more. We spoke--really spoke about our feelings. He allowed me to rehash conversations over and over until I was able to find peace. He made room for unspoken sentiments.

He attributed this in part to the relationship he had after ours. He claimed shortly after we dissolved he was introduced to a young lady whom he then became involved with and allowed to move in. She lived with him for a little less than eight months until her immaturity and lack of cleanliness drove them away from each other.

I was jealous. How could he do with her what he'd forbidden with me? I had to talk it over with Trent to get a better understanding of the male psyche.

"J, it has nothing to do with you really," Trent said, speaking in generalities. "A man's movements are always dictated by timing. She just happened to be in his life at a time where he felt he needed to grow up and make changes. You might have been the one to teach him that. The lessons, when learned, are not always implemented with the teacher."

I learned a while ago not to force a woman's position on a man's logic. Men were often honest with those of us who just listened. So I did. Siete said the same exact thing Trent did when I brought the topic up. As *timing* would have it, he wasn't rushing into anything as residentially binding with me since he'd just come out of a live-in situation with her. Kairos had different plans for us.

In any case I was joyful again. My weight started to tell the story of a woman in a special kind of love. I was filling out in all the right places. My face was rotund and rosy. Siete noticed the changes quickly.

"You look really nice," he greeted me one morning over our FaceTime call. "You're glowing."

I was. I was happy to be with him. Things weren't peachy, though. One night we were having our usual afterwork phone call when he mentioned my mother.

"Where does your mom live?"

"She lives close to me. Why?" My latent suspicions were awoken.

"No reason. I asked because, when everything happened, I was most concerned about my relationship with her. She and I were building a good rapport. She was my basketball and sports buddy. I feel like I need to have dinner with her to smooth things over and clear my name. I'd like it to be just she and I, though. You can't be there."

There was no way in any version of reality I was going to allow him to have dinner with my mother in my absence. My antennae went up. After we hung up, I called my mother.

"Gwen, let me ask you something." My mother had since requested that we call her by her first name and not any semblance of the word *mommy*. I, having a habit of condensing everyone's name to one syllable, called her Gwen instead of Gwendolyn.

"Did you have any of your financial documentation in the safe when it was stolen?"

"Yes, Jacquii." She had a slight attitude. "I had all the quarterly statements of all my investments in there. That's why I had to take additional safety precautions after the theft. Why are you asking?"

"I was just wondering, that's all." I couldn't tell her the real reason for the inquiry. I now knew why the private dinner was a priority for Siete. The keeper of the purse strings, my mother was the new target. I badgered Andrew for spiritual insight.

"Andrew, do you see anything shady with Siete? Are you picking up on any bad vibes?"

"Why are you even talking to that man again?" Andrew didn't know we were in a full-blown relationship. "I don't know, Jacquii. The gift doesn't work like that. It just comes to me."

"I know, but you don't see anything at all? When you go to sleep tonight, meditate on him," I insisted.

"Well, I saw him earlier." Andrew was tapping into the spiteful queen dwelling inside him.

"You saw him earlier where?" I was doubtful and intrigued at the same time. Where was he going with this line of conversation?

"I saw him here. He came to my house." Now he'd crossed the line.

"You're such a cantankerous *bulling* ass. Not every man who sees you wants you, Andrew. You're always going after some woman's man."

Bulla or *bulla man* is Trinidadian nomenclature for a homosexual man. It's our equivalent to the Jamaican term *batty bwoy*, but it's not loaded with the same degree of malice.

The accusation was unfounded, but the concept of the action alone sent me into an ire.

"Really, Jacquii? Really? This is how you're carrying on over this dumb shit?"

"You don't know him. Don't get comfortable to make those kind of jokes about him with me. He doesn't concern you." I was going to shield what I held sacred.

"You're just a dumb cunt! That's what you are!" He hung up the phone.

I called him back several times during the night to curse him out further, but he didn't respond. A simple discussion turned into an argument that would end a friendship. Knowingly or unknowingly, Siete had a way of putting an end to my closest and most antagonistic relationships whenever he came around.

Winter came with a new wave of responsibility. Brynn left her principal's post in Newark and was assembling a board for her newly proposed charter school. She was steadfast on running a school her way, and was determined to have me on her board as president.

Brynn and I were friends from the department of education. We worked as technology staff developers. She was a pretty mix of Puerto Rican and African-American. When we were in the same room, we normally turned heads with our tall statuesque appearance, fierce outfits, and high stilettos. We each had an exotic look distinctively our own.

She was the kind of friend who was perceptive, intelligent, highly opiniated, and ofttimes bossy. In fact, she called herself Miss Boss Lady. She and I bonded after I provided monetary assistance a few times when needed. Aware of my organizational talents, keen work ethic, and ability to turn vision into action, she elected me board president despite my meager attempts of refusal.

Every Monday night, Erica and I had to end our dinner hangs early so I could get on the conference call with the board members. Brynn would take her post as the Queen Boss Lady and administer tasks to us, her servile minions. I was resentful. I didn't want to be president. Nor did I want to give the little free time I had to yet another educational venture. My nine-to-five obligations were all I'd graciously commit to.

With me becoming increasingly disenchanted with the system, my day job only served to provide the financial means for me to do what I really loved, traveling and singing. In allegiance to our friendship, I stayed on the calls, listening to her rant about finding a viable space for the school or fundraising expectations, which it seemed I carried the bulk of as president. It was torturous. I'd vent to Erica at dinner and brunch.

"Find a way to step down from the post. Do you have to be president?"

"Apparently, according to the bylaws, I have to serve in the post for a specific amount of time. There has to be a quorum with a unanimous vote for me step down. And someone has to be identified to take my place because the board can't operate at any time without a president or designee."

"Damn, it's like you signed your life away. I'm pretty sure you can have a conversation with her to tell her how you feel." I put it on the back burner because vacation took the front.

* * *

My mother and I went to Trinidad for Carnival. We were gone for three weeks in March. We stayed in St. James, a district in Port-of-Spain central to Woodbrook and town. We were high on a hill close to Fort George, a fort from 1804 which still had its original cannons on display.

At the very top the hill, one had a broad view of Port-of-Spain and the Gulf of Paria, overlooking festively colored domiciles swaddled by greenery and car lights flickering like lightning bugs in the dark. It was a trek for us to get up and down and hard for some of the natives to find. I made the trip often, going down the hill for fresh coconut water each morning or good Trini Chinese food in the evening. The sun was at its peak at 7:00 a.m. Any attempts to stay cool after the morning walk proved to be fruitless.

My trip was ruined after Carlos's MCM bag with his laptop and hard drive were stolen. We'd just left an all-inclusive fête that he DJ'd in Valsayn and went to the Oval to see Machel Montano perform. The car we drove was broken into and his belongings taken. The thief also stole one side of my favorite pair of red stilettos.

The thievery triggered too many ill memories. I was ready to go home. Lucky for Carlos, he was able to fulfill his contractual obligations by using his other DJ friends' equipment. After all, it wasn't about the music as it was his voice and his spirit. His fiancé bought a new Apple laptop down to Trinidad when she came in a few days later, and another DJ on the island whom he'd forgotten he'd loaned his backup hard drive to came through. He hadn't lost his collection.

I'd go to adjacent rooms in our shared apartment to call Siete and keep him abreast of the happenings. He never expressed his disapproval, but I could tell my constant traveling was beginning to weigh on him. I called him during our stay in Tobago promising I'd come see him as soon as I landed the next day, bearing gifts in the form of Hennessy White. He was ecstatic.

Andrew would email me while I was away to tell me my brother, Lucas, would deceive or betray me in some way. It was a prophecy and peace offering. I ignored them both.

A week after I returned home, I came down with a severe case of bronchitis. I tried to work, but the coughing was incessant. I was on my way home one afternoon when I received a call from ADT.

As the detective said, I never made the slip of leaving my new apartment without arming the alarm first. The dispatch representative received an alert that the patio door was open. I told her not to send any authorities over. I was home and would check it out myself. When I did arrive upstairs, the patio door was indeed open. Strange, it was closed and locked that morning. Too tired and sick to make a big deal of it, I went to sleep.

I was bedridden for a week watching the *Walking Dead* on Netflix. Still vain and afraid to catch anything, Siete kept his distance. He called every day to make sure I was okay but never visited. He claimed I got the bug from *kissing one of those Trini boys* while I was away. I laughed at his idiocy. I spent my days sleeping, eating heavy foods, and watching the *Walking Dead*.

The infection was taking a while to get out of my system. Aside from the balcony door opening, the toilets would flush, waking me out of my sleep. It was confirmed that I had spirits in my home, but I was too sick to care. I just said a prayer asking that they be good spirits protecting me and went back to sleep. I'd come to find out later that the spirit was my maternal grandmother, Alexandrina.

The charter work with Brynn continued. In fact, it picked up with intense speed during my vacation. Brynn was busy meeting with elected officials in various Brooklyn districts to get buy-in for her middle school proposal. As president, she wanted me to accompany her on these meetings.

I had no problem assisting, but in the absence of a written proposal or application, I wasn't comfortable leading the conversations. I knew the mission, vision, and principles of the school but had no knowledge of the innerworkings aside from a school schedule. I needed the full blueprint. Whenever I'd ask Brynn for the written proposal, she'd say she was still writing it or it was close to completion. I've yet to see the written application.

The final stroke was Brynn's expectation that I'd lead a district meeting in Bedford Stuyvesant without her. She didn't give me the message until the day before. She advised the day of, two hours before the meeting, that she wouldn't be attending because she was speaking to another district at the same time.

I refuted the delegation. I don't fly by the seat of my pants, and winging it wasn't my idea of preparation. She had to be there. This was her project and it had to be her delivery. She showed up with an unpleasant attitude, and I knew this wasn't a work relationship that I wanted to be a part of.

When we did meet with the board, they tore into the school proposal. They rebuked us for being negligent in our research as the need of the community was viable high schools, not middle schools. They found the curriculum to be insufficient, citing the school as an alternative after-school program.

Long story short, I couldn't have led the meeting without Brynn present. We left knowing that there was more work to be done, but the work would be hers. I planned to step down from my post as president, but I'd let her know that after the girls' gala I was throwing for my 38th birthday.

Sistah's Sippin' Champagne was the name of the gala. I was hosting in my new apartment. Nearly a year in, I furnished the place almost exactly as my Crown Heights abode. I just added a new entertainment system, rug, red bar stools, and many pieces of artwork. I decorated the balcony with an outdoor rug, two rattan chaise lounges facing each other at a slant, stargazer lilies, and solar-paneled night lamps. My new place was significantly bigger than the last two, so the guest list grew to seventeen ladies. Sixteen showed. This was the biggest and most expensive gathering I'd thrown to date. I gave Trent a maximum budget of one thousand dollars. He in turn, hit me with a sixteen hundred dollar invoice. Even though I'd asked the ladies to chip in, I'd still have to come out of pocket. I was stressed, but the show had to go on, and go on it did.

I created a special, six-hour Gala Tunes playlist for the evening that started with smooth R&B, moved into house, partied into pop and hip-hop, and winded down with calypso and reggae. On the menu there was, Trois Oeufs Farcis (an assortment of deviled eggs), fish tacos, Blu Bird (grilled chicken with blueberry barbecue sauce), garlic confit, duck à l'orange, watermelon salad, crab puffs, bruschetta, lobster cups, finger salad, and red velvet cheese cake. The signature drink was a Grand Marnier Strawberry Mimosa.

Trent's server for the evening bailed at the last minute, so Erica agreed to assist.

My quarters were cramped with sixteen ladies. The buzz of five to eight conversations transpiring concurrently was an earful. I had to restore some sense of order, so I took the floor with my story. I told the story of the second burglary. I was grateful to have Tamia in attendance because she filled in the blanks and reenacted a lot of Siete's body language and movement. Her acting brought the narration to life.

I concluded the tale by saying, "And he's coming here tonight to address you all. He wants to speak his truth and clear his name."

My girls didn't have time to digest the full narrative or their feelings toward it, when in some synchronistic conspiracy of fate, the bell rang followed by three knocks on the door. Siete had arrived on queue. His arrival couldn't have been better planned.

The room exploded in pure pandemonium. All professional women, my Christian friends clutched their pearls and made a sign of the cross, my drinking friends ran to the kitchen to refresh their glasses, my shrewd business-savvy friends strategized, my happy-go-lucky friends laughed their asses off, and my street savvy friends squared up for battle.

Brynn, sitting to the left of Keisha, took an oath of verbal vengeance.

"Oh hell no. It's on. I'm going to light into his ass. I don't care what he says. I don't like how he did my friend, and I don't believe anything he has to say."

This scenario was too surreal to be true.

Siete greeted me with a kiss. "Wow, you look great."

I was eating a lot while I was ill and the extra weight added some thickness to my hips. He strode in with confidence and surety. I fixed him a glass of Grand Marnier and told him I'd just finished briefing the ladies on the events that took place. The floor was his. He addressed the full room of beautiful and baffled women with mastered elocution.

"Good evening, everyone, my name is Siete. How are you?" He paused waiting for the faint *we're fines* to come through. "Thank you for giving me the opportunity to address you tonight. I told Jacquii I wanted to speak to you all because there are a lot of misconceptions floating around about me, and I want to get a chance to clear them up."

I was sitting on a bar stool facing the larger crowd with Siete standing to my left. Out of the corner of my left eye, I spotted Brynn shaking her head and screwing her face. She wasn't having it.

Siete continued. "I'm not going to go over the events since Jacquii already told you what happened; however, I do want to say that I had no involvement in the crime. When I met Jacquii, she was perfect. Well, let me not say perfect because nothing and no one is perfect, but she had and still has a lot of the qualities that I deem suitable. If I'm guilty, I'm guilty of being an absentee boyfriend.

"I promised to protect her and love her, but I fell short. Because of my absence, I was blamed for the event. And rightfully so. I'm not mad at her or anyone else for thinking it was me. Anyone looking from the outside in would say it was, but I stand before you today declaring my innocence. I love Jacquii, and I'd never hurt her."

His opening statement left room for the ladies to interject comments and clarifying questions.

Keisha opened the door with Oprah-like sophistication. "So what's the ah-ha moment that made you realize you weren't a good partner, and what will you do differently in the future?"

Siete, quite prepared, held court. "Well, quite naturally, after we broke up I had time to reflect. I went over the things I'd done and said that I didn't follow up with. And with us being apart, I realized that I had the woman I'd always wanted. I lost my best friend and the woman I wanted to spend the rest of my life with. So, naturally, I found someone else and tried to do right by her, but it wasn't Jacquii and it didn't last. I love Jacquii. I plan to marry Jacquii."

The ladies filled the room with *whens?* Siete and I laughed.

"Very soon." I was surprised by his revelation.

Brynn could no longer hold her silence. "So you said in your opening speech that you were guilty of being an absentee boyfriend and for that reason you were willing to take blame for the incident. Wouldn't that mean that you were essentially guilty of it all?"

Brynn, noticeably aggressive, was using legal tactics she'd acquired as a lawyer to trip Siete up.

Siete, accustomed to arguing for a living, positioned himself behind me, leaning on the bar stool. He rebutted without breaking a sweat, "No, you said I was essentially guilty of it all. I said, as an absentee boyfriend, I could understand people using me as a scapegoat, because I wasn't actively involved in the relationship. It doesn't mean that I confessed to anything other than that."

The ladies held their breaths. This was getting too intense.

Brynn, dissatisfied, came back again. "It doesn't make sense. If Jacquii was the love of your life and the *perfect* mate, as you say, why weren't you involved?"

"For many reasons. I had work obligations. I work long hours. I get home extremely late. I'm physically and mentally exhausted. That's not the energy I want to bring home to my lady, so I take time for myself to decompress. Just so happened, the night of, that's what I was doing. But again, I won't take the blame for the burglary, nor will my friend."

Tamia stood to get a refresh on her drink, with the mention of Siete's friend, her ears perked up. "Which friend are we talking about?" She looked at him askance.

Siete, sipping his cognac, wasn't expecting Tamia's bit of comic relief. He laughed, covering his mouth to prevent himself from spitting his drink on me.

Jeanette, still not sure Siete answered Keisha's questions fully, revisited the first inquiry. "But what was your main takeaway from the entire experience?"

"Siete!" Trent, listening to the interrogation with Erica from the kitchen, had had enough. "Come into the kitchen. That's enough of the Q and A, ladies."

Siete was freed. He stayed in the kitchen for ten minutes giving the ladies time to breathe and digest. In the background, Mobb Deep blared boastingly about being timeless and priceless. Siete came back into the living room just in time to hear them say *Flyness*. He leaned on the wall closest to the speaker to hear one of his favorite songs.

The tone of the room changed after Siete spoke. It was hard to get the ladies focused enough to have heartfelt conversation. We opened the floor to speak about relationships in general. I asked the married ladies in the room to provide guidance and counsel for us who were still single.

Nivea, recently separated, stood up to charge her phone. "Don't ask me shit about marriage. I'll tell you that."

Rosaline laughed. She offered up some wisdom. "Oftentimes, people get married for the wrong reasons. Marriage isn't about the way someone looks or the sex. After time, you get old, looks fade, and the sex is infrequent. There has to be something more substantial that binds the relationship. You have to genuinely like each other's company because you end up more as friends as time goes on." Siete listened to her intently.

Siete stayed around for a half hour more, ate some food, and prepared himself to leave. He, feeling triumphant, made sure to shake the hand of every lady in the room on his way out. Brynn and Belle didn't accept his hand. He quickly moved through to the other fourteen ladies, his eyes resting salaciously on Samiyah, who was beautiful and thick, just as he liked.

Once he left, the room felt lighter. The ladies could truly be themselves again. Most were touched by his gallantry, others circumspect. Belle was among the guarded. Having studied people for the better first half of her life, she suspected him of premeditated, masterful manipulation. She saw a gleam in his eye after he'd spoken that said, *I got 'em!* She wasn't about to get got.

I promised I'd never invite another man, other than Trent, to one of my sister circle events again.

My mother sat in in deep quietude as she listened to my recount of the previous night's events. This was my unveiling of sorts, my pseudo-reintroduction to the new Siete. I relayed in deliberate and careful detail, ensuring I emphasized his redeeming qualities. I spoke of our covert romance.

I rationalized his eagerness to stand before my friends and endure a *sistahs'* inquisition was justification that he was indeed an innocent man. After all, no man who's done intentional harm would continue to reap life's rewards in the form of professional promotions and accolades.

As I presented my defense, Brynn called. I could only guess that she was still fuming over her heated exchange and wanted to contribute her analysis of Siete's speech. I sent the call to voicemail telling her I was with my mother and I'd call her back via text. She urged me to call her back that night. When I rested my case, my mother, not normally the religious type, beamed with unforeseen delight.

"See what God put together no man can put asunder. Things work out the way they're supposed to. Sometimes you have to let someone go to see if he'll return, and if he does, that's love. I was thinking it could've been the super in this case as well."

Still having one eye open on Siete, I wasn't so sure I agreed with that one, but if it smoothed things out for us to be together and for me to finish what I started, then so be it.

I didn't call Brynn back that night. I wasn't mentally prepared to deal with the barrage of pessimism that awaited me on the other side of the receiver. Instead, I called Siete to tell him I'd told my mother about us. We had her blessing. That solace would be ruptured the next morning.

My mother called with consternation in her voice. "J, I was thinking about everything you said last night and something doesn't sit right with me.

"I don't trust Siete. I don't trust that he came back with good intent. And that story he gave you about meeting that woman after you broke up was a lie. He was always with her. They were always living together, and they most recently broke up. I can't tell you how to live your life, but you keep your head on with him. After all, he *is* an actor. Don't forget that. And ... I don't want him anywhere near me."

Just like that--grand opening, grand closing! I wasn't one to argue with a mother's intuition. I had doubts and a mission of my own. I had to see this unearthing through its entirety.

Siete and I continued on despite my mother's caution. While he wouldn't be at the family gatherings and functions, it felt good that I was no longer sneaking around to see him. We became closer and he began to let me in on childhood incidents, family FaceTime videos, and his book collection.

He introduced me, through discussion, to the *Seven Spiritual Laws of Success* by Deepak Chopra. He said the book enlightened him in ways no book before ever had. I ordered the book and read it on my own accord. I'd report back my correlations between the Laws of Pure Potentiality and Detachment to my own spiritual struggles. He marveled at my ability to comprehend and apply the written text. I guess he needed additional indication of my intellectual capacity.

He, being a voracious reader, suggested that we start a book club, the two of us, alternating picks every two weeks. I jumped at the opportunity. Not only would we get closer through our love for words, but I could manipulate his thoughts through my book choices. An ingenious idea, this was going to be fun.

He gave me the honor of choosing our first book. I chose, *The Five Dysfunctions of a Team* by Patrick Lencioni. The book was an easy-to-read fable that detailed the organizational breakdown of teams due to the absence of trust, fear of conflict, lack of commitment, avoidance of accountability, and inattention to detail.

Our relationship suffered from all five dysfunctions. I was hoping, through its purposefully crafted conveyance and exercises, we'd be able to identify the collapse within our earlier attempt, and he'd be motivated to re-establish our relationship based on the five tenets of trust, conflict, commitment, accountability, and results.

We met to discuss the book on Memorial Day evening. We took a walk through his neighborhood while we compared notes. Our approach to reading the book was so similar, we connected over two sentences:

A fractured team is just like a broken arm or leg; fixing it is always painful, and sometimes you have to rebreak it to make it heal correctly. And the rebreak hurts a lot more than the initial break, because you have to do it on purpose.

The majority of our discourse was focused on this one quote. The notion of rebreaking on purpose to promote proper healing was as profound as it was accurate. We inferred that our second coming was the healing after the rebreak.

That evening the lovemaking was divine. We indulged in each other until we were satiated. I can't recall if it was the magic within the words or the lust in the air, but we looked extremely sexy to each other. The attraction was stronger than it had been in a while. We pounced on each other with renewed sexual vigor.

In the heat of the night, I asked that he come inside me. I knew I was ovulating, so the odds of getting pregnant were high. He obliged. Once again, I heeded Halle's advice and propped my behind up on a pillow to assist the semen through the uterus, to the ovary. We'd then wait to see if that union was as viable as ours.

My next pick was going to be transcendent.

I painstakingly scouted for *the book*. I was looking for one that spoke to my heart and my undertaking to uncover the truth. I thought I found it, but I sent it to Siete first since we decided we'd each vet the book before committing to it. He wrote me back quickly.

This book is dope. I ordered it immediately.

Sanctioned by his endorsement, our next book choice was, *Forgiveness: Twenty-One Days to Forgive Everyone for Everything* by Iyanla Vanzant.

I needed to come to a place of forgiveness to fully absolve Siete. Through reading, I realized I needed to forgive myself first. Siete immediately gravitated toward the forgiveness of self. I guess he was silently atoning for his transgressions.

The book was designed for the reader to scan an *Emotional Triggers List* each day prior to tackling the exercises. On the list were many character traits, some of which weren't so appealing. I tried to get Siete to share his emotional triggers list with me. He refused. I wanted to get a scan of his list to compare it to the character traits of the narcissist, but he, always calculated, said I'd use the list against him. I wouldn't have condemned him for his shortcomings, but he wasn't that far off.

It was going to take us some time to get through this book. Each of the twenty-one days was assigned to a specific person or physical phenomenon we had to forgive, starting with the self. It was a deep dive in redemption. We checked in with each other each week, but it would take us a full month, if not more, to confront our respective demons.

A few weeks later, Siete surprised me with tickets to the Mets game at CitiField. I wasn't thrilled about the game, but what I was exhilarated about was the 50 Cent G-Unit concert immediately after. He got us seats in the front pit. When we sat down, he instructed in a gruff and unpolished manner.

"Listen, we're in the front of the field so you have to pay attention. Be aware of your surroundings and don't sit here looking dazed because the ball comes flying into the crowd, and that shit *will* hit you!"

I tried my best. I was bored out of my mind. I focused all my might and telepathic energy on the score board willing it to skip to the end of the ninth inning. I knew I wasn't good company on that outing. Siete sat next to me making videos mocking my ignorance.

"Look y'all, she don't know what she's looking at. She has no idea what the hell she's looking at."

He was right. It wasn't like he was making an effort to teach me either. We decided to take a food and bathroom break before the show. His best friend Quan was also in the stadium, but he and his fiancé were sitting in another section. I was content with the separation, but Siete wanted to connect with them during the break. We ate in separate sections. The food, not up to my standards, was merely sustenance to get us through the long day.

Siete and Quan met up while I was in the bathroom. When I came out, he greeted me pleasantly. I found my place behind Siete. I didn't feel safe, spiritually, in his presence but returned the salutation.

The concert was great. 50 was an excellent performer. This was the first I'd seen him live so I was impressed with his stage presence and ability to connect with the crowd. The G-Unit crew was fine at best. Lloyd Banks held his own, but the others didn't make quite an impression. The night turned cold quickly up in the stands. After all the dancing I could, I was ready to leave.

When we got back home, I asked Siete to drop me off at the pharmacy around the corner while he found parking. He wanted to know why.

"What's the matter? Is your throat hurting? Are you coming down with a cold?"

"No, honey. Not every trip to the pharmacy is for Theraflu or Nyquil. Just meet me in a few minutes."

He did, bringing a much-needed hoodie for me to cover myself. For early June, the weather was still on the cool side. We walked back to his place laughing at his silliness regarding what we'd do if we were under attack and on foot. I was wearing sandals, so I was an easy target. In true Siete fashion, he found a way to shed comedic light on my culture.

"Well, your ass is Trini, so you should be able to take those sandals off and run on the concrete barefoot with Usain Bolt speed."

"Don't you worry about what my Trini feet could do. I'll use them to kick you in the knee-cap."

"That's another thing. Y'all Trinis always like to kick. What's that about?" We laughed all the way home, but the laughter wouldn't last long.

We spoke with his mother and nephew over FaceTime. His family lived in Virginia. He and his brother were the only two in Queens and New Jersey. We told his mother about our book club and the recent book we were still delving into, *Forgiveness*. She was impressed and proffered that she too was a literary aficionado. She, however, preferred books that leaned heavily toward the mentally macabre like *Flowers in the Attic* and Stephen King's most recent works.

After his mother went back to eating, Siete spent quite a bit of time on the call with his nephew. I went into the bathroom to take the pregnancy test I'd bought at the pharmacy. It had been three weeks, and I had an innate feeling I was pregnant. I didn't have symptoms, nor was I feeling lethargic. I just knew. Three minutes later, my instincts were precise. I rushed Siete off the FaceTime call. I wanted to give him the good news.

"Baby," I said excitedly. "Tell Brandon you'll call him back. I want to show you something."

He disconnected. "What's up?"

"Baby, I know you said you had dreams of being a motivational speaker, on stage, with your son and I in the front row of the audience. Well, you're one step closer. You're going to have your own Brandon."

I showed him the pregnancy stick with the positive results. He moved away from it, afraid of the urine.

"It's covered with the plastic cap. You won't touch anything unclean. Geez," I said slightly annoyed by his revulsion.

"So what does this mean?" he asked in outward shock.

"It means you're going to be a daddy."

He wasn't happy at all. This wasn't the reaction I anticipated. I allowed him some space to process. He walked out the room and immediately got on the phone to return a friend's call. I must have waited for half hour. He didn't acknowledge me or what I'd just told him. Rather, he confined himself to the living room, speaking loudly about trivialities. I waited some more, went into the bathroom, washed my face for bed. I waited some more, put my sandals on, packed my things, and headed to the door. He ended the call.

"Hey! Yo! Where are you going?" He intercepted my exit by placing himself in front the door.

"I'm going to Brooklyn," I answered indignantly.

"What's in Brooklyn?"

"My crib! Where *I* live. Since you obviously need time to process this. You can do it without me." I kissed him and moved out of his way. I left his apartment, ventured back into the frigid June air, and drove home.

Timing my travel back home, he called as soon as I entered my apartment.

"Baby, I know my response wasn't what you were hoping for. It's just that I'm shocked. I wasn't prepared to hear that. It's just a bad time right now and I don't know how this fits."

"Siete, there will never be a *right* time to have a baby. You said you wanted one. We're both thirty-eight years old. We aren't getting younger, and I'll have more complications as I get older."

"I just need time to think about it. That's all. My reaction doesn't mean I don't love you. Because I do--love you."

Dignified as the ultimate mantra of love, I found myself tiring of those three words.

Calling Brynn back wasn't as immediate as she'd hoped. Consumed by the unforeseen twists of life, my attention was occupied elsewhere. Erica moved out to Trent's place. She still hadn't found the ideal apartment, but she didn't want to cramp my style. I was fine with her staying as long as she pleased, but she felt as though she was overstaying her welcome.

It didn't help that my mood swings over Siete probably made her feel unwelcomed. It wasn't about her. He was a conundrum of magnanimous depth. I did, however, call Brynn and text her. She didn't answer. Considering all the newborn stress I was under, I had to write her a note telling her how I felt.

Subject: Charter School Updates
From: Jacquii
To: Brynn
Date: June 10, 2014 at 11:57 a.m.

Hey, Brynn.

I sent you a text and called but haven't heard back, so I'm sending this to you via email. I hope all is well and that you're in good health and spirits. I wanted to let you know that I will be stepping down from my post as president of the board. I do love and support your dream to be principal. But to me, it's just that ... your dream.

I have no desire to work outside of work hours on building a school. I expressed this to you when you asked me to be your business manager in Newark last summer, when you were writing your proposal for the charter school, and at the first board meeting in your home. I've just reached a point in my life and career that I want to do what makes me happy.

I've worked at various levels in the DOE and have seen enough bureaucracy and politics to know that this work is definitely not fulfilling. It's a means to an end that allows me to devote my time honing and crafting my musical talents. I value our friendship too much for it to end over a business venture; and with every conference call, community meeting, fundraising request, etc. I find myself growing more and more resentful. I'm resentful of the process, resentful of the work, and resentful that I'm not being true to myself.

So I hope you can receive this well, as I don't feel that I'm doing my just due to this post or your mission. I appreciate that you value my work ethic, but I can't slave after slave hours on something that's not mutually beneficial. I apologize in advance if this presents any inconvenience to you or your work. I will be sending my official letter of resignation later on this evening.

Love Always,

Jacquii

Subject: Re: Charter School Updates
From: Brynn
To: Jacquii
Date: June 10, 2014 at 11:12 p.m.

Hey, Jacquii.

First, let me say that the fact that you included in your email a reference to *this business venture* possibly ending our friendship, gives me *pause* in that there may be some *subtext in the text*. But since I don't know what it is, where it may be coming from, or if my assumption is valid, I'll just include two facts:

1. If you think that this email may have that potential, then you don't truly know me, and/or there's no validity to our friendship, as this isn't a deal breaker.

2. I'm going to be just as candid as you were in your email, so please don't assume I'm angry. I'm only expressing my feelings.

I appreciate you being candid about your feelings, but to send this via email is an insult to me and to our friendship. If I didn't return a phone call, that probably means that I didn't get it. If you sent me a text and I don't respond, that probably means that I didn't get it. I **ALWAYS** return any and all correspondence from you. That has never changed.

So I'm not sure how vigilant you were in trying to reach me considering that I called you several times and the last text message that I received from you indicated that you would call me later that evening; a phone call that I never received. So I know you like to write out your lengthy soliloquies 😊, but we've never had them between us, so please let's not start now. Again, why I think there may be more to this email than meets the eye, but I'll address that if you so choose.

By the way, you don't need to recount the positions that you've had in the DOE to me. I know your work history and I have my own so that felt a bit *shady* to me. Why are you going there? You're talking to ME, not some newfound friend off the street who doesn't know you or what you've done and been through. Really?

As far as my dream to be principal, it's not a dream. I know and hope that you know me better than that. I have already been a principal. This vision isn't just a position but a legacy that will live beyond me. It's to give children the opportunities that they wouldn't have considering the climate of education and the bureaucracy that you speak of and that I too am sick of seeing prevent real education from happening.

Therefore, I'm not looking to repeat bureaucracy but to move beyond it and in spite of it. But I say this, not to change your mind, but to make clear my intention; one that you once shared in the past. If you're feeling *resentful* of this work, then I never meant to inconvenience *you* or burden *you*, my *friend*, with wanting to share in that vision; if only for a moment, because it meant something to *me*, your *friend*. I'd do the same for you if the situation were reversed, even if I didn't share the same level of interest, enthusiasm, or dedication.

To me, you support your friends in whatever they choose to do because you see that it brings them joy when you do. I have asked you repeatedly for an invite to one of your shows, but you refuse to allow me to show my support to you on that front. Hopefully, one day soon, you will change your mind.

I ask repeatedly because, as your friend, your success is my success, and vice versa. That, to me, is what true friendship is about ... making sacrifices for those who you allegedly care about and consider close to you. So again, maybe I'm reading more into our friendship than there seems to be, but again, you let me know if you so choose.

Is the fact that you want to resign now, an *inconvenience*? No. It's beyond inconvenient. It's a disappointment. Disappointing because one of my alleged *good friends* is abandoning me right at the eleventh hour because at this moment, self-interest is more important than self-sacrifice. But like everything else, *this too shall pass* ... meaning, I will work it out like I normally do. No worries.

By the way, when we discussed your joining the Board, we did speak about you only going as far as the interview in Albany and receiving the charter. Then we both agreed that you could *exit stage left* at that time, and I'd have someone replace you. Because, according to my recollection, we agreed that this wasn't something that you wanted to do long-term, but you agreed to assist until that point, then step down. There was no agreement for it to ever be any longer than that; all of which end in early September.

Additionally to be clear, I never thought that the few things that you assisted on over these past six months were that burdensome to you. If they were, we should have had this conversation long before now. If you felt like you were *slaving* in this endeavor, then it was never my intention for you to feel like a *slave*. Again, only thought you were supporting your friend.

Last, there will be no need to send an official resignation letter, as I'd not want to add any further unnecessary tasks to your plate or life. To be clear, it wasn't your work ethic that I appreciated, considering that 95% of the work, I do. It was mostly our relationship that I valued and respected, and I wanted people who supported me to be the closest to me, so that I can remain clear, focused, and see things from different angles with objectivity and clarity. Those are things that only my friends can give me.

However, as I type this, I feel like I may need to reevaluate the friendships that I have. The latter isn't said as a slight to you, but it is what it is at this point and seems to be a reality check for me.

Regardless, I respect your decision. Thank you for informing me. Hopefully, you too receive my response to your email well. After all ... it's just an honest exchange between friends. ☺

Best,

Brynn

We continued for about three email exchanges more. I told her that she was way too intense, and she tried to pay me back for a brunch she felt she owed. We never did meet up for that brunch on the 21st of June. I, too overwhelmed with the pregnancy that I was determined to keep, the rocky relationship with Siete, managing work that was no longer gratifying or worth mentioning, maintaining presence of mind and spirit in my singing, gave up on the relationship.

I scoffed at her interpretation of sacrifice. I was plagued by self-sacrifice--a sacrifice of self for professional recognition, the sacrifice of self for love, the sacrifice of self for family, and now the sacrifice of self for the sake of friendship? Never would I subject myself to building someone else up, leaving me undone.

Who, in this entire narrative, was sacrificing themselves for the realization of my goals? What Brynn viewed as a legacy, I regarded as egocentrism too often misconstrued as work done in service of others. It was about building a name and reputation for *herself*. My pursuits were frowned upon by academics like Brynn because it was intangible, impractical, pie-in-the-sky, considered too risky; but it was in direct line of sight and alignment with who I really was at the core.

My art was a form of healing. I needed to heal myself *first*. In that healing, there were wounds too fresh to expose to others. They needed time to fester, drip, and ooze, then form a new layer of skin. I wasn't going to allow my friends, as much as I *did* sacrifice for them, to guilt me into changing my course or rush me into sharing what was solely mine. Not until *I* felt I was capable, and it was right to do so.

Because of this persistence, the sunset had fallen on yet another season.

I regarded her audacity with derision. *Sacrifice?* With all that I'd suspected about Siete, I was subconsciously sacrificing relationships for the sake of saving my own with him.

11

PREGNANCY HAD A WHOLE NEW MEANING THIS TIME AROUND. IT WAS AS IF a wave of selflessness came crashing over me. I felt the urgency to share everything I'd learned in life with the fetus growing inside me. I understood why my mother looked at me with tender eyes. I understood her need to make sure I had all the tools I needed to be great, and I was ready to do the same for my own child.

So mother and daughter set out for an impromptu afternoon saunter through Prospect Park. It was one of our dedicated pastimes, but fluctuating hormones and mood swings of extreme magnitude caused me to be awfully short-tempered. Knowing how and when to maintain peace, my mother placidly held her corner, taking her social cues from me.

On this Sunday afternoon in June, however, I bowed my ego to her matriarchal tutelage with the humility and eager receptivity of a misguided student in search of a long sought out master. We walked the first quarter mile in stillness along a winding, naturalistic watercourse fringed by a belt of opulent trees, breathing the fresh prana into our lungs and souls, enjoying the syncopated beats of the runners' footfalls that landed between the rhythms of African drumming in Drummer's Grove. I started out gently.

"Gwen, I asked you to walk with me today because I'm struggling with something and need your maternal insights."

"I knew you needed something," she declared with adamance. "You've been nice to me of late."

"What do you mean? I'm always nice to you." I knew this wasn't true.

"Hmm. Whatever, Jacquii. Just tell me what's going on."

"Well," I said disinclined to go on, "I'm pregnant for Siete and I've decided to keep the baby."

"Whew," she said, sighing with relief. "I was thinking you were going to say that the two of you eloped. I was getting ready to take your name off all my documents."

I nearly fell out with amusement. Always the financial planner, she had her sights laser focused on her bottom line, and no one would get in the way of that.

"You laugh, but I'm dead serious."

"No, we're not married," I confirmed, "just with child."

"But you always said you didn't want to have children. What happened now?"

"I don't know. I suddenly feel different. I feel like I have so much love and knowledge to give a child right now. I see the way you look at me, even at this age, and I want to feel that love for my own.

"The problem is Siete isn't as excited as I. He wanted a son at first. But now that I'm pregnant, he's shut down. He says he's not ready for a child. He's so strange sometimes. He said now he'll have to learn a whole new person and get to understand if his or her personality meshes with his. Who says that about his own child?"

"Hmm. That's a strange reaction, but he's right about that. Many of us don't stop to think about the personalities we bring into the world. But leave him the hell alone--that jackass of a man. Always up to something.

"You're at a point in your career that you can afford to take care of a child. It's not the ideal situation. You know I'm not a huge promoter of marriage, but raising a child alone isn't easy. You'll have to sacrifice some things and alter your lifestyle a bit, shop and travel less, but it won't be a financial strain.

"If this is what you truly want to do, then do it. Everything will work itself out. I'll help out when I can, but I'm not taking on any full responsibilities. I raised the two of you, so you will raise your own."

"Yeah, that's what all grandparents say before the child comes."

"Ha! You know me better than that." Three times a grandmother on my brother's side, I really did, and she meant every word.

My mother hushed, inwardly in thought for a bit, before she spoke again.

"Just know," she said, "once you have this baby, that man will forever be in your life whether he says he wants it or not. You need to prepare yourself for that."

As we journeyed along on our three-mile walk around the park, the heaviness of single motherhood dissipated. I was going to be just fine.

Siete was mad when the positive results were confirmed by my gynecologist. He didn't want a child. The pipedream he'd sold me was another of his illusive fantasies written for chumps and the naïve. He believed I was making a choice for both he and our unborn son.

I knew this one was a boy. I could feel his calm in my spirit. I sang to him when I was home. I sang with a vibrancy that I'd been missing. It felt good to extend and contract my abdominal muscles with every breath, supporting each note. I was breathing and birthing life simultaneously.

Siete and I fought every night we spoke. With each argument he'd gradually get angrier and angrier. He was annoyed that he didn't have the power to control me. This was a pronouncement I didn't have to run by him. It was my body, my decision. He was rendered helpless, and that toyed with his alpha male ego. Trent assured me Siete was simply scared and needed time to come around. I'd have to consider going through the gestation period alone. I was considering going the entire life cycle alone.

"Listen, Siete, I'm not having this baby to keep you or to hold you down. If you feel this is too much and you don't want to be in our lives, you can leave. It would be sad to raise a son without you, but we'll be fine."

I never imagined myself as a single mother. That wasn't how I was raised. It wasn't what I grew up seeing in my household, but I wouldn't deny myself the joy I felt. He'd become still at my declaration of independence.

Despite our differences, we had two major events to attend that neither of us wanted to miss. The first was a basketball game. Siete's pal organized a game among friends at the world-renowned Madison Square Gardens. He rented the space for four hours, and the guys had access to play on the same grounds as their icons.

This event was in progress for months. When Siete called to tell me about it, I told him I was waiting to see who he'd take as his plus one. The idea that I'd even have to compete with his friend was disturbing to me, but Siete assured me that I was unequivocally his first and only choice.

I nagged Siete for months about his preparation for the game.

"Honey, are you practicing? Did you go to the courts? Can you even move the same with that extra bulk?"

Each time he assured me that he was so athletically adept, he could bounce back easily. After all, he was in the gym every other night.

He came over to my apartment the Saturday night before the game. We ordered jerk chicken, oxtails, and Rasta Pasta from Footprints Express and again, the topic of conversation was the baby.

"I just think it's selfish of you to make a decision for two other people; one, *me*, who's telling you he isn't ready, and the other who can't even fend for him or herself." He was trying to implore me to reevaluate my right.

"First of all, it's a *he*. Second, it's my decision to make. I'm sorry, my love, but in this court, the man has no say. You originally told me *you* wanted to have a child. Now that I'm pregnant, you want out. What that says to me is it's not that you don't want to have a child. You don't want to have one with *me*."

"How can you say that? I'm with you. I love you. If I was ready to have a child it would certainly be with you. It's not the right time. I'm not where I need to be financially."

"Siete, you'll never be where you want to be financially. Like I said, if you don't want to be here for us, you don't have to be."

"This is the third time you told me to leave."

I didn't know he kept count. That night we broke one of our cardinal rules. We went to bed angry. I slept on the farthest side of my bed. I didn't even want his feet to touch mine. There would be no sexual exchange that night. If he didn't want our child, then he wouldn't indulge in the act of making one.

The next morning, Siete sat on the couch watching Michael Jordan videos via the smart TV's YouTube channel. He was a pompous man thinking he could telepathically acquire masterful skill with no physical application.

"Siete, what are you doing? Are you going to eat before the game?"

"Nah, I'm good. I'm watching some of Jordan's plays."

"So, you're thinking you can study and learn his plays through osmosis?" He didn't respond. He was too submerged in Magic Mike.

Being in the actual Madison Square Gardens on an off day with access to the full court was amazing. The home of the Knicks was too much for the guys to handle. The teams were comprised of old heads, most on the heavier side. The slimmest person there was Siete's younger brother Knox. They were on a brief hiatus, and this was their chance to unite as brothers and make amends.

I was finally meeting a family member in the flesh. Siete was in shape, but he was built like the Hulk. It took the guys a minute to get used to bouncing the ball on the hardwood flooring. Not having the same rigidity as concrete, the ball wasn't bouncing as high on the wooden surface. They had to bounce the ball harder, which required more effort.

I sat on the sidelines recording the game. From the lens of my camera, I was disappointed. Siete missed every basket he shot. His breath control was weak because his workout consisted of heavy weight lifting and not intensive cardio. Knox made one two-pointer.

Siete insisted his team won, but the player to score the most points in the entire game was the fattest one on the court. It was the irony of all ironies. I found it hard to believe this was the same person who bragged about his physical prowess like it was something to marvel. It was an embarrassment. His athleticism as a basketball player was yet another figment of his fantasticated imagination. I never let him reconcile what I considered to be a huge loss.

Tuesday, June 24, 2014 was the second and most iconic event ever planned. We went to see Dave Chappelle and Nas perform at Radio City Music Hall. The Nas concert was monumental for me because his documentary, *Time is Illmatic* was shown as a special event at the Tribeca Film Festival on my actual birthday.

I, employing a man to do a woman's job, sent the information to Siete to plan. In true Siete fashion, he neglected to follow through. I thought I'd missed out on the opportunity. Elated was I, one day at work watching Jimmy Fallon's *Tonight Show*, to see Dave Chappelle announce the addition of another booking starring Nas as his special guest.

I immediately jumped on Ticketmaster and bought three tickets; two for Siete and me because we were both huge Nas fans, and one for Lucas, who was a big Dave Chapelle fan. It was also a way for Lucas to get an accurate read on Siete from one street dude to another.

Dave's standup routine was tolerable for a comeback. It was reminiscent of Bill Cosby. Most of his jokes revolved around his family life and fatherly quirks. He made a few social commentaries on the Paula Deen and Donald Sterling controversies, but his humor didn't have the same edge as it once did.

Lucas and I felt his performance was lackluster. Siete thought it genius. The two men excused themselves during the intermission to get drinks at the bar. They had taken a genuine liking to each other. I was still very much pregnant and irritated by the marijuana smoke in the aisle behind us.

The highlight of the show was Nas's performance. Nas was majestic in an all-black outfit topped with a red velvet jacket. When he performed, he did so with ease. He didn't strain his voice or have an entourage to create an artificial hype fest. His microphone was adjusted to complement the timbre of the full orchestra backing him. The backdrop of the orchestra in front of the widescreen display of Illmatic stills was incredible. The concert was classy. It was grown and sexy. We revered Nas in divine exaltation.

Siete went back to Queens that night. I drove Lucas home to get his opinion.

"He's a cool dude. Funny as hell. I don't know, J. I don't know if he did that shit." He had his doubts.

Our moment of camaraderie and peace would come crashing down the next night on our routine phone call. Siete was still incensed about the prospect of being a father. I was tired of having the same dispute. I was emotional. We yelled. We screamed.

This was the first time we'd ever spoken to each other in this way. He threatened to leave me and the baby if I went through with the delivery. I told him he lacked empathy and was incapable of loving anyone, even himself. Again, I encouraged him to go. He threatened to do me bodily harm.

He never finished his statement, but the intent was in his words, "I swear if I was there right now, I'd ..."

His incomplete trail could've been finished with "put hands on you," "strangle you," "fuck you up." Who knew? I wasn't phased in the least. Nor was I afraid. This baby was being had. My adamance put us on the precipice of war.

I sent him a subliminal shot via text. 50 Cent's *Irregular Heartbeat* christened him a scared pussy whose fear pulsated resoundingly across the boroughs. He ignored it.

We didn't speak for many days after that. He sent me text messages saying, *Hey*, testing the waters. Refusing to acknowledge him or his texts, I said a prayer.

"Ancestors and guiding spirits, I pray to you today because I don't know what else to do. I say a prayer to the spirit of my baby, I love you. If I'm not supposed to have you right now, I ask that you come back to me when I should. If I'm not supposed to have you with Siete, I ask that you peacefully go and come back to me with the man I should. Ancestors, please let the baby pass easily. I don't want to have another abortion."

I said that prayer on the Friday morning. I was in the emergency room Sunday afternoon.

Sunday morning, I drove out to Far Rockaway to hang out with Trent and his girlfriend Laura. It started out as a beautiful day. I was feeling especially pretty, dressed in bright colors. I needed to lift my spirits. Siete and I were still at odds. He tried to contact me a few times, but I was despondent. I didn't have the energy to fight anymore. I wanted to revel in the expectancy of motherhood.

Trent made a breakfast of buttermilk waffles, fruit, vegan sausages, and fresh squeezed orange juice. I was fine until the afternoon. Not one to have morning sickness, I began to have lancing pains on the right side of my pelvis. I took to the couch in hope the pain would subside.

Trent and Laura went to a neighbor's house for a get-together. Trent gave me the address and told me to come get him in the event the pains worsened. An hour into my rest, I was jolted by a sharper pain. Feeling like I wanted to regurgitate my breakfast, I crawled to the bathroom. I was bleeding. I knew I was miscarrying the baby. I half-walked, half-crawled from Trent's house to his neighbor's.

"Trent," disoriented by the agony, I pleaded, "I need you to take me to the hospital immediately. I think I'm losing the baby."

We drove to Beth Israel Hospital on Kings Highway. I laid on the back seat of my truck giving Trent directions. He didn't want to take me to a hospital in Queens because it was too far from my mother. His girlfriend Laura followed us in her car. She'd drive Trent back to the peninsula later that evening.

We sat in the emergency room for what felt like two hours and I still wasn't admitted. I made several trips back and forth to the bathroom to throw up. On my third trip I stopped at the front desk.

"I've been sitting in this room for two hours. No one has called me. I'm pregnant and bleeding. I could die on your watch. I need to be admitted right now."

The admissions clerk got the nurses to clear a cot for me. It took several sonograms to find the fetus stuck in my right fallopian tube. I was having an ectopic pregnancy.

My mother came as soon as she could. Trent called her from the waiting room. She walked in with a grace and calm that was refreshing. She was dressed prettily in a silk floral summer blouse and culotte jeans. Her locs were swept in an updo.

She greeted me with a smile. "You look so pretty."

"Thank you," I said, blushing through the pain. "I was going to tell you the same thing."

She sat with me for the entire night into the morning. The emergency floor was overflowing with patients without rooms. I was grateful to have my mother at my side. She looked at me with the sagacity of a mother who'd seen it all.

"God is too wise to make a mistake. You would've had that child, and he would've come out looking and acting just like his father."

The doctor came in around 2:00 a.m. They operated on me at 3:00 a.m. I was in recovery at 4:00 a.m. My mother stayed until the operation was over. She'd return later on that day with a fresh change of clothes.

I awakened later that morning feeling the residual ache of the breathing tube that was lodged in my throat overnight. I texted Siete from my hospital bed.

"You don't have to worry about the baby. I'm no longer pregnant. You can leave now."

He wrote back immediately, "What? What do you mean, you're not pregnant. I'm not going anywhere."

"I'm in the hospital, I can't talk now. My mother is taking me home. I'll call you when I get there."

"Please do."

I stayed home from work for the next two weeks on the doctor's order. My core was in severe pain. I couldn't walk much or sit up. I laid down for most of the day. I refused to take the Percocet or any other medications. I chose to experience the full spectrum of natural healing.

I was healing quickly on the outside. On the inside, I was hollow. I mourned the loss of my son. For him, I had many hopes and dreams. I cried a lot during my time alone. Every day I held my stomach with tears of anguish, trying to reconcile the void that took the place of my joy.

Trent visited me a few days to walk me around the block for lunch. Siete ordered food and had it delivered to the apartment. He never came to see me during the recovery period. He said he talked to his mother a lot while we were on break and, through her consolation, he was warming up to the idea of being a father. Considering the Siete I'd met during the pregnancy, I wasn't swayed.

Martine was very sympathetic to my loss. She encouraged me to take the time I needed to get well. I used that time to get well *and* interview for a new position. I'd reached out to a colleague to inquire about any available positions in his wheelhouse. A week and two interviews later, he called to let me know a senior director position was mine if I wanted it. I answered affirmatively. Once again, I was officially back in Tweed Courthouse.

Siete and I still hadn't seen each other. I told him about the new position. He was happy for me but wasn't impressed with the lateral move. I wasn't either, but I knew the money would follow eventually. We were dancing a delicate tango. I was losing interest in the relationship. He seemed to want to hold on. I sent him links to articles listing the attributes of a narcissist.

Does any of this resonate with you?

He wrote back, *Some of it but not all.*

Don't you think you should see a professional therapist or psychologist to learn how to manage it?

I'm afraid I may be too far gone at this point.

His pure, unadulterated truth gave me pause. I retreated within myself to mull it over for a few days. Noticing my absence, he sent a text of his own.

What happened? No love for the narcissist? He was mocking me.

Work was new again. It was by no means challenging, but there was something about being in a new office around new people that reinvigorated my soul. I made friends within my team. Oscar, in particular, was quickly becoming one of my closest confidantes at work.

Oscar and I went to lunch together every day. We liked to sit in the park and talk about life, spirituality, dreams, and future aspirations. He often spoke about his wife, a poet and artist with whom he was still madly in love after twenty years. I often spoke about Siete, the boyfriend who never was.

We sat in the park one Monday in late August. I was at the end of the rope with Siete. I was determined to end the relationship that weekend. No longer able to sustain the façade of commitment, he fell back into absenteeism. Oscar tried to talk about it. I told him there wasn't anything to discuss. Come weekend, it would be done.

During our talk, the phone rang with a blocked number. I normally avoided blocked calls, but I answered this one for some reason. On the line was a man with an indecipherable accent. It sounded like it could be Spanish, but it was jumbled.

"Hello, is this Jacquii?"

"Yes," I said, hesitating, "this is she. To whom am I speaking?"

"Yeah, I'm calling because your brother got into an accident with my cousin. He was backing his car out of a gas station and hit my cousin's BMW. They got out the car to assess the hit and it's twenty thousand dollars in damages. Your brother tried to call the cops to the scene of the accident, but my cousin took his phone and is holding him at gunpoint. We're holding your brother hostage until you wire us the money for the repairs."

"What? What the fuck are you telling me right now? You're holding my brother hostage until I come up with twenty thousand dollars?"

I was yelling in disbelief. Oscar was all ears now.

"Yes, ma'am. We'll give you the information to wire the money."

"No, first of all, I don't understand what the hell you're saying. I can't even decipher your accent right now. Second of all, I don't have twenty thousand dollars to send to anybody."

"Well, ma'am, if you don't send the money, you'll lose your brother."

I hung up. I was pissed to the highest degree. The call didn't make sense to me for a myriad of reasons. One, my brother would never call the police to any accident for which he was responsible. As a man of the streets, that's not his first reaction to anything.

Two, the twenty thousand dollars set off alarms in my head because that was the same amount Siete claimed he owed the IRS back in 2012. Three, the caller was insulting my intelligence by quoting me a figure that was assessed on the spot. I had a body mechanic on speed dial for fourteen years. There wasn't anything anyone could tell me about the cost of body work. I'd crashed and fixed cars in the past. If the damages were really worth twenty thousand dollars, the car was totaled. It wouldn't serve any benefit to have body work done.

Four, the fact that they called me to tell me about my brother was dumb. I wasn't budging a finger for him. Yes, I loved him, but I was done rescuing him from any dangers. If he was really being held for ransom, he wasted his one and only life line. He was on his own. Furious, I called him anyway.

"Yo, what bullshit are you into now? Somebody just called my phone telling me they're holding you hostage for twenty thousand dollars ransom."

I was so mad, I didn't even make the connection that he'd answered his own phone.

"Yo, J. What are you talking about? I'm at work. I don't even know what that's about. Somebody called you saying they're holding me for ransom?" He was mad.

I ran down the full details of the call. Lucas was livid.

"I don't know nothing about that. You need to check with that dude you're with. I'm in Staten Island at work. As a matter of fact, when you finish work today, come link me." We hung up.

I called Siete.

"Where are you right now?"

"I'm at work, honey. What's wrong?"

Again, I ran through the details of the call but made a slight modification to the ending of the conversation with the caller. After the caller said I'd lose my brother if I didn't wire the money, I told Siete that I said, "Okay, well, lose him then."

Siete took the bait.

"You told the man to lose your brother?" He was clearly comparing my version to what he'd heard. "Hm. What's your brother into now?"

"No, see that's the thing. My brother isn't into shit. The question is, who else is into something? My brother is fine and at work. I don't understand why those assholes would think I wouldn't call him first."

"See, here we go again. I can't be the blame for every crazy thing that happens in your life, Jacquii. I don't have anything to do with this. Call me after work so we can talk about this. I can't talk now."

I told Oscar the full story. We both agreed it was crazy. The redeeming factor was I'd scheduled a random reading with a psychic on Wall Street. She was a Staten Islander who came highly recommended to me by my girl Natalie. I wasn't planning for this call to be a part of our dialogue. Nor was I ready to hear what would ultimately be revealed.

I met with the reader at 5:00 p.m. sharp. We convened in a rented office space in the middle of Wall Street. My search for spiritual guidance in the dank, soul-selling atmosphere of the financial district was ironical. The room was barren with the exception of a table, two chairs on each side of the table, and a massage table to our right. In her thick Staten Island accent, she began.

"There's a voice I'm hearing. That's the energy coming in. The way this works is I use these cards, but I'll still be seeing and hearing things. And in my head, I'm talking to what we call counsel. He'll give me more information."

"Okay."

She shuffled the cards as she cleared the phlegm in her throat. The reading began.

"Here we have the chariot card. You're at the point in your life where you have to figure out what direction you want to go in. You drive the car, you don't just let it take you wherever like whatever happens, happens. This is a change." She pointed to a new card. "But the change is down. This isn't good. Is there anybody who would stand in your way who would try to prevent you from moving up and forward?"

"A lot of people," I confirmed. I'd heard this from readers often. "I can't say specifically, but I've always been around people who try to impede my progress."

"It's like a jealousy, and it looks like you're going to run into more of that. But you don't have to accept that in your life. Have you read--uh, I sound like a parent--have you read the book *Ask and it is Given*?"

"No," I said unknowingly, but I was ready to receive anything that would help.

"Get that book. The authors are Esther and Jerry Hicks. Now they do what I do. They channel the spirit and tell you how to create what you want in your life. It's excellent. I can't begin to tell you. I've tried it and it works. There's like twenty exercises in the back of the book. So when you come up against this, you'll know how to deal with it. You should start it before you run into that."

She flipped through cards, placing them on the table. "Is there a man in your life who maybe will try to stop it or would be jealous?"

"Well, I got back with my boyfriend. We broke up for nine months and I wanted to know ..." I paused because I didn't want to say too much. I wanted her to reveal his guilt. "He'd be the only one. I mean, he hasn't really displayed jealousy." I was hesitating in my speech.

"Is he controlling in any way? Because what I'm picking up is, this man, in his head he has plans. He sees you a certain way. He may be trying to make peace with the way you really are and what he'd like. So, uhm, let me see what it says." She flipped through more cards, analyzing each one. "You want to stay with this guy? Cause I don't think so."

"I wanted to know if it made sense to."

"Doesn't look like it." She flipped through the cards some more. "Actually there's somebody else. There's somebody new. It's saying, like you have so much more. See this woman? She's breaking the chains. She's changing her whole life. And you'll meet someone--there's another man who will be very, very supportive.

"If you look at this card," she said, pointing to a card with two roads meeting. "There's one road coming this way and another coming this way. You'll know how to work through things and solve problems together. And you'll see things the same way. But it doesn't feel like it's this guy you're with now. It's upside-down, so you haven't met him yet. Why'd you take this one back?"

I sighed heavily. To explain my warped sense of logic would be too lengthy.

"Because he told me ... Well, we broke up because I thought he did something that I'll ask you about later. And I took him back because he came back to me asking for forgiveness. He said he wasn't the person I thought he was."

"So this is the best card in the whole deck," she said, continuing with the reading. "It's reversed, and I want to know why. Did you give him a lot of attention?"

"Mm-hmm!" I'd given him too much attention.

"And he needs that. But here the cards are saying this relationship is morphing him. Like it would be you supporting him, you understanding him."

"Yes, and that's exactly how it's been."

"So I'm asking you, why would you stay with him? There's somebody better. And even though it says end this, you don't have to go home and do it now. You can enjoy it in the meantime but know that it's just for now."

"But would it get in the way of me meeting the person I'm supposed to be with?" I asked.

"No, it won't get in the way."

She flipped through the deck that seemed to be never ending.

"This is a jealousy card. There's a heavy energy around you. So you have this a lot?"

"My whole life. My entire life. No matter what I do, to the point that I get headaches because I'm fighting the energy."

"Do you sage your apartment? Do you do stuff like that?" she asked.

"I smoke out my apartment with frankincense, myrrh, and charcoal every month," I stated.

KNOCKING FROM THE INSIDE

"If you like crystals, carry a Black Tourmaline. That's good for you. That will absorb negativity. What you can do every day, there's something called St. Germain's Violet Flame. When you get up in the morning, you picture a violet flame around you. Its taller than you are and it's all around you. You're inside this, and as you're walking around during the day, it's just there around you.

"What happens is St. Germain says that this violet flame protects you from any negativity. If the negativity somehow gets through the violet, that violet transmits it. By the time it gets to you it's powerless. You have a lot of this negative energy around you. Did you notice this when you were small?"

"Yes I did. I've noticed it my whole life."

"But you'll get your power back, and there'll be no more worries. Yeah, you'll get your power back," she said.

I wrote down the name of the crystal she suggested. She opened the floor up for questions.

"So, my apartment was burglarized twice, two years apart, two different places. I want to know who did it."

"Do you have names so we can ask about a specific person?"

"Well, the last time I thought my current boyfriend Siete had something to do with it."

"So you want to know if he's involved?" she asked. I nodded.

"This is a little tricky. If he was involved, it's not that he did it, but he'd know the people who did. And he may have tried to stop it. He tried to talk them out of it. He's somehow connected, but I don't think he did it. He couldn't stop it. Yeah, you need to get away from him. Does he work?"

"Mm-hmm."

"Does he have money problems?" she asked.

"I don't know. He acts like he doesn't."

"This looks like he does. He's got money problems that you don't know about. Yeah, he does. And these are like demons. Again, money problems. This says get out of it. Get out of this relationship.

"And even if you decide to stay, this is like don't have a child with him, don't marry him. It's not good for you. Is there really something that you want to stay for?" She couldn't understand my reasoning.

"Well, I guess I was trying to see it through."

She changed topics abruptly. "Do you have any brothers?"

"Yeah, I have one. I was going to ask you. Today I received the craziest phone call. Some guy said he got into an accident with him and he was holding my bother hostage for twenty thousand dollars. I called him and he's fine. But I wanted to know if there's anybody in my immediate circle who would be behind that call."

She flipped though the cards once more. "It's somebody you trust."

"Really?" I asked more out of irritation than shock.

"Somebody you trust. You should be wary about what you say around people. Who do you talk about money with?" she asked.

"I don't really talk about money with people at all. The only people I trust would be my family and this guy that I'm with."

The truth was, I didn't talk money with Siete. I didn't trust him with that information. Little things, yes, but nothing financial.

"The guy you're with now, does he have one friend in particular that he's really close to?"

"Yep." She saw Quan. I didn't have to mention him. She justified my dream.

"Yeah, be careful there."

"That's the person I don't like. I told him it was his friend who was behind the burglary."

"I think you hit it. I think you're right. Now it's showing me your boyfriend with this one guy. This is like get out immediately. When the cards keep saying the same thing over and over, it means this is really important for you. You have to get out. Just get out. Especially now that we're seeing it's your boyfriend and this guy.

"Yep, it's the friend. It's him. Well, now you know. And it'll happen again if you don't. You have to break all ties with this guy."

Before I left, I asked her one more question.

"You mentioned my boyfriend is trying to make peace with who I really am and how he'd like me to be. How would he like me to be?"

She looked at me and said, "Submissive."

Lucas and I met up after work. He couldn't believe the events of the day. Siete was calling my phone non-stop. This time around he was playing the role of the concerned boyfriend. I kept telling him I'd call him back.

Lucas and I strategized. I didn't tell him about my meeting with the Wall Street psychic. He wasn't too keen on readings. He didn't like the idea of being exposed himself. My plan was to say as little as possible to Siete about my reaction or next steps. I'd keep him guessing.

When I returned home, I gave him a call.

"What took you so long to call me back?" He wanted to know my every move.

"I went for a drive. I had to clear my head."

"Hmm." This was a new one coming from me. He didn't know how to interpret that.

"So what happened exactly?" He asked me to tell him again what I said earlier.

I gave the exact rundown with the added line.

"And you told him to lose your brother?" he asked. He was still stuck on that manufactured line.

"You know, I find it strange every time you come around something illegal happens."

"Jacquii, I had nothing to do with this. I'm not going to be the scapegoat for your problems. Somebody is clearly after you, but it's not me."

"It still doesn't excuse the people you hang around with. Your friend Quan is a bitch. And I don't trust him. I don't care what you say. I don't want that man around me AT ALL."

"How am I supposed to maintain my relationships when the two people I care about the most don't like each other?"

"I don't know. That's on you to figure out. I already stated my piece. He's not to be trusted. And as far as I'm concerned, he doesn't have a reason not to like me. The fact that he does further verifies that he's a bitch."

Out of nowhere came a strange shift in discourse.

"Yeah, I never mentioned anything to him about this, but when I got bagged by the police in the drug bust years ago, I always thought he was the one who snitched on me." Now he was willing to sell out his beloved to gain my trust.

I was over it.

"I have to go. I'm tired of talking about this. I just want to clear my head. I'll call you tomorrow." I hung up without waiting for a response.

Tomorrow came, and the next day, and the next. I didn't return Siete's call. He decided to FaceTime me at work. I answered, exasperated.

"Yeah, what's up?"

"Where are you? That's a nice building," he said, marveling at Tweed's interior.

"Yeah, this is where I work now. It's an old courthouse. What's up?"

"Nothing. I just wanted to see if you were okay. Tell you hello. Let you know I love you."

"Thanks. I'm good. I have to go back to work." I ended the call.

The next morning I woke up resolved that I was done once and for all. I'd found what I'd gone back in to discover, and then some. I called him before he went to work. He didn't answer. I left a voicemail.

"So, I wanted to have a conversation with you, but you're not answering. I'm tired of you coming for me. And to think I gave you an out. I sat and waited nine months for you to come clean about the burglary, and you decide to pull *this* stunt? Well, this is it for me, champ. I'm done. Deuces."

I blocked his number. I deleted his texts. I deleted all his emails. I closed my Facebook account and fell off the face of the earth. In a matter of minutes, I disappeared. There'd be no more contact. As the Wall Street reader advised, I'd broken all ties. I met with Rosaline for lunch.

"So you left a break-up voicemail and blocked him?" she asked incredulously.

"I sure did." I was feeling lighter by the minute.

"Jacquii, this isn't good. He's going to be very angry with you once he realizes you're gone."

"Please. Nine days, he'll be fine." I borrowed the saying from Andrew, unaware that nine represented the full cycle of completion.

Little did I know, Rosaline was absolutely right. This was only the beginning of a long battle.

12

FAINT WHISPERS OF PARANOIA TEASED MY SUBCONSCIOUS AS I MOVED through the subsequent days after *the ghosting*. By week two of my split with Siete, my armor of strength and surety slowly chipped away every time I replayed my lunch conversation with Rosaline. There wasn't any physical indication of danger, but in the recesses of my mind laid the foreboding sensitivity that I was being watched. Perhaps it was purely a suspicious instinct, but the seeds of doubt had been planted.

As the Wall Street reader advised, I purchased a Black Tourmaline pendant. A novice to crystal healing, the stone made me light-headed and dizzy whenever I held it in my left hand, the hand that receives energy. Nevertheless, I wore it daily around my neck and between my bosom for spiritual protection.

I made the stone my study, seeking a greater depth and understanding into its metaphysical properties and uses. Black Tourmaline was one of the most powerful protective gemstones historically used by Shaman for physical, mental, emotional, and spiritual protection.

It had the ability to absorb negative energies or physic attacks and repel them, sending it back to its sender. I'd later discover that the dizziness I initially felt was my body's reaction to the stone's cleansing attributes. Regular wear eventually grounded and acclimatized my energy to the stone's frequency.

Holding my spiritual and mental welfare sacrosanct, I also asked Lucas to move in with me as an added safety precaution. It was an arbitrary Friday evening at the barbershop when I made the call.

"*Yo!*" he answered with his customary greeting, elongating the y for emphasis.

"Hey, what's up? I was thinking with everything going on with dude, I'm not sure if or how he'll retaliate. I think it would make the most sense if you moved in with me for a while."

"Word. That'll be a real good look. I'm staying in a room at my boy's crib right now and it's not the best situation. I'll give you a nervous buck-fifty a week. And dude ain't about to do nothin'."

"Alright, but I don't want any of your people in my place. And I don't want your boys to know where I live. My space is the *Harmony Hut*, and I'd like it to stay that way."

"Nah, I'm not bringing anybody over to your place. People don't really know where I stay anyway."

"Okay. Let me know when you're moving in. I'll get you the spare key." In the quick of an instant, I had another roommate.

My brother was still working at the silkscreen printing company in Staten Island. As both a diurnal and nocturnal male, he'd leave for work at dawn, get out early afternoon, hang out until dusk, and come home during the wee hours. In Trinidad, they'd say he was *haunted* for keeping such long days. For us, it was the ideal setup since we weren't in each other's way.

He had his own sleeping and bathing quarters, and I had mine. Having been raised in the same household, he was relatively tidy save for the sickeningly sweet odor of leftover nicotine that lingered in the seams and fibers of his clothing.

I'd planned to buy groceries on a consistent basis with the extra money he was giving since he had a voracious appetite for all things food, but the plans would come to a screeching halt by second week's end of our living arrangement.

The phone call received on that Friday evening was one of a heart-wrenching kind. Lucas, being overly emotive since childhood, wasn't one to hold back tears in any situation that wounded or angered him. While it was poignant to witness a man confident in his masculinity to be free with his tears, my brother unleashed his so often that for those closest to him, his weeping bordered more toward the grotesquely tedious. Used to the sad stories and completely unphased, I braced myself for what was to come.

"What happened now?"

"Yo, J, I went to work today and these dudes are telling me not to come back to work. My assignment is done, and they'll give me my check on Tuesday." He cried between each perceptible word. "Why do they have to wait until Tuesday to give me my check, though? If they knew they were letting me go today, they should've had it ready."

"So did they fire you? Or did they lay you off?" I needed to understand the full breadth of the release.

"I was working temporarily. So they're saying they didn't get the contract they were expecting and no longer have a need for an extra guy. The timing is all fucked up. I just moved in with you and only paid a week's rent." That was the absolute truth, but I couldn't dwell on that in the moment.

"Hm. Don't cry. These things happen on a daily. I know you weren't expecting this but you can find something else to do. When you come home we can talk about it some more."

We hung up, and I went back to cleaning, which was my normal Friday evening routine. This was the first Friday in October, and as a rule I swept and mopped the floors of every room; dusted the furniture, and burned charcoal, frankincense, myrrh, three kings, dragon's blood, and sage throughout the entire apartment.

I waited for Lucas to come home before I smoked the apartment out. I needed him to be cleansed as well. He was already starting off on the wrong spiritual footing and disturbing the ethereal equilibrium of my place. My space had to maintain its lightness. He came home even more distressed than he'd been over the phone.

"So tell me what happened exactly."

"So remember I was first working there full-time and they changed management. They laid me off for a while, and I was collecting unemployment. About a year after the change, my boy took over as manager. He called me back to work as a temp because the company was getting a lot of contracts and needed someone extra who didn't have to be trained.

"As a temp, I'm entitled to four sick days. I called out sick on Monday because I was out drinking on the Sunday and woke up late. I figured I could use one of my sick days and go to work for the rest of the week. I go in this morning and the owner tells me I called out too much and that the work was slow. At first, I was going to make a scene and ask them why they were letting me go now, but I decided to chill. I just asked them to give me my last check before I left, and that's when they tell me some shit about *come back on Tuesday for the check because they weren't able to cut the checks today.*

"So now I have to travel all the way back to Staten Island to get my check when they should've given it to me before I left."

The tears came again.

"Yo, sis, this shit ain't right. I swear every time I take one step forward in life, something happens to keep knocking me back down. I'm trying to stay on the right path. I'm trying to stay out of these streets, but it's always some shit."

I sat, listening intently. I paused knowingly before I spoke. He wasn't going to like what I had to say.

"They were absolutely neglectful to not have your check ready today. Especially since it's the weekend and you normally get paid every Friday. You have every right to get upset about that, but ... you were working as a temp. The unwritten rule for temporary employees is that you don't have privileges.

"They gave you four sick days, yes, but the implicit expectation was that you took none. Until you're working full-time, you're to be on your p's and q's. There's no leniency for the temporary worker. And then, you take a day off because you were hungover. The problem with you is you get too comfortable too quickly. Your priorities are all wrong. No one owes you anything. You came to work, they paid you. You weren't guaranteed a position because you were a temp. Is it fair? Probably not. But what in life is?

"You walk around acting as if the world owes you something. Everything I've done was earned with blood, sweat, and tears. The trips I take, the days I call out, all came after twelve years of honing my craft, proving myself, and paying dues. There are no handouts for us. That wasn't in our cards. Somehow, you think people are just supposed to give you things.

"And stop the blasted crying. This is a minor setback. You take time to reflect and go back out and find something else to do. It may take some time, but you can't let this break you."

"You're right. You're right. They should have given me my last check today, though."

"Yes ... they should've, but stop telling me I'm right! I don't need to be frigging right. I need you to hear and understand what I'm saying."

In accordance with street vernacular, the words *you're right* served as a pacification to get the other person to shut the hell up. It wasn't an acknowledgement of fault or ownership but an act of placation geared toward the ignorant. I hated to hear those words, especially from my brother who had a habit of saying them whenever he was tired of being reprimanded.

As the story goes, I'd only receive one week of rent. Still adamant about not preparing meals, I started out buying food for the two of us. I'd text to find out what he wanted to eat and bring the food in on my way home from work.

I wasn't sure how the job search was going, if it was even being conducted at all. With the natural cunning and duplicity of a conman, my brother always had a story readily concocted, shaped in such a way that you'd best accept it. He always needed money borrowed to see about *a job*, but there was never any follow-up. I'd never hear about the application or notification process.

Eventually, his days would consist of him hanging out all evening into night and coming in around two or three in the morning, at which point he'd put the living room television on at a volume that ranged within the sub frequencies and binge watch Netflix shows until 6:00 a.m. Miraculously, what I'd lost in hearing as a baby, he'd gained tenfold. While the TV was inaudible for me, the reflections of the picture bouncing off the walls in the dark would wake me up. I'd have to sleep with my bedroom door closed, a practice that was foreign in our childhood household and mine.

By the time I'd awake to go to work, he'd have trudged to his bedroom where he'd sleep off the remainder of the day until an hour before I came home from work. At 6:00 p.m., I'd come home to find the carpets vacuumed, the furniture dusted, and the dishes washed. Noticing his indolent pattern, I discontinued his food supply and the restocking of the fridge. I reckoned, being hungry, he'd act out of desperation to find something fiscally constructive to do with his time.

It went this way for months. I often called our mother to complain.

"Gwen, he does absolutely nothing but sleep all day and hang out all night. I don't even think he's looking for work. At least the place is clean when I get in. But now he has a strange way of waking up and not saying good morning. He'll just pass me straight with no acknowledgement whatsoever."

"I'm not getting between you and your brother." My mother always played the role of a distant diplomat when it came to my brother and me. "The two of you made an agreement on your own. I have nothing to do with that. But I'll speak to him about living in your place and not speaking to you in the morning. *That's* disrespectful, and I don't like that at all."

He continued with his uncouth behavior until my mother did get a chance to speak to him. His greeting shifted from perturbed silence to an unintelligible grunt of a "morning."

I'd had enough. The shit was going to come to an end.

"Listen, I don't know what your problem is, but you walk around here every day like I did you something. You don't wake up and walk past me saying nothing. That's not how we were raised."

"I SAID GOOD MORNING!" he yelled at me belligerently.

"NO! You have an attitude and I DON'T LIKE IT!" I raised my voice in return. "You said, 'morning' for the first time today. And the only reason you said it was because Mommy told you to. I'm not one of your *niggas* in the street. You're not going to disrespect me in my shit, contributing nothing. And even if you were contributing, you're not going to disrespect me in *my shit*. Period!" He remained silent.

In all actuality, I really didn't need his money. I rationalized to myself that had I been in my apartment alone, as I usually am, I'd have to bear the weight of everything solely, as I usually did. Though, there was something to be said about an able-bodied man who allowed rejection to fester and become dejection, dejection to fester and grow into inactivity, inactivity to fester and rupture into unproductivity, and unproductivity to solidify a longstanding condition of bankruptcy.

I observed the gradual progression of his spiritual, moral, and financial decline. Six years my senior, he'd experienced slight rises to prominence and grander plummets to destitution several times over in his lifetime. The lack of income and sustenance coupled with his proneness to self-medicate eroded his soul. He, subjecting himself to this trifecta of disaster, began to lose weight rapidly.

I didn't consider that he too had had his fill of failures and thus, chose to plant his flag of defeat on my living room floor. Rather, it incensed me to see a grown man wallow in self-pity. As a single woman who'd been independent for fourteen years, I was never afforded that luxury.

At maximum, there was a two-day turnaround time designated to getting over my *woe is me* moments. It was my predisposition to generate a contingency plan in parallel to my bereavement. Because of that, it was hard to accept the authenticity of his downfall. I felt duped, taken for granted, and bamboozled once again. I, main breadwinner and host to a bespoken parasitical roomie, became complacent, acquiring yet another liability.

With every reversal of fortune, I found myself analyzing past relationships and my hasty inclination to discard the people I cared about most. While it's true that people come into our lives for a reason, a season, or a lifetime, I had to wonder if my relationships were merely seasonal? Or if avoidance was the easiest coping mechanism to manage?

I knew, in my heart of hearts, I craved the familiarity of my roots and the closeness of friends who saw me for who I was. I longed for laughter without judgment and pretense. I needed to be around those who would tell me what I needed to hear as opposed to what I wanted. I decided to get a haircut.

On this specific day, however, I sat next to Andrew in concession to his prophecy. I'd seen him at the barbershop during previous visits. Still fuming from our last phone conversation resulting in the *cunt* misnomer and successive phone disconnection, I ignored his presence.

"You were right about my brother trying to deceive me," I conceded. "Thanks for sending me that message."

"Please, you know how long ago I sent you that email? It's only now you decide to acknowledge it?" He wasn't letting me off the hook easy.

"Yeah, I know. I had an attitude still."

"Well, I said to myself, nine days and she'll get over it. But it's like it took you nine months." We laughed at my stubbornness.

"And Andrew, you won't believe everything that happened in those nine months either."

I willfully disclosed the goings-on about my reunion with Siete, his appearance at the girls' gathering, the pregnancy, the phone call, and the final break-up. Andrew sat in dumbfounded astonishment.

"All of you women are something else, *oui*."

A pragmatic Virgo, he found it hard to digest the senseless determination of the female species.

"So, not only did you make back up with the man, you went and made a baby with him too? I swear, y'all women are just dumb. You weren't afraid for your life? Well, as they say, God protects children and fools, so you had your reasons."

"Then call me a child of God. Shit!" I laughed at my snappy comeback. I wasn't going to accept the moniker of a fool.

"Girl, speaking of which. That book you told me to get by Lolita Files, *Child of God* was the shit. It's like everybody was *bulling* everybody in that story. The mother was *bulling* her brother, the son was *bulling* the sister. The father denounced his son for being a *bulla*, only to find out he too was one and was molesting his own brother, who was also gay. I said to myself, *Nah man, this is too much bacchanal.*"

Bulling, a derivation of the aforementioned slang *bulla*, meant engaging in the sexual act, straight or otherwise, depending on the context in which it was used.

I chuckled at Andrew's colorful synopsis.

"I told you it was good. But it was more than sex, though. The story has a strong spiritual element. It speaks about love, loss, persevering in the face of adversity. It also shows the division in families. That book is powerful."

"I told everyone to get that book. The *bulling* was just too much."

I couldn't stop laughing. Leave it to a Trini to become fixated on the salacious aspects of art.

We couldn't fit our entire conversation in at the barbershop. I drove Andrew home, after which we called each other to continue. We proceeded with my retelling of Carlos's bag being stolen in Trinidad. I wanted to hear his perspective.

"Carlos called me from Trinidad after it happened," Andrew said, sharing details I wasn't privy to. "He called me crying that same night. I told him it was that blight, Kamal. He set the whole thing in motion out of jealousy. But he didn't tell me you were in the car too."

Kamal was the owner of the car which was broken into.

"Yes, I was there for the entire thing. Now that you mention it was his friend, it kind of makes sense. They had a big argument over his car door on the way over to the Oval. He was mad because Carlos didn't protect his car door from being dented. It was so bad, Carlos told him to pull over and let him out on the Beetham."

The Beetham was a major highway running through one of the most dangerous parts of Trinidad.

"But why would Kamal have someone break into his own car?" I couldn't understand the logic. "And the crazy part about it was when we came out the party and opened the back door of the car, I completely missed the window frame sitting neatly on the back seat. It took me a while to notice it. So they used my stiletto to break the glass then?" I asked.

"No! Why would they need to use your shoe to break the glass when the frame of the window was taken out clean? Kamal made the call when all of you were at the Oval. He told whoever did it exactly where the car was. They removed the window of the back door, stole Carlos's bag with all his DJ equipment, some small money that was in the car, and one side of your shoe. The shoe was red, right?"

"Yes, it was. My favorite pair of red stilettos--one side gone."

"Exactly. What you didn't know was later that same night, after they went to the police station and dropped you off, Kamal took Carlos to an obeah woman to supposedly find the person who stole the bag. But when he took him, he went in to speak to the obeah woman first, leaving Carlos unattended for an hour. What do you have to talk about for an hour when the theft wasn't aimed at you?"

"Damn, that's diabolical, Andrew."

"He went in to cover his tracks so the woman wouldn't let his name slip. Then, he gave her *your* shoe because red is the color of sex and passion.

He went to bind you to him so he could *bull* you. But whatever that obeah woman did, that shit didn't work."

Initially, when this exposé settled into my consciousness, my ego wanted to curtsy in flirtatious reverence to the base instincts of a man so stricken with desire, he'd resort to employing mystical guerilla tactics to conquer me sexually. But my spirit crumbled in violation at the potential of getting caught in the crosshairs of a neophyte's spiritual conflict. For his ineptitude, I was gratified.

"That's why I always say when you fall on misfortune, you hardly have to look far to find the culprit. The person is usually right in your camp, under your nose. Huh, people get caught up with this thing called *friend,* yes."

Andrew's words, raw and unfiltered, were dead on target.

My affairs of the heart were at a stage of quiescence. Three months celibate, I had no appetite for distraction or histrionics. This didn't dissuade my girlfriends from checking in on me frequently to ensure my mental health was intact. Keisha, especially, was integral to my recovery. She called offering jewels at the most opportune times.

"Hi, Jacquii, I'm just calling to make sure you're okay. Have you heard from your ex at all?"

"No, not at all," I answered, relieved for the reprieve.

"Good. How are you otherwise?"

"I'm fine for the most part. The only thing that frustrates me is Lucas living here."

Keish remained silent. She wasn't venturing on familial ground. Having been with him for three years, she knew what I was enduring and would be sympathetic. She snickered. "Have you noticed any of your forks missing?"

It was an odd question, but I went to the draw filled with cutlery to count. I had a set of eight large forks, but the smaller set had four in the draw and two in the dishwasher. Two of my small forks were, in fact, missing.

"Wow. That's crazy. Two of my forks are missing."

"Mm-hmm. He has a habit of throwing the forks out when he empties his plate in the garbage. I lost so many forks because of him. I don't have much to say about him being with you, but you know what you can and can't deal with.

"I called to tell you two things. First, I want you to see my friend Tansey Tang. She has a jewelry store on Nassau Street around the corner from your job. Get yourself a crystal bracelet. Tansey makes jewelry of all kinds, but she specializes in gemstones. She has a large selection, and what she doesn't have, she'll find. You need a bracelet for your spiritual, mental, and emotional protection."

I understood what Keisha was explaining. To date, I only possessed the Rose Quartz pendant she'd bought me from a vacation in St. Lucia and my Black Tourmaline pendant. I had no idea which crystals or gemstones to choose for the bracelet. Keisha sensed the uncertainty in my silence.

"You want to put Tiger's Eye. Tiger's Eye is good for releasing fear and anxiety and prevents people from draining your energy. You want Lapis Lazuli. Lapis Lazuli will boost your self-confidence and inspire you to speak your truth. Add some Agate. Agate cleanses and stabilizes your aura. You definitely want some Jade for protection, good luck, and abundance.

"Citrine combats negative energy and is the stone of prosperity. Carnelian is a protective and grounding stone. It will clean all the others in the bracelet. Put some Rose Quartz to attract unconditional love, some clear Quartz for power and energy. Amethyst is a good one to add for psychic protection. It'll also protect you from theft.

"And the last stone should be Black Obsidian for protection, healing, and truth-telling. Once you get the bracelet made, buy all three *Crystal*

Bibles by Judy Hall so you can learn as much as you can about crystal healing. Crystal healing changed my life. I guarantee you'll see the difference.

"The second thing I called to tell you is, I'm getting married next July. I'll be sending you a *Save the Date* for your refrigerator soon, so be on the lookout for it."

Keish was never fond of marriage in the past, so this news came as a complete shock to me. I was elated. She deserved a man who would honor and provide for her. The man she was dating did all of that and more. After the riotous relationship she'd had with my brother, this was the peaceful devotion she needed.

The next day, during my lunch hour, I walked from city hall to Nassau and Fulton Streets to meet the Tansey Tang that Keish spoke so highly of. The shop was small and quaint. It didn't carry the same superficial air that many other jewelers in the Financial District did. What it lacked in fanciful interior design, it more than made up for in character and warmth.

Tansey was a middle aged woman of Chinese descent. Although she lived in America for several years between the West and East Coasts, her Chinese accent was thick. She had a sassy spunk and flare. I could see why Keisha chose to befriend her. I introduced myself as Keisha's friend and gave her my list of gemstones. Tansey measured my wrist and told me to come back that evening to collect the bracelet. A mixed bag, the cost would be sixty dollars.

I thought the price was steep for what appeared to the human eye as colorful beads but made the investment. I sent Keish a picture of the completed piece. It wasn't as aesthetically pleasing as some of the others I'd seen in the shop.

With so many different crystals in one bracelet, Tansey did her best to match the sizes. Some were small, others a bit larger. She added two of each crystal type. The stones, although of the same family, sometimes had different shades. One citrine was faceted and round, the other amorphous.

I didn't complain. It was created for an express purpose, and that purpose wasn't beauty. This would be the first of many crystal bracelets and gemstones to come.

December 2014 was a defining moment in my vocal development because I performed with my workshop group at Smalls Jazz Club in Greenwich Village. We performed an ensemble piece, but Fay allowed us to perform one solo piece as well. Bearing the past year's events in mind, I chose an obscure song written and performed by George Duke called *So I'll Pretend*.

Over the years, I fought to emote my vocal expression. Most times I'd feel disconnected from the lyrics. With this song, however, the lyrics rushed out of me like a broken levee failing to contain the overflow of the converging dams. My ribs expanded, allowing my diaphragm to push the breath down into my abdomen. I began to sing the complicated melody of an unrequited love that compelled me to endure some strange things.

Using my core muscles to pull the melody out from the depths of my cervix, I flooded the audience with overwhelming emotion. Fay came up to me when my piece was done.

"Jacquii, your performance was great. You touched me. You almost moved me to tears."

I was willing to accept Fay's *almost* as a huge win. The audience felt my heartache hanging in the balance, floating within the tessitura of an unreciprocated love.

Contemplatively, until that point, I'd been party and prey to many *strange things*.

$$2015$$
$$4 + (2 + 0) + (2 + 0 + 1 + 5)$$
$$4 + 2 + 8 = 14 / 5$$

Five Personal Year

Dramatic changes, freedom, travel, turning point. You'll get a second chance now: This is the halfway point where you'll sense a change for the better in all your affairs. Life lessons will seem easier to learn, and you'll find yourself more mentally alert.[6]

The obstacles that stand in your way shall become the stepping stones to your elevation. Release the anger, put to death the worry. The stormy winds will not destroy you, but will clear the path before you.[7]

[6] (Strayhorn, 1997)
[7] (DannyTarot, 2020)

"Together still,
Going against my own will,
Spells are made of lavender love.
Thief of my dreams,
You came to me,
To steal my fate and destiny with your lavender love!"

13

THE PRACTICE CAME ABOUT MORE AS A RESULT OF A PROMISSORY indulgence than true enthusiasm. Natalie launched her new passion-based venture in January, and as a woman who loved supporting female business owners, I decided I'd be an early adapter. I postponed my commitment for weeks until it became increasingly difficult to face her because she was one of my direct reports in my previous position. To my team, I often emphasized the importance of demonstrating initiative.

After expending all the *flake-out* coupons I was allotted, on a cold Sunday morning at the end of January I convinced Gwendolyn to attend a restorative yoga class with me at Stacked Yoga. She and I practiced Hatha yoga sporadically for a year when I was a vicenarian. Almost twenty years later, and each in great shape, we figured we could hang.

Traditionally, a restorative yoga class consisted of deep breathing exercises used to hold five or six basic poses that were supported by props such as blocks and a bolster. The intention was to work through stress, relax, and rest. Natalie's rendition of restorative was more of an upbeat Vinyasa flow to EDM and House music.

We were overwhelmed by the chair poses, the trees, the warrior ones, twos, and threes. The erratic flow of movement and shifting poses caused my brain to short-circuit. *Utkatasana what? Uttanasana how? Sun Salutations why?* My body cried out for more Tadasana and Child's Resting Pose. My biceps and triceps burned from planks, three-legged downward dogs, and merely holding them suspended in the air for two minutes at a time.

Gwendolyn was finished with yoga after the first class. She elected to exercise her basic poses in the comfort of her home. I built a practice. Every Sunday morning I'd drive from Flatbush to Stacked Yoga in the middle of Bedford Stuyvesant. There was truth to that old *Bed-Stuy do or die* adage. I'd go after work with my yoga mat in hand. With weak upper body strength, the mat was vital. The more stick and suction my hands and feet had on the mat, the better my performance.

This wasn't to say my practice had improved exponentially. It was definitely a gradual process. I'd literally go through entire sessions with a stank attitude. Especially when a pose was first called to be held for a count of five but ended up being held for twenty because Natalie often stopped to assist students in the middle of the count. Vinyasa represented the antithesis of a Zen experience. Natalie, familiar with my personality and completely unbothered by it, would move through poses with ease.

"Jacquii, stop giving me the screw face and breathe. Mind your mat's business, people. Don't worry about your neighbor. This is your practice at your pace. Make this hour and a half count," she'd say, to which I'd suck my teeth, pout my lips, and step my game up.

Yoga was meditation through channeled movement. It was the locus of the stilled ego, the breath, and the body choreographed in a series of intentional postures. It opened my chakras. Even though I'd have to sleep after every class, my third eye chakra would open up and be activated for days. I was always clairvoyant in a dream state, but yoga made me even more so. The core exercises opened up my sacral chakra, which enhanced my creativity and emotions.

The practice assisted me with the technical aspects of singing. The expansion of the rib cage, deep breathing into my core, and building up of stamina all made me stronger. I felt more relaxed, could support the notes better and sustain them longer without feeling winded. All the initial resistance I put up was transfigured into healing energies and physical gain.

* * *

It was a Friday in March when I'd learn the true healing of crystals and gemstones. I left work early to take my nephew MacBook shopping. It was a birthday gift four months deferred. Nevertheless, we went shoe and technology shopping in Soho.

I parted ways with my nephew, he heading home into Flatbush and I heading into Crown Heights for the routine haircut. Carlos's shop was always brimming with excitement on a Friday evening. By this time the drama had died down. Grayson was replaced with another barber who was also a DJ. The omnipresence of Soca, Hip-Hop, and Reggae mixes told the stories of digital turntablists who possessed the skill of soul transcendence and the less experienced who served as their apprentices on the come up.

Andrew wasn't in the shop on this Friday. I sat next to Carlos's chair waiting for my cut. When my turn came, I stood to take off my cotton and fleece trench coat. As I removed my left arm from the coat's sleeve, the armlet Tansey made snapped and the crystals went scattering all over the shop's floor.

"What fell?" Carlos looked on the floor when he saw me looking bewildered, trying to recover all the crystals.

"It was my crystal bracelet," I said, salvaging the crystals I could find.

"Just so the bracelet broke? I just heard the snapping noise. I didn't even realize it was crystals that made that noise."

"Yeah, Los. That was strange. I just had it restrung the other day too." I stuffed the crystals I found in my bag. I'd have Tansey piece it back together and supplant the crystals that were lost.

I sat pensively in the chair while Carlos shaped me up. When I first purchased the armlet, Tansey strung it with strong elastic. She doubled the elastic for durability. Over time, due to frequent use, the elastic stretched. Every time it would loosen I'd go by Tansey to change the elastic. Finally, I asked her to string the bracelet with wire to mitigate the stretch of the elastic. This last adjustment took place two days before. The wire was too new to break without physical force. I told Andrew about it when I got home that evening.

"Eh heh, so your metal bracelet snapped when you took your coat off? That's not good."

"Yeah, there's something spiritually wrong in Carlos's shop. I don't think I'm going back, Andrew. Carlos is my boy and he'll remain that way, but I can't subject myself to that energy. I've been working hard to remove myself from that."

"I told Carlos he should have me clean the place down spiritually. It's been feeling heavy for months now. If you're not going back, neither am I."

I had to find a way to tell Carlos I wasn't coming back. He and I were especially close, and I'd come to love him like my brother. The next Monday during lunch I took the bracelet over to Tansey's shop for repair.

"Jacquii, this no good. Bracelet stretching too much. I just change for you last week. You around negative energy. Metal breaking means crystal protect you from something heavy. You have to stop going there, Jacquii." Tansey pleaded with the concern of a mother of three. I made a verbal agreement that I would.

I had one of Collin's barber friends recommend another barber who was just as skilled, if not more so, than Carlos. He turned me on to Phil. Phil, Collin, and Carlos all worked in the same shop back when Collin and I were together. He recognized me as soon as I came to see him for a cut.

"You know he told me a Jacquii would be coming. I asked myself which Jacquii he was talking about? But when he sent your picture, I said I remember her. It's been so many years and you look the same."

I laughed. I'd been around the barbershop scene for so long, I didn't even know I'd made such an impression on the barbers. Phil sounded truly honored to be cutting my hair. Having cut it once before, he knew exactly how to shape me up. He knew not to go too far down on the sides, and he blended my hair perfectly all around. His first attempt was the best I'd ever received after Collin.

After a month of not going to Carlos's shop, he called to find out what happened.

"Hey, Jacquii, I'm not hearing from you. Like you gave me up?"

"Los, I'm sorry for going MIA on you. I've just been dealing with a lot. That bracelet that broke at your shop was a spiritual bracelet I wore for protection. It was held together with metal. The metal snapped in your shop after two days of being rewired. Something isn't right, Los. There's a lot of negative energy around you and in the store."

"Yeah, I know. I took some time and closed the shop down. I changed all the furniture and someone came in to clean everything out. I did the woman's side over too. It's looking nice now."

"Yeah, but you need to change the people working in the shop. It's not the physical shop itself. It's your employees. They don't have your best intentions at heart. You're my boy for life, but I can't be there, Los."

He understood. Nothing was forever. All good runs have an end, albeit unforeseen and abrupt.

TORMENT (tôr′mĕnt′): *to cause to undergo great physical pain or mental anguish.* How does it feel to be trapped in a skin afflicted with dis-ease? Dis-ease concocted by a figment of one's imagination, causing another to bring her mental capacity into question. I can tell you how.

It started in spring, in the middle of the day, at work. I felt them crawling in my eyelashes at first. I flicked. I thought, my mascara must be old. The crawling moved to my eyelids, then to my head. I swatted and swatted until I scratched, transferring grease to my eyes, mascara to my head. Imagine the gnat that accidentally flies into your eye on a hot summer day multiplying by five in each eye, writhing their way through the hair follicles of your eyelashes and under your skin. I blinked.

Fluttering, my eyes winced in reverberations of physical displeasure. No reprieve. I closed my eyes meditatively and took a deep breath--inhale, hold. Ex ... hale. In ... hale, hold. Now ex ... hale. I opened my eyes. Still there. I'd recently developed allergies. This had to be an allergic attack.

I got up from my desk and went around the corner to Duane Reade. I scouted the shelves maniacally for eye wash. It seemed every Duane Reade in the city was undergoing a sanitorium-esque interior redesign with all their vivid white aisles and classic soft white lighting.

The remodeling made it difficult to find basic items. Why were the snacks on the ground floor and the cosmetics up or downstairs? Who thought it was a good idea to reorganize the damn aisles, grouping cough medicine with eye drops? WHERE WAS THE BLASTED EYE WASH?

I finally found one solitary eye wash left, paid for it, and ran to the first floor bathroom at work. Flushing my eyes gave me intermittent respite but didn't ameliorate my predicament.

That night, after washing my eyes and throwing away my mascara, I went to sleep. A few hours into slumber, I was jolted awake with crawling on my legs and arms. I felt the sensation of pin pricks under my toenails and fingernails. I shuffled my legs around to find a different spot.

I respread the duvet to shake whatever was under it off the sheets onto the parquet floors. I shook the duvet even heavier yet again. I tried going back to sleep. The crawling and pin pricks persisted. This must be a bed bug infestation, which would explain why it started at the office. Someone at work has bed bugs and transferred them to me. I turned the bedroom lights on to see the time. It was 3:30 a.m.

Crazily tearing off the bed sheets and mattress protector, I pierced the mattress with a detailed eye for anything moving. Nothing apparent to the naked eye. I grabbed my phone, entered *feeling bites in bed nothing there* in the Google search. The query yielded results pointing to bed bugs, mites, dust mites, termites, gnats. I moved the bed. I swept and mopped the floors. Nothing to be unearthed beside dust and lint.

This persisted across days of disquieted work and nights riddled with restlessness and sleep deprivation. On a Friday evening I asked my most trustworthy doorman upstairs to help me inspect the mattress for bed bugs. With him, he brought two large plastic bags for the mattress. We undressed the mattress, inspected every crack, crevice, and corner. We flipped it over and did the same. We looked under a magnifying glass at my platform bed's metal and wooden frame. No sign of termites.

"There's no sign of bed bugs, Miss Jacquii. Your apartment is so clean, we'd have spotted them easily. They're brown with flat backs."

"So what could be biting me in my sleep?"

"I don't know, but let's put these plastic bags over the mattress and put the mattress protector over the bags to seal whatever it is inside."

We laboriously covered the double foam mattress and I tipped the doorman for his time. I stripped everything in my apartment down, starting from the bedroom, to both bathrooms, out to the living room. I swept. I dusted. I mopped with apple cider vinegar and hydrogen peroxide, then mopped again with Florida water.

I washed every dish in the cupboard. I washed and vacuumed the area rugs. I cleaned under the furniture. I trashed all the bed linens, pillows, and blankets I owned. I drove to Sears and purchased brand new bed dressings from the ground up. There wasn't a living, breathing organism visible to the naked eye in my apartment besides Lucas and me.

The next day I went to the extermination store to explain my plight.

"Do you have a sample of the bug in a jar for us to inspect?" asked the exterminator.

"No, that's what I'm telling you. I can't see whatever it is. But I feel things biting my legs and arms while I'm sleeping and stinging me under my toenails and fingernails."

The exterminator, a young and friendly young man of Indian descent, looked at me baffled.

"At first description, it sounds like flees. Take this spray. Spray under and behind your bed. Close the door and leave the apartment for a few hours. When you come back in, wear white tube socks. If it's flees, they'll jump onto your feet and you'll see them on the socks. But I'm afraid that's only as high as they can physically jump. The other agitation might be something else."

I did as advised. There was no sign of flees on the socks. I called Andrew. I divulged my latest despairs.

"Hm. Sounds like somebody has your name in a calabash, girl."

"Andrew, you think so?"

"Yep. I do."

"Like right now, as I'm speaking to you, I feel like something on the couch is biting me. Andrew, I cleaned this apartment from top to bottom. I stripped the mattress, threw away all my linens, bought new bed treatments, sprayed the place down for bed bugs and flees."

"Bed bugs? In *your* apartment? Jacquii, please. There's no dust in your apartment on a normal day. Your place is the only place I can wear white socks and leave with my socks just as white as they were when I came. Stop. It's not bugs. It's obeah in your cunt." He laughed uproariously.

The preceding evening I called Erica to tell her what I was going through.

"I'm going through the same thing." Erica was still rooming by Trent in his spare bedroom. "I feel mine in my head and on the back of my neck, though. It's so aggravating, I think I'm going to cut my hair off. I called exterminators over here and had them treat the rugs throughout the entire house. I went to the doctor and he gave me a cream for my scalp. I've been using sulfur too. It's been working. Try the sulfur."

I ordered the sulfur from Amazon and, when it arrived a few days later, lathered it on my skin in desperation. It did nothing but smell up my new sheets. I discarded those and purchased a new set.

A few days later, I called Trent.

"Yo, Jacq. Talk to your girl. She's bugging the hell out. She swears I have bed bugs. She got exterminators to come treat my rugs. She's sequestered in her bedroom because she's convinced that whatever it is originated down in the living room. I haven't hosted a dinner party in my house in weeks because I don't want to subject anyone else to what might be bed bugs, but I don't see or feel anything. Neither does anyone else in here. It's just Erica."

"T, I'm telling you, it's real. I'm going through the same thing here, but nothing is working. Erica is at least saying the cream the doctor gave her is working. I'm beginning to think I might have multiple sclerosis."

"Well, I don't know what the two of you have going on, but keep that shit away from me and come get your girl." We laughed and hung up.

The nagging feeling of an unresolved ailment tortured me. There was no way I could function under this duress. Everything was affected. My head exploded in fragments of pain every time I sang at my weekly workshops. If I wasn't fidgeting or swatting myself at work, I'd sit in a dazed gaze.

I walked to the neurologist's office on Broad Street in the middle of the Financial District. She was a young female doctor and appeared to be likable enough. I told her what I was experiencing.

"How is your vision? Are you experiencing any blurriness in sight? What about numbness, weakness, or stiffness of your hands, feet, or joints?"

"No, doctor, none of the above. Just the crawling and biting under my eyelids, in my head, arms, and feet. I feel pin pricks like I'm being stuck with needles under my fingernails and toenails. The pricks happen when I'm asleep."

"You feel crawling in your head, you say?" she quipped with the condescending, half-smirk of a mindful skeptic heavily steeped in the pharmaceutical teachings of Western medicine. "It could be poor circulation. Are you sleeping in a cramped position, preventing the proper flow of blood?"

"No, I can't get to sleep long enough for my muscles to cramp. And yes to the crawling in my head! Trust, I know what I'm telling you. I'm fully cognizant of my feelings and experiences. Are there any tests you can run?"

At this juncture, the tests were just my way of ruling out all possibilities before I finally settled on the most plausible--the dark arts.

The doctor did the easy exams first. She had my blood drawn and tested to see if there were any traces of substances pointing to the presence of MS. Except for high levels of B12 and B6, my blood work came back within the normal range in every type.

She had the lab technician conduct what they dubbed *Evoked Potentials*. He adhered wire electrodes to my scalp to test my brain's response as I responded to a series of clicks, electrical pulses on my arms and legs, and visual patterns via video--all normal.

The last was the MRI. She wanted to get a closer scan of my brain to see if there were any changes caused by multiple sclerosis, like signs of inflammation in the brain or spinal cord. The MRI came back normal except for a small cyst the radiology technician spotted on the image. She had me scheduled for a detailed CT scan of my brain.

Andrew was my closest confidant through this phase in my life because he'd provide the spiritual guidance and comic relief I'd need to get through some hard days.

"I don't even know why you're bothering with all those tests. They'll show nothing. You're perfectly healthy. All these damn MRIs and CT scans for what? What's unique to Trinidad is the doctor would've said, *Miss Madam, I'm afraid there's nothing else we can do for you here. You might want to see a bush doctor.* But with all these medical malpractices and lawsuits hanging over doctors' heads in America, they wouldn't dare say something like that to a patient."

Needless to say, the CT scan results proved the cyst was benign.

Erica had head lice. Everything at Trent's house was restored to some semblance of normalcy. I asked my mother about the probability of me having head lice as well.

"Seriously, Jacquii? Please! Your hair is cut in a Caesar. It's too short to have lice. You would've seen it moving." Her tone turned reminiscent.

"Back in Trinidad, the little Indian children would get it a lot and you'd see them sitting in the front gallery between their mother's legs as she went through the scalp and squeezed the lice *snap* between her fingernails." She imitated the characteristic snapping sound the lice egg made as it was squeezed to its death. "You're fine on that score. Find something else. That's not it."

That evening, I went to sleep early. I was able to deduce that the biting generally started around 2:00 a.m. and lasted about two to three hours. It would behoove me to get an early start. It was the best sleep I'd had in weeks. My dreams were lucid and vibrant. I saw, standing over my bed, an apparition of Siete magnified.

He stood majestic and triumphant. He wore a shirt with the Superman *S* on the chest. He had both hands balled up in fists, arms akimbo, as if he really was a superhero. He looked down on me laughing, crow's feet smiling, eye's affirming, *Yes bitch! I got you back!* It was the divine prophecy for which I yearned. Andrew was right. I now knew who the mastermind behind my artificial hell on earth was.

"Andrew, you were right again." I said, confessing my previous night's dream. "It's Siete doing this to me. He's angry that I left him."

"I told you someone had your name in a calabash. Ha! Oy! I can't. That man had your ass hop-pin', girl. You were the house cleaner, the exterminator, the everything in one. Oh shit. This is too much. My boy said, 'Hold that, bitch! Take that in your *rook-kook-a-tun-tun*'." He cackled a high-pitched laugh.

"Andrew, I'm going to need you to help me clean this place spiritually. I need to remove this negativity so I can watch TV in my living room and sleep in peace."

"Yeah, remind me when you're ready. I'll tell you what to buy."

"I'm ready *now*, shit!"

"I have to tell you what to buy and my mind isn't on that right now. Once it comes, I'll call you and you'll have to write it down, because as soon as I say it, I'll forget what I said."

It was the most unorthodox lesson in spiritual contact I'd received to date. One would think a male suitor riveted his eyes lovingly on his woman to capture the quiver of her lips when she was scared, the squint of her eyes when she smiled, or the soft hum of her snores as she slept. Never would she imagine he'd keep tally of the things that brought her the most peace and pleasure, only to use them against her in acts of a twisted and demented ilk.

If there was anything I loved more than music or food, it was sleep. It was my time to recharge, my time to rebuild my strength and get in touch with spirit. Siete knew these things about me. It would annoy him to FaceTime me from work, he stuck in the office and I in the comfort of my bed. It became customary for him to find me there. He'd be the only one to know my Achilles heel.

I never went back to the neurologist's office. It was a futile endeavor.

There was a silver lining in my dark cloud, however. Lucas was moving back upstate with his girlfriend. I could only guess he grew tired of seeing Keisha's *Save the Date* magnet glaring at him from the refrigerator. Settling for his second best, he longed to be romantically yoked as well. I, so excited to have my space to myself, volunteered to drive him back on my birthday with plans to meet Tamia, Tyra, and Samiyah for brunch.

We left Brooklyn at 6:00 a.m. We were making good time, with a half hour left in the journey clocking us in at 8:00 a.m. I was driving an easy ninety-five miles per hour when I spotted the state trooper's car ahead scanning my speedometer. By the time I came upon him, I'd managed to get my car down to seventy-five miles, but it was still far beyond the fifty-five mile limit. We were pulled over and I was summoned to court in Saugerties, NY for speeding. Every time I acted altruistically toward my brother, I wound up the loser.

KNOCKING FROM THE INSIDE

I sat in the Wall Street psychic's office. I needed confirmation that my dream was real. She discerned my discomfort.

"Your chakras are all closed, honey. Are you feeling good? You don't look that good. If you want, instead of a reading, I can put you on the table and do some Reiki Healing on you."

"NO! I don't want any reiki healing today. I want you to sit down and tell me what's going on! Please." She was stunned by my hostility. I needed her to feel the urgency of my suffering.

"What's going on?"

"I don't know, that's why I'm here to see you. I think I might have bed bugs."

"Bed bugs? Your home is just as pristine and put together as you. I'd be surprised if *you* had bed bugs." She didn't have to step foot in my apartment to state the obvious. "Do you have any bites?"

"I have this small pimple on my arm." I pulled up my sleeve and raised my arm to show her.

"No, that's not a bed bug bite." She shuffled the deck three times, pausing for my cut.

I cut the deck in three and watched her place them back in one pile.

"Who's working black magic on you?" She paused, looked at me, and carried on. "The cards are showing me there's a man working on you, but he's working with a woman. She's doing the actual work."

"Well, remember, I came to you last August to find out about my ex. After your reading, I left him."

"Yeah, I'm seeing a man. He's angry. He's hurt and lonely. When people do things like this, they're crying out to be heard. He wants you to suffer and hurt in the same way you made him suffer when you left."

"Still? Doesn't he have someone else by now?"

"No, he's tried to replace you, but the relationships don't last. He can't find anyone." She paused at the cards for a minute.

"He's disturbed, this man. Mentally disturbed. Didn't you see this when you were with him?"

"He is, isn't he? Is he psychopathic?"

"He may be something like that. I'm seeing he has mental issues. He's around you, you know. He's around, but you can't see him. He has a lot of time on his hands. Is he working?"

"I don't know. It's funny you should ask that because I've been going on his company's website to see if he's listed as a staff member, and he isn't. Was he fired?"

"It seems like he was. He has nothing now. He's hit rock bottom. He's depressed. He's sad. He's lonely."

"He doesn't have a job, but he's using his spare time to make my life miserable. Wow!"

"But you're giving in to him. You're giving up your power. You have the ability to fight him, but you've given up. What happened?"

"I'm tired. I feel like I'm always fighting. I have a show to do next month, my head hurts every time I try to sing, and I choke. I don't have the physical energy or strength to fight right now."

"You *have* to fight this. Get a blue scarf for your neck when you perform. You need to activate your throat chakra. See, if we did the reiki you'd be relieved of that."

"We'll do that the next time I come. I needed a reading today."

"You need to file an order of protection against him."

"Can I? He hasn't physically done anything to harm me. How can I prove he's harassing me?"

"Tell the police he's stalking you. Tell them you see him outside your apartment and give them dates. You have to protect yourself."

I left the Wall Street psychic's office disillusioned and dispirited. Siete was using his life's force to destroy me when all through our separation all I ever wanted was to love him. At night, I prayed for his internal happiness. Sleep being a loathsome task, I stayed up asking my ancestors to send him missives of love and blessings. For light would eventually overcome the darkness. His darkness, however, was one of a gritty type.

It was odd being back in the headquarters of the 70th Precinct. I didn't know what case I was going to make, but I was going to make a good one. I completed a written report. The report itself felt like a violation. Where does the assailant live? Are there any distinguishing marks on his skin? What were the exact incidents of harassment? When? What time?

The officer at the front desk told the officer in charge of abuse claims to speak with me.

"Ms. Leveine, I understand you're filing an order of protection today?"

"Yes, Officer, I am."

"Describe what's going on."

"My ex is stalking me. I broke up with him last August and he's been harassing me." This was all true, but I couldn't prove any of it.

"When you say stalking you, have you seen him outside of your home?"

"Yes," I lied. "I've seen him parked in a car in front of my building."

"Do you remember the color, make, and model of the car?"

"Yes, I think it was a silver Nissan Altima."

"Did he try to speak to you?"

"No."

"Did he approach you?"

"No."

"Has he tried to text you?"

"I have him blocked on my phone. He can't reach me."

"Ms. Leveine, we need a strong case against him. You may not want to, but I ask that you unblock his number. As soon as he texts you, we can make an arrest if the report is filed with the courts."

"Would he be notified that there's an order of protection against him?"

"Yes, he will."

That was the last thing I needed. This was an all-out war. I couldn't reveal my hand to my opponent. I couldn't go against an army with a hand gun. The penal system left me uncloaked and ill-equipped in these streets. The absurdity of the justice system to put so much faith in a piece of paper. Would this court order prevent him from retaliating with stronger spiritual force once he learned of its existence? Excuse me, Your Honor, may you please send your guardian angels to stand forth while his demons ambush?

I told the officer I needed more time to think about filing. He was a man of Caribbean descent. My heart yearned to tell him the attack was spiritual, but I was fearful of being ridiculed. Back to square one, I unblocked Siete's number in case he decided to text.

Andrew finally came through to assist me with the cleansing of my apartment. It was the middle of May when I picked him up. I'd just traded my GLK in for a 2015 ML 350. I was holding out for the GLE Coupe, but the release wouldn't be until August and the dealership was anxious to get me out of my current lease six months early.

I had all the ingredients he told me to buy. We had two cleanings to do: one to clear out the negative energy and the other to usher in the positive. He stood in the kitchen running down the list of ingredients to make sure I'd purchased everything as instructed.

"So for the first bath we'll need the blue soap, Jinx Remover Oil, Go Away Evil Oil, Run Devil Run Oil, some sea salt, blue cubes, two cut limes, and pennies or quarters."

"Check, we have all of that."

"Okay, let's start in the back in your room and work our way up to the front door."

Lucas, greeting us, walked out of his bedroom as we were heading to the back. Unable to get along with his girlfriend for more than two weeks, he'd moved back to Brooklyn into my spare bedroom. He didn't want to be around while we performed the exorcism of the space.

KNOCKING FROM THE INSIDE

"That's your brother? I know you told me he was a street dude, but he's a straight thug."

"He's actually much nicer than he looks. He's not unapproachable, just has a resting *mean-mug* face."

"Hm. If you say so. Jacquii, I have to say," Andrew changed the topic as he wiped the window sills, door handles, and floors with the mixture, "I'm cleaning this place and I don't feel anything negative in this space. Right now I feel like I'm making more of a mess than anything else. This apartment is physically and spiritually clean. I don't feel anything biting me."

"Lucas doesn't feel anything either. He doesn't have any ants in his bedroom. They're only in my bedroom and living room. The other morning I found an ant crawling in my bed. In my bed, Andrew! Let's just finish. I have to cover all bases."

"Fine, but you'll have to come behind me and clean up this lime pulp we're leaving on the floors."

Andrew began to pray as he finished working in each room.

We were exhausted after the first go round. My two-bedroom wasn't humongous, but it was much larger than the average New York City two-bedroom. Because I had a minimalist approach to interior design, we had a lot of unoccupied square footage to cover.

"Okay, throw this old water outside into the sewer. You don't want any of this water emptied out in your place." I did as I was told and returned while Andrew rested.

"Now, get a new bucket and let's mix the new bath. For this we'll need, Jasmine Oil, High John the Conqueror Oil, Prosperity Oil, Uplifting Oil, Magnet Oil, milk, and Florida water."

"Yep, I have it all here." We mixed the new bath and began to wipe and mop everything again from the front door to the back of the apartment.

When we were done, I smoked my apartment out with charcoal, frankincense, myrrh, three kings incense, dragon's blood, and sage.

The crawling and biting continued. It wasn't as incessant as it was when it first began, but it wasn't completely eliminated either.

I'd stopped by the Smoke Joint for some smoked barbecue the next Sunday after yoga when a text pinged my phone, "Hey, Beautiful! You've got a text message."

It was from Siete. My hands shook uncontrollably, my stomach sank as I retrieved the message.

Hi, Beautiful. I was remembering that today was the same day in May when we went to El Patron and you made me take my sneaker off in the restaurant to smell if it was new. I know you don't want to hear from me or speak to me. But know that I will always miss and love you, queen. I'm sry [sic] *for everything.*

I didn't know which was worse, the fact that he sent the text after everything he was doing or the fact he sent a text message plagued with errors because he knew I'd want to upstage and correct him by texting back. Instead, I relaxed the ego. I did nothing.

The truth of the matter was, El Patron was the last time we'd seen each other in August of 2014 right before his birthday. It wasn't a pleasant dinner. We argued over the pregnancy, his lack of involvement in our relationship, and I may have mentioned his obsession with sneakers. I didn't remember making him take them off to do a sniff test. He was clever. I didn't bite.

A week later, as I readied myself to leave for yoga, my fingertips were suddenly inflamed. It was as if my hands were spread over an open fire. The burning was so unbearable, I dropped my mat, wincing in pain. I refused to scream. I wouldn't give him the satisfaction of a reaction, a text, an email, or phone call. I took an oath of silence. I'd stay resolved in my fight. He wasn't going to cause me to burst under any form of pressure.

I stood erect in my martyrdom, but I wasn't completely erect. I bent head over torso, fine and fragile, marveling at the profundity of animal instincts linking the beast to the beauty.

* * *

In the meantime, I purchased more crystals. I found a beautiful Larimar pendant at Tansey's shop. Larimar, a stone indigenous to the Dominican Republic, was named by the Dominican explorer who re-discovered it. He named it after his daughter Larrisa, and "mar" which means "sea" in Spanish.

A blue stone reflective of the tranquil sky and powerful seas, larimar is a singer's stone. It harnesses feminine energies and empowers the wearer to sing her divine feminine truth from the heart while protecting the voice. I added a Larimar bracelet to my collection.

I asked Tansey to make me a Carnelian bracelet. She added Tiger's eye for self-confidence and Onyx for physical strength and stamina. Carnelian, the true singer's stone, illuminates the voice and promotes confidence on stage during live performances. It's the stone best suited to make timid speakers become eloquent and bold. I also bought a citrine bracelet for additional self-confidence because I was at a deficit.

For our summer workshop performance in mid-June, I got up on the stage at Small's Jazz Club and delivered a rendition of Horace Silver's *Doodlin'* that surprised me and my workshop members. Fay, fully knowledgeable of all the spiritual ailments I was fighting against, was convinced I could pull it off. She stood in the audience with a nod of acknowledgement when I sang the vocalese tune from my lower register to the top of my upper register.

The song was an especially difficult blues tune, having the upbeat chromatic progressions of the solo substituted with words. To sing this song meant I had to have every single note crystallized in my body because the original solo was tight, there were avid musicians in the audience familiar with Horace's piano solo, and the delivery had to be spunky and soulful. To pull this performance off in the midst of my brief descent into madness was no small feat. It was just one song, but it was an enormous victory.

14

AS GWENDOLYN AND I DROVE FROM THE DUTCH SIDE OF SINT MAARTEN TO the French side of St. Martin, I reflected on Keisha's nuptial day. She, not one to exclude any detail, put on the ceremony of a lifetime. It was an outdoor wedding in a ritzy Long Island country club. She had a project plan for every aspect of the wedding. From the Hip-Hop violinist playing on the side of the altar, her choice of Kem's *You Are* for her processional entrance to the endless food options at the tasting and reception, the execution spoke of elegance personified.

I'd never seen Keisha so radiant. She exuded exquisite vivacity. She'd kissed many a bullfrog before she'd found her prince. I was humbled that one such frog just happened to be my brother. My devotional sister for lifetimes, she bestowed upon me jewels too great to be repaid by the cost of two plates. I knew Lucas would always have a special place in her heart; however, she needed the calm, stable strength of a settled man.

Our new travels would take us to the RIU Palace in the remote and mountainous Anse Marcel. The property was situated at the end of a twisting, steep, hilly road, surrounded by patches of dehydrated grass and weeds. Our van purred up a mountaintop of hiking trails, opening to dry forest that was less than panoramic; cerulean skies blanketed this sleepy, nonfragrant town.

I was prepared for our stay at the secluded resort with an arsenal of books on my Kindle and enough bathing suits to last six days. Gwendolyn, more of the adventurous type, was longing to see the world teeming outside of the confines of the resort. She wanted a taste of what St. Martin had to offer. While each Caribbean island was similar to the next, they individually possessed an inherent vibe and pulse unique to its inhabitants and their ancestral anecdotes. She wanted to hear the tales this foreign land had to tell.

She'd resign herself to keeping me company on the beach, reading, while the entertainment staff could be heard meters away holding water aerobics classes to the latest Soca tunes.

"So this is what people do on a vacation? Lie around and eat or drink on the beach?" she asked, looking across the shore line at the long expanse of sunbathers. "After a few days of this, I'd be ready to go back home."

"It's called a vacation for a reason. Vacate the mind and all activities for rest and relaxation."

"I don't have a job anymore; every day is a vacation for me." She laughed.

"So, I'll hire a cab one of the days for us to go into town. This way we'll see what the island looks like outside the resort. We didn't see much on the drive over, and I'm not that interested in going to the Dutch side. I believe that's where the majority of the shopping is, and we didn't come to shop."

"Okay, I'd like that. Break up the monotony a bit."

For three days, almost by rote, we woke up at 8:00 a.m., made our dinner reservations at one of the RIU restaurants, read on the beach beholding the azure waters until midday, ate lunch, made conversation with the kitchen staff and locals, ate some more until sundown, showered for dinner, ate again, and ended the night watching the evening show.

By the third iteration of this daily programming, even I longed for a change in routine. I looked forward to seeing something different. We asked one of the young ladies we'd befriended if she could get us a driver to take us into town to Grand Case where the shops and restaurants were located. I had a request of a peculiar kind. I wanted the driver to make a pit stop at a local spiritual reader.

"Hmm. I have a friend who'll know where to take you," she said coyly, hinting to the idea that this friend would be especially inclined to do her bidding. "He's my special friend. I'll make sure he treats you well. Don't worry. You'll be in good hands. I'll call him now." The young lady left to make the request.

"Jacquii, you're going to another reader? You're not tired of seeing these spiritual people? I keep telling you the power is in your mind and in your control. Didn't you read the *Science of Mind*?

The *Science of the Mind* was a book written by Ernest Holmes which described how one can control the faculties of the mind to fully realize her life's purpose.

I rolled my eyes more from recognition than defiance. I'd heard this rant several times over. We were two different women. She believed that all of life's occurrences were in her sphere of control, that she had the internal ability to shape a reality free from unsolicited spiritual interference.

I knew in my soul that I had a symbiotic relationship with the universe. It was an interdependence between the self and higher spirit. Yes, many things were in my internal control, caused by my own choices, but others were influenced by my karmic connection to this life and others past. I also believed that moments of physical exhaustion or mental weakness could make a normally viable body susceptible to arcane forces.

My mother had ceased to open herself up in that regard. Her resolve, being as strong as it was, blocked her from the natural clairvoyant gifts of our ancestral lineage, the gifts she once had. I was fine with her defense mechanism as long as she accepted my heeding to a higher calling beyond myself.

"I did read the *Science of Mind*, and I still want to see a reader tomorrow. I'm paying for the cab, so just come along for the ride and enjoy the vacation. All this back talk. Goodness." We laughed as the young woman returned to our table.

"Everything is set ladies. He'll meet you in the front lobby after breakfast tomorrow and take you into town to see about *that*," she said, dipping her chin and raising her eyes to accentuate my esoteric intention, "then he'll take you into Grand Case for lunch. You'll organize the payment with him tomorrow when you see him."

We thanked her, wishing her a good evening since her shift was ending. Tomorrow would be a grand adventure, and so it was.

The road in was the same road we drove to get out. An unpaved twisting hill, we drove down the dirt road until we were at the bottom. Our driver, a smiling man, seemed thrilled to be taking us on the odd trip. We drove through the French side for some time, looking at the minimal vegetation the island had to offer. Perhaps it was dry season.

Gwendolyn sat looking out the window, shaking her head at me as if to say, *if this is what you want, then so be it.* I was determined to discover something; what that something was, I wasn't yet sure. Ten minutes into the drive we stopped at a blue and white house repurposed as a business storefront. Our smiling driver got out of the driver's seat, walked the perimeter of the front office, looked toward the stairs standing akimbo, deep in thought. He finally settled upon walking up the stairs to ring the bell. We waited until he came back out.

"Should we come out of the car?" I asked in eager anticipation.

"No, the house is now a real estate company. The lady has moved," he answered thoughtfully, perusing his mind for another option.

"If you don't have anyone else, no worries. We can just go to town." I was beginning to think the ancestors were telling me my journey was unnecessary.

"No," our driver, no longer smiling, responded. "I may know another place." He got on the phone with one of his friends. "Hey, where are you now? You're at the shop? Remember that lady you told me you saw on the

Dutch side? She's still there? She is? Okay, I'm coming over there now. Give me about twenty minutes. Okay? Okay." He hung up.

Twenty minutes later and on the Dutch side of town, we were parked in a lot surrounded by a barbershop directly in front and a library to our left side. Our driver, smiling again, walked toward the barbershop.

"Wow, Gwen. This is turning into a big production. Perhaps I shouldn't do this again?"

"Well, you were adamant that we make this trip. Now the young man is going out of his way to make sure he pleases his friend. Depending on what he says when he comes back, just tell him you've changed your mind."

He returned ten minutes later with a younger man who had an amused look on his face.

"So we have more company, I see?"

"Yes," our driver said, getting into the car with his friend. "He speaks English and Spanish. The woman we're going to see is from the Dominican Republic. She only speaks Spanish. My friend here has her number and knows where she lives. She's home waiting for us. He'll translate for both of you."

Now, a real prospect, I was unexpectedly anxious about receiving this reading.

Contrary to the land on the outskirts of the island, we arrived at a house recessed behind lush banana leaves, palm trees, and tropical plants of all types. The porch had a young woman sitting out front. We all exited the car. My translator asked the younger lady for the actual psychic. She went into the home, leaving us out front. A moment later, a heavy set, unsociable woman came out beckoning us to follow her inside.

"Jacq, I'm not going inside there with you, you know. I'll stay out here with our driver friend." My mother wanted no part of the spiritual dabbling.

"I know. I didn't think you would. I'll be right back." My younger translator companion and I ventured inside.

Upon my entering the front door, I overheard my mother say to the driver, "One thing about my daughter; when she makes up her mind to do something, there's no talking her out of it. She's very determined." I could only assume our smiling driver smiled some more at her admission.

The home's design was a decorative fusion of your grandmother's living room stuffed with plastic-covered floral furniture and the digs in a seventies blaxploitation film with plastic beaded curtains adhered to the door frames, suspended over shaggy carpet. The elder guided us toward a bedroom at the back of the house.

Congested with statues of both African and Catholic saints, skulls, and sundry spiritual paraphernalia, the room had the dim, dank feel of one that hadn't been exposed to fresh air in a while, smothered by candle wax. We crouched around a small table in the center of the room, she on one side with my translator and I on the other. She lit her cigar and began to pray in Spanish.

My younger translator sat in willing deference, waiting to be summonsed on my behalf. She got her deck of cards and began to shuffle. She stopped to ask my translator my name. I told him, he then told her. She shuffled again and lit a candle. She handed it to me. Taking it back, she mounted the candle on a statue adjacent to her. Talking through my translator, she began.

"You met a darker skinned man. He lives far away from you. He likes you, but he has someone where he lives. He's not sure if he should stay with her. She has a child. He's not ready for that." She was referring to a young man I'd met at Keisha's wedding.

Keisha cunningly arranged for us to sit at the same table knowing we were both single. He was her good friend from her doctoral program. He was almost ten years my junior. While he was great company at the wedding, he wasn't anywhere in my immediate plans.

The reader continued, "There's a lighter skinned man around you. He's lighter than you. He's angry. Very angry. He's doing this to you so you won't find another man." She raised her hand to exemplify the spiritual ambiance of the room and the potential power of his work.

"How old are you?"

I told my translator to tell her thirty-nine. My translator, readying himself to respond, nearly choked on his words when he realized what I'd said. He was expecting me to be much younger. Tipping his head with the approving nod a man gives a woman who's taken good care to preserve her youth, he gave the psychic my age.

"You're supposed to be married by now. You get into relationships, the men love you immediately, then about a year or so after, they go. This has been the pattern. Someone has put a generational curse on you that hasn't been removed. I see you've been to several people in your hometown, but they don't help you. They just take your money. You need someone with my abilities to remove the curse."

She stopped to appraise my interest in spiritual work. I sat quietly waiting to get the rest of the reading. For sixty dollars there was definitely more to come in this reading. Sensing my determination, she continued with what she could.

"This man who's working against you loves you very much. There's just something about you that brings out his bad side. He's sad. His anger makes him want to control you. You have to do something to remove his work. Again, let me do the work here and I promise you it'll stop. It'll be $250."

"No," I said, speaking to my translator, "I'll find someone in New York to work with." I thanked her for her time.

We got up to leave. Two hundred fifty dollars was an investment when we were in the same city. It would be a huge loss to me since we weren't. Checking up on the results of a spiritual job via phone and Google Translate made no sense. We walked back out of the plastic bead curtain onto the front porch. My mother looked up and smiled, relieved to see me out and in one piece.

"How'd it go? Was it what you expected?" she asked.

"I'll tell you later."

"Okay. Look, Jacq, she has the Wonder of the World plant growing in her yard. I don't want to take a piece without asking. You think she'll give me a leaf?"

"Let's ask our translator friend to ask her." Just as I turned to ask my younger companion, the elder came out and stood on the front porch looking down on us, a stern look in her eyes.

My mother pointed to the plant and looked up at the elder woman in hope she'd acquiesce. The elder shook her head no. My mother, persistent when it came to fruits and plants, asked her directly.

"Please, may I have a leaf of your Wonder of the World plant? I didn't want to take it without asking you first."

The older woman looked my mother once over as if she was appraising the purity of her intent. She bowed her head one last time, her eyes askance, and moved slowly off the porch to find a piece that she considered worthy. Carefully breaking a leaf from the plant, she handed it over. Gwendolyn was elated. She, captivated by the Wonder of the World plant, had tried once before to grow it in Brooklyn to no avail. I was glad she received some form of reparation from my deviant excursion.

The Wonder of the World plant, scientifically termed Kalanchoe Pinnata, is a miracle medicinal plant used to cure almost every ailment from infections and inflammation to treating boils, skin ulcers, cancer, epilepsy, and earaches to relieving muscle pains. It's a wonder because the plant literally sprouts new growth without having to be planted in soil. If one left a leaf of the Wonder of the World shrub in an enclosed book without tampering with it, she'd return to see new buds sprouting out from the many spikes around its perimeter.

We four, piling into the minivan, headed back into town to drop our young translator off at the barbershop where we'd retrieved him and upset the order of his day. I thanked him profusely for his time and gave him a twenty dollar bill for his services. He was surprised and grateful for the gift. He'd have come along for the ride with no expectation just for the excitement of it all.

Our driver, smiling still, dropped us off on familiar grounds in Grand Case on the French side of the island. Giving us two hours to walk around and eat, he'd pick us up at the local souvenir shop at the corner of the strip. We, free to ourselves to roam the small town, decided to have lunch at a Caribbean seafood restaurant called The *Talk of the Town*. We took our seat on the blue benches facing the street and passersby. I told Gwen all that I could remember.

"Wow, that man is still thinking about you almost a year later. I have to say, though, when you two saw each other on that dealership floor, you were instantly drawn to each other. There was no way the two of you weren't going to be together. This sounds like a past life connection. But he's possessed now," Gwendolyn said recalling Siete and my encounter four years prior.

"Possessed? You mean obsessed. He won't let it go. He's determined to make my life a living hell."

I told her about the torment I was suffering with the bites and crawling which hadn't yet subsided even though we were across the Atlantic, close to waters that intermingled with the Caribbean Sea.

"You have the internal strength to change that. Never forget that," Gwendolyn said, resolute about the power of the mind. I had a hunch that getting rid of Siete would be a Herculean task.

Two hours and three hundred dollars later, our driver dropped us back to the RIU Palace with his plastered smile. He'd have stories to share with the locals for days. We thanked him for his services, albeit pricey at $160. We went to see our lady friend in the kitchen to thank her as well.

Walking back to our room, Gwendolyn turned to me. "Tonight, after dinner, ask the bartenders at the resort club for some lime wedges. Tomorrow morning, wake up at the crack of dawn, go to the beach, and scrub yourself down with each lime wedge as you pray for removal of the negativity. When you're finished with each wedge, throw it as far as you can over your shoulder without looking back. Go as far into the water as you can standing. Make sure to wet your entire body, head and all."

Six o'clock the next morning, I circumspectly walked out to the beach. The ground keepers were beginning to come out to wash the beach chairs and place the umbrellas. It was customary practice on resort grounds for patrons to come on the beach around 7:00 a.m. with their towels and bags, securing their prototypical spot for the day. I wanted to avoid the rush.

I walked to the far end of the beach, out of direct sight, and did as instructed. I dunked my entire body in the sea water a few times to get acclimated to the water, ensuring my crystal bracelet was cleansed as well. Taking lime wedge after lime wedge, I scrubbed my face, neck, shoulders, under my arms, stopped to gaze up at the sun, and took the rays in while I prayed.

"Ancestors, please watch over me. Please enclose me in your love and strength. Grant me the discernment and intuition to see all things. Remove all negativity that's cast upon me from Siete and others of whom I may not be aware. Allow my aura to be cleansed and my chakras to be opened. Allow me to live in love, positivity and light no matter my circumstances.

"Ancestors, I ask that you use me as a vessel to heal others who are in need. Allow me to use my voice and words to heal the hurt. Allow my voice to transcend hearts and souls. Allow me to sing from the depths of my soul with the words and lyrics needed to heal the listener. Please allow me to step righteously into my life's purpose."

It was the first time I'd ever made such a request. I didn't know what lured me to say those words. They just came with an intuitive knowing that this was where I was supposed to be and that healing was my life's mission. I wanted to heal the world with the power of song. I left the sea feeling refreshed. I wasn't sure the negativity was completely removed, but I had to believe in something greater than myself, a power greater than the dark.

* * *

Lucas was still living with me. It was coming upon the fourth month of him being back and the eleventh month of him inhabiting my spare room. He swore the end of every month was the last. At the end of August he'd still not found someplace to go. It vexed me to cast my eyes upon him. I was still feeling the financial sting of the $375 retainer I paid to the traffic lawyer in Saugerties.

With no interest in driving back upstate, it made more sense for me to retain a lawyer more familiar with the county, its courts, and judges. He'd be better able to fight my case, proving it was my first speeding offense, in that county at least. Aside from the retainer, I was still bracing myself for the cost of the actual fine and consequential points on my license.

"So ... when are you planning to leave now?" I asked to get the new date.

"Yo, I'm working on something with my boy. I'm moving back upstate. He may have a job lined up for me back there. By the end of the month I should be out. Please, Sis, just bear with me until the end of the month."

"Okay. The end of the month." I don't think he recognized the gravity of my tone.

I pondered over the quandary I was in with my brother.

I sat quietly at my desk, the voices of all my former male bosses coming to the forefront of my psyche in unison. *Jacquii, you're not his sister. You're his mother. You enable him. The only way a man learns how to be a man is to be treated like one. You can't coddle him and expect him to grow up. He'll have no reason to mature unless he's put in an uncomfortable situation or hits rock bottom. It's the only way.* From adolescence onwards, there were years of *Jacquii saves Lucas* stories in the historical archives. He was my prodigal son.

It was 2:00 p.m. when I left Manhattan. Still leaving right before I got in from work, the plan was to get to him before he departed. It would take approximately an hour to get there. My adrenalin rushed for the entire train ride home. I'd have to be firm in my stance. There was no room for sympathy or back-pedaling.

Lucas was startled when I came in at 3:00 p.m. I found him in his bedroom--my spare room--getting his clothes together. Apparently, he'd just finished doing his laundry.

"Yo. What's up? Why are you home so early?" he asked, his eyes assessing my body language.

"I came home early because I wanted to see you before you left. I want my keys back."

"What? Yo, whatever." He flippantly went back to folding his clothes. "I told you I was leaving at the end of the month."

"You said that last month. I gave you a whole month extra. This is now a full year you've been here. You haven't contributed anything beyond the first $150. I have to pay $618 for a lawyer and speeding fine that I got driving your ass back upstate and you're still in my face every day. You have me talking way too much. Just give me my keys please."

"GIVE YOU YOUR KEYS? HOW AM I SUPPOSED TO GET BACK IN?" he yelled before catching himself and hushing his tone. "How am I supposed to get back in?"

"That's the point. You take your things with you on your way out today. Time's up. You have to go today. Now. It's a good thing you washed your clothes. You'll have them when you leave." He ignored me.

I went rifling through his jacket pocket, looking for my keys. He grabbed the jacket away from me before I could get my hands on them. Eyes enraged, mouth pursed, fists clenched tightly onto the jacket, he breathed heavily through his nose as if he'd charge. With the display of disrespect in my apartment I was now ready for a fight.

"If I don't get my keys back now," I enunciated each word measuredly, "I'll call the cops and have your ass escorted out."

I fixed my unblinking stare on him to let him know I was dead serious.

In the current social climate there was no way I'd call the police on my only brother. The chances were too risky that he'd either get locked up or seriously hurt, but desperate times called for desperate measures. I secretly hoped he wouldn't call my bluff.

To my surprise, he reached into the jacket pocket, retrieved my keys, and slapped them down in the palm of my hands. He excused himself to shower. He'd be out of my hair, if only for the night. He needed to decompress.

As he left the house, I called out to him, "So when are you coming back to get your stuff?"

"I'll be back tomorrow." He slammed the door on his way out.

When I'd return home that evening, there would be no call to pick up his belongings. I texted to find out if he was on his way. I received no reply. I waited until the morning. Still no reply. I called out from work. I neatly folded his clothing and packed them in the suitcase he had in the closet. I packed all his shoes in a large plastic bin he had stored in his closet. Not wanting to relegate his remaining clothes to black garbage bags, I packed them in my biggest suitcase, a fancier four-wheeler.

After all was packed, I deflated the blow-up mattress, threw away his linens, swept and mopped the floor. I cleaned the scuff marks off my white walls and wiped down the windowsills. When the room was stark and spotless, I smoked it out with charcoal, incense, and sage. I moved the suitcases and bin to the front foyer. When he called, whenever that would be, he could quickly remove his items without having to come back in.

He called me the next morning before I went to work. The timing wasn't ideal but would have to do. I relished this final farewell.

The sight of his possessions neatly packed in bags jumbled his thoughts. Lucas was expecting to shower from the night before and take his time getting ready. This morning there would be none of that.

"Yo. Why'd you pack my stuff?"

"What do you mean, why'd I pack your stuff? I told you to leave. You never came to get it, so it's here waiting for you. You should be grateful you didn't meet your clothes in a garbage bag."

"You asked me to come here!" He was using his only trump card.

"That was a year ago. You've been promising to move since January. That ask has worn out its welcome."

"I can't carry all this with me," he said, his confusion surmounting.

"Oh, well, I don't know what to tell you. You're not coming back in here, and everything you own is right here."

He frantically began opening the suitcases looking for his items.

"What are you looking for? I folded everything up and packed them neatly. You're messing up the clothes and making me late for work."

"Yeah," he said, throwing clothes out of the bags and onto the foyer's floor, "because you didn't pack my stuff right. I don't know where everything is."

"What do you really think this is?" I asked incredulously, "When I packed your clothes, I wasn't coordinating outfits for you to go to school in the morning. I packed your shit so you can leave."

"Yeah, but I can't find anything. I can't think," he declared, his confusion turning into bewilderment.

"This isn't calculus. There's nothing to think about. It's easy; put your clothes back into the bag and go." He was raising my blood pressure by the minute.

Tired of my snarky comebacks, he chuckled slightly to himself. "I hear *that* hot shit.

"I can't think BECAUSE YOU'RE STANDING OVER ME LIKE YOU'RE MY WARDEN!"

He clenched both fists as he sat on the floor rummaging through his own belongings, matching shoes with outfits. It took every ounce of my being not to fall out laughing on the floor. Even in dismay, he was the comedian.

"That's right. I'm the warden of *this* apartment. This is cell block C6. And today's your lucky day. Today you get your get out of jail free card."

He began to place his items back into the bag. I, tiring of his procrastination, threw the extraneous items back into his suitcase. He got up from the floor, squaring off with me. I pushed him toward the door. We tussled, slipping on the foyer's mat. Realizing that I was provoking a physical altercation, I let him go.

He opened the door, removing the bags. He'd leave the bin behind.

"You're going to die," I declared matter-of-factly.

"You're gonna wish death on me?" His eyes, blood-shot red, teared up with sadness.

"I'm not wishing anything on you. I'm saying, if you don't change the way you're living, one day I'll get a call that you're dead."

A solitary tear ran down his dark face. He turned his back on me and walked down the carpeted hallway pulling both suitcases one behind, the other on his right side. I closed the door behind him, walked to my bedroom, my heart weeping a sorrowful lament of catharsis as I got ready for a late workday.

I'd permanently set the prodigal dove free.

$$2016$$
$$4 + (2 + 0) + (2 + 0 + 1 + 6)$$
$$4 + 2 + 9 = 15 / 6$$

Six Personal Year

Duties, responsibilities, arts, commitments. During this cycle you'll be
known to have a magnetic personality and an ability to read people and
situations accurately. So much so, you may receive money, gifts, and
favors from others.[8] This is a time associated with music; you'll be
inclined to further your studies, as you'll have a greater capacity to
learn and retain new skills.

On the shadow side, you may be willing to engage in any form of
necromancy to fulfill your desires.

---

[8] (Strayhorn, 1997)

"Hello, let me tell who I am,
Just in case you were wondering,
Got a bit a style and grace that I may share with you.
Follow me as I'm Jacquii-ing!
Got a natural do that is fly. Attitude is so diva,
I'm the kind o' girl who doesn't give a damn or two.
Don't judge me. I'm just Jacquii-ing!"

15

IT WAS A COLD NIGHT IN EARLY FEBRUARY, AND I WAS ON MY WAY HOME from work with takeout when Nivea called my cell.

"Yo, J. This year is our fortieth. We need to do something big besides going to dinner. Did you have anything planned?"

"Not really," I said casually. "Natalie sent an email invite to a yoga retreat she's having during my birthday week. I think she told me she's having it in St. Lucia or Antigua, one of those islands."

"And you're saying this so nonchalantly. That sounds like fun. Were you planning to go?"

"I didn't give it much thought. I'm leaving to go to Amsterdam in the Netherlands at the end of the month, so I've been concentrating more on that. But if you want us to go to the retreat, I'll send you the invite. Do you even do yoga?"

"No, but I'll do it for the week. Anything to get away and do something different for the big forty."

"Okay, hold on. Let me find the email in my phone. She sent another reminder sometime late last month." I searched my Gmail account for the email, pausing when I saw the actual destination.

"Girl, the retreat isn't going to St. Lucia or Antigua. It's going to Santiago de Cuba. It's a week of Salsa dancing and yoga." I forwarded the email to Nivea.

"Cuba? Well, let's go. This is a once in a lifetime thing." Nivea sounded more and more enthusiastic.

"Okay, we have to make the first deposit by the fifteen of this month. So I'll see if I can pay it off before I leave for Amsterdam."

"Okay, I'll make the first deposit by then." We hung up with a renewed sense of urgency.

Moving money around in my head, I planned how I'd prepare for Amsterdam and pay for the trip to Cuba in the same month. One thing singledom had taught me was how to rob Peter to pay Paul, still leaving enough in Peter's supply so he wouldn't feel the weightlessness of a lighter reserve. I plugged away at my monthly spreadsheets reallocating and repurposing funds, determined to accomplish both.

One of the greatest gifts Lorraine had given me before our relationship dissolved was the gift of budgeting. She taught me how to split monthly expenses over a month so I'd pay half of everything on the fifteenth and the remaining half on the thirtieth. Rent would be split in half, and the bills would also be equally distributed over two biweekly periods. The due dates, however, would always be on the thirtieth or the first of the next month, giving me leverage to change the order of the bills in case of emergency. This freed my funds up for savings, provided a fixed amount for miscellaneous spending on day-to-day expenses, and alleviated the pressure of having to pay everything at month's end.

The saved half of the rent also provided a cushion in case events unaccounted for arose. In those cases, I'd take the balance owed out of my fixed spending money at the end of the month to make up for the deduction. It was a method I'd grown to adapt and perfect. That and adjusting the tax exemptions on my checks for a few weeks to get extra income up front. It was a single woman's game of monetary chess, the queen having all the power and leverage to move money horizontally, vertically, or diagonally without falling prey to financial debt or tax evasion.

The trip to Amsterdam would be a special one. I'd been asking Fay for months to assist me with finding a vocal coach overseas who could help me fine-tune my vocal technique. She often had student-visitors from other parts of the world who'd study with her for a week or so, and I wanted that experience in reverse. I longed to study my craft in the day and be a cultural voyeur at night.

She'd come through by connecting me with her own vocal coach from the Netherlands who was still teaching privately. I arranged for Gwendolyn and me to spend eight days in Amsterdam and one in Berlin, Germany. We'd fly into Amsterdam on the Sunday, spend the entire week, fly out to Berlin on the Saturday morning and back into Amsterdam that Saturday night. I'd perform in Amsterdam on the Sunday and we'd fly back home to New York on Tuesday, March 1st. I booked two-hour long lessons with the master vocal coach every day except the Saturday we'd be in Berlin.

We checked into the swanky Ink Hotel Amsterdam three hours earlier than our scheduled check-in time. Amsterdam was six hours ahead of New York, and our bodies felt the heaviness of a 2:00 a.m. slumber at 8:00 a.m.

The Ink Hotel was a printing house for a Roman Catholic newspaper before it was remodeled into an artsy boutique hotel. The rooms were designed out of thick concrete walls that muffled the sounds of neighboring guests and were decorated with cartoonish soft atlases of the Dam Square in the historical center of Amsterdam.

The drawings were narrated with cute commentary about the union rights of the sex workers in the Red Light District and the unsuspecting tourist who's wallet was stolen by the crafty pickpocket on the backstreets of the canals. With the help of the maps on our hotel room walls, we were able to walk to all of the major landmarks with ease.

The dampness of the dewy rain hit my face as I walked fifteen minutes along the Central Station on Prins Hendrikkade to get to the vocal coach's home. I passed the narrow canal houses and the picturesque boat moorings for touring boats along the river Amstel, dodging overzealous cyclists and bus trams at every intersection, thankful for the flats I wore.

The Gothic architectural design of Central Station dominated the city's landscape. The metropolis bustled with international accents of pedestrians and their carry-ons rolling over sodden, cobblestone streets. Cannabis loitered in the clouds. A few furtive glances to my right would lead my sightline into the simple Mac-adorned office spaces of advertising and writing firms.

One such glimpse led me to the glass of a working girl reading a book as she waited for the arrival of her morning clientele. In the irradiation of the morning gloominess she seemed ordinary, uneventful almost. Her captive stare peering upward and into me, intuiting that this was indeed like any other job during its downtime.

Arriving at the flat five minutes early, I stood outside, looking stumped at that the sophisticated bell system which took the full five minutes for me to decode. When I finally did ring the bell, the sliding door automatically disengaged from its lock and slid to the left, allowing me in.

Onno, my vocal coach for eight days, was a tall and strapping man at six feet four inches. He was built like a lumberjack and had an operatic voice just as big and powerful. He spoke with a distinguished Shakespearean lilt and carried himself with a similar majestic air. He looked down at me, taking me all in.

"That's a beautiful coat you're wearing. Very beautiful, I should say. You have a look of an English trapper. I'd caution you, however, that Holland is filled with animal rights enthusiasts. You wouldn't want someone spilling paint on such a lovely garment in protest." He laughed at the imagined sight.

"No, I wouldn't," I admitted, "and neither would they. Trust me." I winked at him jokingly. I understood the passion behind the cause.

We walked into the living room of his two-story flat which had the warmth and artistic flair of an antique thrift shop filled with ornaments, clocks, and tables of all sorts.

"Before we begin singing today," he said with the articulation of an ancient English teacher, "we'll start with breathing exercises. The towel exercise is good to control the expansion of your rib cage.

"Wrap either a towel or a belt from a robe around your rib cage, hold each hand on the opposite side of the towel, and cross the towel over your chest with your fists facing downward like so, breathe in, expand your rib cage, and pull the towel slowly, letting the air out of your mouth in a hissing *s* sound. Hold it for forty-five seconds if you can."

I could only sustain for thirty seconds on every try.

I did various breathing exercises, first with the towel, then push-ups against the wall, and finally, stepping up and down a footstool. We then did a lesson on resonance.

"How are your resonators?" he asked with certainty.

"What are my resonators?" I asked without a clue.

"When you sing, you want to open your soft palate to allow the sound to come out. Your throat should just be lying there. Never force the sound out of the throat. The resonation in your lips, in your nasal passage, and face supported by your breathing and abdominal muscles will propel the sound forward. There are resonators above your eyes, around your nose, and over your mouth.

"If you ever find you're flat, raise the ears like so," he said, using his face muscles to bring both his ears up. "And suddenly you're back in tune.

"The reason we do exercises like the towel exercise is to practice keeping the rib cage expanded against resistance. Once the rib cage is wide and open, the diaphragm is free to move up and down, supporting the breath. Now breathe in and expand your ribs, opening the nostrils. You should feel the diaphragm pushing the air down.

"We use the abdominal muscles to control the pitch and sustain the notes. Never try to create a pitch from the throat. Pitch originates in the stomach."

I was amazed at the mechanics of singing. I was getting a different lesson in anatomy. This was the anatomy of creating sound. I really liked Onno. Not only was he great at explaining the concepts, he'd take my hand and put it on his back or stomach so I could conceptualize what the movements should feel like in my own. He was truly a master at his craft.

Our lessons would continue over the next three days.

Gwendolyn and I spent the afternoons at museums or walking through the canals, and the evenings in search of good food. Holland wasn't particularly the town for indelible cuisine. It was hard for us vegetarians to find food that was filling and tasty. We settled on one Italian restaurant for breakfast, a choice of a vegan or Indian restaurant for lunch, and one specific Chinese restaurant for dinner.

At night, I'd practice in my room. It was a great place to practice. Since the walls were so thick, I could sing loudly without disturbing my mother and others in the adjacent rooms. It was the first in a long while I'd been able to sleep in a bed without any spiritual disturbance. I fathom crossing the Atlantic Ocean and being by the North Sea lessened the potency of Siete's spells. I welcomed the respite in my deepest repose.

It was during Thursday's lesson with Onno that my leisurely vacation would turn into a working one.

"So now you're going to sing your first song," Onno said, sitting down to assess how the technical work transferred to my singing.

"First song?"

I'd practiced one song for Sunday's showcase and had another in my arsenal as backup, but I thought I was only singing one.

"Yes. For Sunday's show you'll have five song selections. You'll perform two in the first set and three in the second."

Completely unprepared, I was getting a dose of what it meant to be a working singer on the road. Panic set in, but I told myself I'd been through worse in life and definitely worse in the past year. I'd have to pull it together.

"Okay, let's keep it simple with standards then. I have the backing tracks of *Misty, Cry Me a River, Bewitched, Bothered, and Bewildered,* and *My Funny Valentine* on my phone. We can add those four." These songs, although not eclectic enough for my normal repertoire, would have to do for the time being.

"Good. Let's do two today. Tomorrow you'll come out to my beach house in Zandvoort for our lesson, where we'll run the other three and set up for the show."

I was short on time. I had that Thursday night to practice. Gwendolyn and I were going to see Fay, who was also in Amsterdam, perform at the Bimhuis on the Friday night. We'd be in Berlin all day Saturday and fly back into Amsterdam late Saturday night. The show was Sunday. I technically had two nights to get my act together.

Nonetheless, I set out for Zandvoort the next day.

Taking the metro in Amsterdam was as easy as it was comfortable. With WIFI-enabled, double-decker trains traveling above ground out of the city center through Haarlem and into Zandvoort, the views were filled with houses situated on the sea, some square and modernized with glass walls, others more cottage-like. Onno met me at the Zandvoort train station where we walked through the quiet beachside town back to his house.

We ran through the week's drills before we started with the songs, singing each one to ensure for proper pitch, resonance, and articulation. Two hours seemed to go by in a nanosecond with Onno, and I had the added pressure of leaving ten minutes earlier to catch the train back to Dam Square Central Station. I shared my burdens with Gwendolyn over lunch.

"Gwen, I'm enjoying everything that I'm learning. But I feel like it's too much in a short space of time. I can't even imagine how I'm going to see Fay tonight, practice when I get back, fly to Berlin tomorrow, and be ready for the show on Sunday."

"You will," she said matter-of-factly. "You've always risen to the occasion, and this is no exception. You'll do what has to be done and perform as best you can. That's all you can do. This is what you want your life to be, right? You want to be a Jazz singer. So jump right in and embrace it."

"Yep. You're right. This *is* the life I want. Might as well claim it now."

"So stop stressing yourself unnecessarily."

That evening we walked from our hotel to the Bimhuis. It was a longer walk than I'd anticipated. I tested the walk out from Onno's Amsterdam flat to get a sense of its location so we wouldn't be lost the day of. Walking from our hotel directly there was tricky as it was long. We had to cross a park, walk down several flights of stairs behind a tunnel of sorts, up more stairs through a restaurant, and over the train station to get to the suspended Black Box of Jazz on the edge of the water.

The Bimhuis is the most prominent venue for Jazz and improvised music in Amsterdam. Fay was performing her set of music inspired by the late Herbie Nichols, who was widely known for his composition of *Lady Sings the Blues*, but his musical catalog had more of an avant-garde sound fashioned after Monk's Caribbean stylings. She'd written original lyrics to many of his songs. She and the instrumentalists used their instruments to bring out the sentient side of Herbie's composition using free vocal improvisation, prepared piano, and keen auditory interpretation.

The show was one to rival any traditional Jazz set with its versatility and fresh approach to the artform. I aspired to use my voice in these dissonant ways that allowed for authentic expression beyond scripted melodies and harmonies, touching the intimate depth of the audience's heart. Fay's set was met with a standing ovation. I couldn't stand around in wait to bid my farewells. We'd have to catch up Sunday night at one of the local Jazz houses by the canals after my performance.

In the thick of the Amsterdam night, the scent of sinsemilla wafted in the air. My mother and I walked back to the hotel, where I practiced for two more hours before I passed out from physical and mental fatigue.

* * *

The brilliant sun did little to warm Berlin's temperament on the successive Saturday morning. Not only was it frigid in weather, it was frosty in personality. Overwhelmed by the turn of musical events, I didn't have a planned agenda arranged for our brief excursion. We ad-libbed by taking the standard bus tour around Berlin to see the historical sights.

Where Amsterdam was close, densely populated, and the travel facile, Berlin was expansive, detached, and sparsely occupied. Even with the demolition of the now graffiti-laden wall, the separation was still apparent in the city's architectural design and feel. I slept through most of the tour, too uninspired and unmotivated to get out at any particular site.

We got off in the luxurious shopping district along Kurfürstendamm Avenue, the Champs-Élysées of Berlin. The streets were barely populated on a Saturday afternoon, so we ate lunch in the only Asian restaurant we could find. There we sat drinking tea, killing time before we caught the bus back to the airport. Had we stayed for a night, we may have had a better experience with the night life, but the day left a lot to be desired.

Anxiety greeted me on Sunday morning, my stomach a gassy mess as I thought about the show later that afternoon. I rehearsed my songs as much as I could before breakfast, not wanting to sing on an empty stomach.

After breakfast, I ate the green apples I'd bought from the Albert Heijn supermarket since Onno advised that they, having the optimal level of acidity for the digestive tract, were the best to eat before a performance. The malic acid found in green apples washed the mouth, purging it of excess mucus. They also served to be good lubricants for the mouth, allowing the tongue and cheeks to have unobstructed mobility over the teeth and gums.

I ran through the resonance exercises, vocal drills, and warmed up to ensure my soft palate was lubricated and open. Always aloof before a show, I sat in silence on the metro to Zandvoort. Gwendolyn paid me no mind. She was used to my pre-show madness.

I arrived an hour before showtime to practice with Onno. We started with the humming drills.

"I find that you're particularly flat this morning. What happened? You were doing so well all week. What's changed?" he asked with genuine concern.

"I don't know. I have a serious case of the fantods right now. Maybe my nerves are causing me to go flat."

"What have you to be nervous about? You know the songs. You have the pitches. You have the expression. There's a world of people out there who are just waiting to love you. Let them," he pleaded.

It was the most salient announcement of all announcements I'd heard all week. I relaxed in the construct that I'd be loved by the audience now coming into the beach house in pairs and trios.

The show was a mashup of performances by Onno, Onno's partner Wout, and me. We each took turns on the stage showcasing our different artistic styles. I started out with *Misty*. *Misty* was never my favorite song, but my voice resounded so clearly over the mic that I fell in love with my own sound. It was the first time I'd heard myself with my outer ears, as Onno would say, each word articulated clearly. I guess the enjoyment of my own sound encouraged me to express myself more freely. The second song was Rachelle Ferrell's *I Forgive You*. It was my ode to Siete. I had to put the energy of absolution into the universe in hope he'd stop his relentless antagonism.

We paused for the second set while Onno, artist turned host, served his guests a choice of wine, black tea, or soup. It was a sublime experience, reminiscent of my girls gatherings but with live music and homecooked food instead. The living room was filled with people of all ages sitting on antique furniture. I drank tea while I waited to end my set.

When the second set began, I found myself running to the bathroom almost every five minutes. Gwendolyn looked at me with an irritated look.

"What happened? Are you that nervous that you have to go to the bathroom so often?"

"No, I'm not nervous. I think it's the tea that has me using the bathroom."

"No, it's your nerves. You need to relax. You're doing fine."

"No, I'm telling you I'm not nervous," I whispered, exasperated.

I began the second set with *Bewitched, Bothered, and Bewildered*. I began with the verse. As I sang on through the chorus, I saw Onno sitting in the back of the room carefully listening to each note. When I sang the first three words of the chorus, his arms went up in the air to let me know I was getting flat on the word 'again'.

I quickly reacted, opening my soft palate and raising my ears to get the note back in tune. He nodded with a look of satisfaction. The next three songs went by so quickly and with so much ease, the experience seemed ephemeral--short-lived. The audience was loud with applause at the end of my set. I was indeed loved. I pulled it off, five songs in two days. It felt great to live up to the challenge and live life concurrently.

All my life I'd lived in close proximity to seriousness, barely leaving room for the joys of risk-taking. Perfectionism was my mental ailment of choice, its pursuit being as fleeting as it was impossible. My quest for it, knowing the full extent of its nonexistence, was what induced the anxieties I continually imposed upon myself.

It was a twisted tango between the mind and intellect, my mind the lead, my intellect the follow. This trip taught me to let my hair down a little and let life happen. Every experience preceding this moment was a setup for a successful completion of the latest lesson, and there would be a lot more on the horizon.

I met up with Fay and her husband back in the city center. We met at a local Jazz club located in what seemed, from the outside, to be a house but was a bustling club on the inside. The room was packed with Jazz enthusiasts. The contrast between New York's local clubs and those in

Amsterdam was alarming. What appeared to be a dying genre under siege on the East Coast of North America was taking on a whole new life in Holland.

"I didn't even see you after the show last night," Fay said through the crowd. "I looked for you after the performance, but you were gone."

"Oh, girl, your performance was amazing, as always. I had to go back to the hotel to practice for my performance today. I thought I was singing one song, but I had to learn four more in two days. Sorry for running out, but if I stayed later I'd have been distracted."

"Oh, yes, the show in Zandvoort. So how'd it go?"

"It was great. Onno is an excellent teacher. It was the clearest I'd heard myself sing ever. The whole concept of using the resonators made such a huge difference."

"Yes, Onno is one of a kind. I told you he'd be able to teach you many different things. I even took a few lessons with him myself because certain things you forget over time."

"Thank you for everything, Fay. I'm so grateful for this experience."

"Absolutely. This is what Jazz is about. Bringing others in and paying it forward. I'm glad you enjoyed yourself. You've put the work in."

We closed the night at their favorite coffee shop. A non-smoker, I went along to see how the weed houses operated. It was a quaint coffee shop with roots and culture reggae blasting on both floors under dim green lights. After an hour, I departed to go back to the Ink. One day of rest remaining had my heart homebound, high with euphoria.

I took time off from work in the mornings and early afternoons to fix my spiritual life. I took the opportunity to visit a Bronx Botanica after one of my routine school visits. The coincidence of this visit was I'd worked around the corner from this Botanica for two years and never ventured in.

Here I was in mid-March looking for some magic spell, potion, or amulet to help ward off the residue of Siete's hex. A half hour later, I left the store with a dressed uncrossing candle that had Siete's name etched in it, a bath, a promise to come back once the candle finished burning, and an appointment for a reading by the Priest of Ochun.

Seven days after, I went back to the botanica early in the morning to have the glass of the burned candle read. The priest took the candle in his hand.

"Who was this candle for? A man?"

"Yes," I answered, unsure of what he'd say next.

"It worked. See his face in the glass here? The glitter is showing you his head, his eyes, his nose. He has a bald head, yes?"

"Yes, he does."

"Yeah, here it is. You see it here?" The image was so apparent. It was astonishing I hadn't recognized it myself.

"Get another candle and let me dress it again just to make sure there's nothing left over from the work he's doing. And throw this one into the garbage outside. Don't keep this on you any longer."

The old candle discarded and the new one in my bag, I set back out to city hall for another day of dormancy.

The second candle wasn't as fruitful as the first. The wick disappeared in the wax and stopped burning halfway through the candle. I discarded the candle outside my apartment building and waited two more weeks for my reading with the priest. I suspected there was nothing more for the candle to do. There weren't any signs of black soot on the glass. Nor did it shatter. Besides, it was April in the city, and I had Santiago de Cuba on my mind.

In the storefront window of the Botanica I sat across from the Priest of Ochun. One would expect this highly anticipated reading to be conducted within the confines of a backstairs chamber; but here we were, unpretentiously exposed for all to see as they walked along their merry way.

"So today is April 15, 2016. I'll be giving you this inspired reading. Thank God. He gave me this beautiful gift to help people, and that's exactly what I utilize it for."

He prayed over the cards as he shuffled, asking the spirits to remove all negative beings and forces from infiltrating. He stopped for me to cut the deck in half and asked for my full name.

"Don't ask where the story comes from. Just listen."

"Alright." I didn't have much of a choice as I was completely beholden to his testimony.

"Okay, here we go." He shuffled the cards some more. "My friends like to ask me, 'Why you do this for a living?' Because I like to gossip."

I laughed loudly. "Yes, you like people's business. I see you."

"You know? I've heard some stories. Whew."

"I know you have," I confirmed.

"We're at the beautiful age where we should be in a more financially stable mode. And we know we have to work every day to provide so we have food and a roof over our heads. Ain't nothing changing that. But in the midst of getting to that place or keeping that place, we sometimes think that things are always going to be flowing. That everything is always going to be good. And all of a sudden shit happens--BS. Stupid, tedious things.

"I feel you're a person who will share love with anyone who comes across you. You have a lot of spiritual angels and deities around you that are of love and energies of goodness, which is great. You have a beautiful history of spirit next to you because in your bloodline it shows that there are people, especially the women, who have spiritual gifts like yourself. There's that thing, you know, *let your conscience be your guide*. Sometimes, our spirit tells us something ..."

"And we don't listen," I interjected. I knew the feeling of self-doubt all too well.

"We ... do ... not ... listen. You have a beautiful gift I'm seeing here. You pick up energy. You feel things. Especially when you feel people's energy, you can determine whether they're bullshitting you or not. So that's a pretty sharp gift. It doesn't come to everybody, but you have that. You have to utilize that beautiful spiritual gift. If you feel like something isn't right, there's a 90% chance that it isn't.

"And sometimes, it's people we come to trust, care for, and love who start doing the sneaky shit. You're getting to see people for who they truly are, and that's the most important part of this path that you're on right now. Because I do see that there's a shift, a shift in everything. I'm talking about your career, love, the home. It's part of the process of your life. It's more of a step up from where you are currently."

"Okay. That's good to know." I was calmed.

"Don't tell me what you do for a living just yet, but I want to tell you that I feel you should've been a psychiatrist or something. You're always giving people advice, even on a spiritual level. In this shift that you're in, you're going to reinvent the *you factor*. You're in the process of this reinvention. It's like the bible says, *I'm the way, the truth, and the light.*

"The words *I am* are becoming a part of you right now. *I'm seeing me more now, than I ever did before.* And it's a beautiful thing because you're embracing your femininity on a higher level. I see that you're communicating your higher self to a higher being. You're growing a new spiritual relationship, which is a blessing. And you're projecting a new sense of peace."

"Mm-hmm," I chimed in agreement.

"Because what I'm seeing is you've taken quite a bit of hits in the last couple of years. When you finally decided to restructure, you said to yourself, *wait a minute, this is just too much. I need to talk to you, God. There's some dark places I've been in, and I don't want to go back there.* And God is saying, *I'm listening to you. I got you.*

"In life, some things that are damaging had to happen. And you're no longer asking why. You're saying, *I've accepted it. It damaged me a bit, but it's alright. I'm not going to let this take me over.* You know why?" he asked.

"Why?" I asked in anticipation.

"Because you have the power of the pussy," he confirmed.

His unpolished pronouncement took me by surprise, and my loud guffaw knocked me out of my seat.

"You're a woman and you're not going to let anything muddy that. That's the best way I could put it for you to understand." He shuffled the cards some more.

"I see something brewing. Something in the midst. I see that it's more work-related, to be honest. I'm seeing a pattern of people shifting. And you're saying to yourself, *I have to be careful. I don't want to lose my job either.* He saw the current climate in the workplace. "And that feeling of, *Damn, why do I have to be on my toes with all this shit?*

"Beware those people who throw others under the bus. And that'll be some shit because, when you see it, you'll say to yourself, *If this bitch can do this to that person, I know damn well she's going to do it to me.* So you already know. The flags have been put up for you to see what's what."

He changed gears.

"Going back on the spiritual grain, you been down those dark roads already. And my spirit says there's this shift, the higher self, the higher consciousness is going to be your maxim. You're going to see things in a different way. It's like an awakening, almost like, *Oh, I got it now.* And people are going to notice you differently. And when I say there's a shift, I see new things coming to you. It doesn't necessarily mean that you're going to lose something on a grand level. But even if you do lose something, it ain't going to be anything bad. Understand what I'm saying?" he asked.

"Yes, I do."

"Because I see people who are going to try to be undermining. You know you can only take but so much. You'll ask yourself, *Is there something on me? Why am I being crossed?* You know you're already getting to the point where you don't want to be there anyway. But you know you gotta do what you gotta do because you've worked so hard to get to that place, man.

"Ain't gonna let this shit go after you put all this blood, sweat, and tears into this gig. But I'll tell you, the moments that seem so dark, actually might be the blessing. You already know what's going on. Prepare yourself for the next level. You understand?" he asked.

I nodded in consent.

"Uhm, I feel that with this new inner-you, you want to build a home. Build a family. That's where we're at now. You're projecting the American fucking dream. You're projecting the *I want a roof over my head, my beautiful three children, and that stinky foot husband of my mine. But I love his ass anyway.* That value of a quality lifestyle.

"You produce this energy because you shine like that. It's who you are. But for you to get there, you have to start letting go of certain other things. Things that aren't really doing right by you. If you're getting red flags from certain people you're with, you have to let them go. But my spirit tells me you have much bigger things ahead. I don't know why you didn't get into real estate, to be honest."

"Why? I'd have been successful at real estate?" I asked.

"Extremely. Anything in the business field. With the energy you have, people will buy whatever you're selling." He chuckled at the witty double entendre. "I'm gonna tell you a quick story that will pertain to where I'm going with this. It's a true story."

"Okay." I nestled in my seat, ears peeled in anticipation.

"There was a lady who came to me. She lived in New Jersey. This individual, she was white, blonde hair, blue eyes, the whole nine yards, looking fine as hell, God bless her. I sat with her to do a reading. And I knew what I was saying when I told her, *You know what? You're going to lose everything you have.*

"But she looked at me and said, *I doubt that, sir. I'm a CFO at a large firm in Manhattan.* I said, *Okay,... no problem. Take your money back. I don't want it. All I want you to do, is when something happens ...*"

He stopped the story abruptly to rap his knuckles on the glass fervently, getting the attention of the local man selling ices.

"Hey, Moe, let me get a cherry icy." He turned to me. "You want one?"

"No, thank you." The hilarity of the scene was like no other.

"So. I'm sorry. I was dying for that cherry icy. You know when you have an urge and it comes right at you?

"So, anyhow, I told her, *Take the money. This is what I really want you to do. If something happens and you know you're going off course, just sit with God. You don't need anything. I'm in the business of helping people. You don't need anything else but God.*

"And then she says, *Well, I pray to God.*

"And I'm like, *No, baby, you're probably thanking God, but you're not praying to God.* Tell me why, three days later, I get a phone call, *You fucking so-and-so.*"

"She thought you did it to her?" I asked, enthralled with the story.

"Yes! I said, *Let me tell you something, sweetheart. One, you don't call me like that. Two, relax yourself! Now what happened?*

"And she said, *I don't know. They're telling me they want me to file some papers, they have an investigation going on, and I should go home.*

"I said, *Okay, pray to God.*

"No, you don't understand.

"I said, *Okay.*

"She kept calling the job. They kept telling her to wait. She kept calling. Wait."

He stopped to eat his icy with relished delight. "Mm-hmm.

"They called her a few days later. *Listen, we know you need some money. Why don't you come in? We'll give you a check.*

"The check was a lot healthier than it was supposed to be. She signed these papers. And finally, she signed for a severance package. Fired. After twenty years. By her own people.

"Not done, though. She got depressed over all of this. She and her husband were married for a long time.

"He came to her and said, *Baby, you know what? I think you need some time. I'm going to take the kids over to Grandma's house. Do your thing. We'll give you some space. I'll see you next week.*

"He came the next week. *Baby, you look really down. I love you. Take some more time.* Third week, *Baby, I love you, but this isn't really working out for me anymore. I love you, though. God bless.*

"Divorce."

He paused to eat more of his cherry icy.

"She's flipping out. She's crying. Then all of a sudden her friend came from Manhattan to stay with her. She started praying with her friend and something happened.

"She called me and said, *I think, I felt God.*

"I said, *Okay, there you go.*

"She said, *I understand! I'm okay!*

"I said, *There … you … go. Go ahead now.*

"She called me again the next day because I felt compelled to this lady. She's on the phone in the morning and I'm like, *Leave me the fuck alone now, lady.* You know, playing with her.

"And she said, *I woke up this morning and the sun was coming into my house. It felt like God was touching me.*

"I said, *Amen! Amen! Good for you.*

"And she said, *Something's going to change.*

"I said, *Of course.*

"Just then, there's a knock on the door. It just so happened that she went to church. To make a couple of extra dollars, she and her friend made some cupcakes, and the church started buying weekly servings.

"Have you ever seen a man you just look at like, *Mhm?* You know, *Mhm.* Never mind her dirty ass had been closed up in the house all day.

House must've been all musty and shit. But she opened the door, looking down. She said the man was wearing a pin-striped suit. She could smell the cologne coming off his socks. She looked up, and there was this beautiful black man.

"He said, *Are you the lady who makes the cupcakes?*

"She said, *Yeah.*

"He said, *Call your best friend up. She's down the block. I need you to get in your car. Call her. You'll understand.*

"Now, I'm on the phone with her while all of this is going on, and I'm like, *Girl, get into your fucking car. Follow this man!*

"She said, *Why? What's going on?*

"He said, *Don't worry, come with me.*

"She goes down the block, meets up with her friend.

"The guy said, *I understand you're the lady who makes the cupcakes. I have a big event coming up. It's going to be my grand's birthday bash, and I want you to make the cupcakes.*

"She asked, *How many do you want?*

"He answered, *I need 50,000 of them.*

"She's like, *What? Stop playing.*

"He said, *No, ma'am, I'm not here to play. So here's the deal. Take these keys to this old restaurant that just closed down. It has enough stuff that you can utilize. I have the lease here that's already paid for a whole year. I also have another check so you can hire some people at the local church that you attend. You can open that up, help them out, and pay their salaries. But I need this to happen. Take this as my down payment.*

"She said, *What?*

"He asked, *Is your name so-and-so?*

"*Yes it is.*

"*Okay, here's a nice healthy check for you. Call this an advance. You can buy whatever you need.*

"She said, *This isn't freaking true. Who are you? Some rich bigwig?*

"He answered, *Oh, yes. I'm very healthy. I'm good.*"

The priest paused to chuckle.

"In the midst of the conversation she asked, *Why are you doing this?*

"He said, *Well, ma'am,* and this touches me every time I say it, *Ma'am, I was in church. I was praying to God, saying I wanted something sweet. And I got your cupcake.*

"Now they're together." He concluded the story, licking the tail-end of his icy with a smile.

"Wow, that's so beautiful." The prophetic recountal pulled at my heartstrings.

"Now the reason I told you that *whole* story is, even if you reach that darkest moment, and you've been in that place--we all have. You aren't going to be there anymore. Just know that God is listening to everything. And you do pray to him. I know you do.

"Just leave whatever is bothering you in his hands. Because you have some stuff that you want to get off, and it's hard for you to communicate it to people who sometimes aren't even listening. But God has some surprises for you. Just like that. God has something in store. I don't know what it is. I just know that something *huge*, is going to happen for you. And I have *no* clue what it is. But if you know how to make cupcakes ... you might as well start baking, honey.

"And *don't* forget me, please!"

16

WHILE THE WORLD GRIEVED PRINCE'S CELESTIAL ASCENSION, OUR flight from Miami disembarked at the Antonio Maceo International Airport in Santiago de Cuba. A group of twelve women from different walks of life, we chose to extricate ourselves from the distractible din of social media and information overload for the sake of introspective fellowship.

Having cleared customs, we stood outside the arrival gate as onlookers of a family who'd been reunited. A circle of arms formed securely around a woman gone far too long. The lineal sobs resounded, touching the hearts of us gazers with raw sentiment. Nivea was poised closely by, transfixed by the outward display of filial love. When the outpouring of ardor became too much to process through sight alone, she herself joined the encircled homecoming speaking in the limited Spanish she could recall from college.

"*Aww, lo siento mucho. Tu Tambien me haces llorar,*" she relayed her sorrow and offered her tears.

The family paused a bit to evaluate their amiable intruder. When they discerned she wasn't a threat, they too extended their warmth by opening the circle to make room for her arms and offered their own explanation.

"*Nuesta hija ha estado ausente durante diez años. Esta es su primera vez en casa.*" The mother explained that her daughter had been abroad for ten years and was returning home for her first visit.

While Nivea hugged her new family, I felt the ancestors hugging me. Their presence was too powerful to ignore. My feet were grounded to the pavement as they reached up to embrace my legs. Our travel companions, awe-struck by Nivea's impulsive behavior, looked at me for clarification.

280

"Does she even know them?"

"Nope," I answered casually between my chuckles. "Meet Nivea. This is who she is, and who she'll be for the rest of our week together."

The group was split. Some of the ladies laughed along with me while others looked away in exasperated shock. The division made clear who we'd be organically drawn toward for the duration of our stay. Nivea's perceived faux pas established a natural clique of a fabulous five, Sharon, Sahara, Sahara's daughter Ula, Nivea, and me.

Sharon was one of my subordinates who, after two years of discovering she was horrible with technology, left the department to become principal of a Queens charter school.

Sahara I met back in 1996 when her name was still Drisa. We both worked for Bloomingdales, she in the bridal registry department with my mother, and I in table top. We were the youngest of the lot with plenty of style and attitude to match. She was model-esque with a blonde Caesar. I was model-like with colorful locs.

We didn't take to each other immediately. She liked my mother instead. We passed each other straight for weeks. On one fateful day, we did our habitual eye-roll, turned our heads, paused, looked back at each other, and laughed. We were inseparable until I was fired from the gig for likening my colleagues' competitive, backbiting ways to *house nigger* antics at our lunchtime communion in front of the boss. Shortly thereafter, we lost contact.

Nineteen years later, we met again at the Soho Apple store on a random Monday night in the winter of 2015. Now a unionized electrician, she traded in her coveted Isaac Mizrahi threads for Dickies, her Kenneth Cole pumps for steel-toed construction boots, and her birth name Drisa for Sahara.

We stayed in contact sporadically since she occasionally suffered from episodes of depression. I tried to convince her to come to yoga class with me, but she skillfully refused by way of postponement. It wasn't until her hairdresser, who happened to be my yoga mate, mentioned my name in conversation that she followed the trail back to me. Now, a year later, she was a regular yoga student and on the yoga retreat with her twenty-three-year-old daughter at her side.

We piled into our caravan of throwback Buicks, Fords, and Chevrolets from the 1950's. The cars typified a graceful era long expunged by the advances of technology. I reveled in their preserved beauty but reviled the acrid fumes from the exhaust consuming my nares. I thought a solitary match would've been the car's demise--and ours, for that matter.

We ventured on to our stay at the Casa Particulares, a series of concrete row houses of varying heights, painted in bright colors of peaches, yellows, burnt oranges, and reds, built on slim, gravelly streets. Aromas of roast pork exited our handler's gate to greet us, masking the aftertaste of fuel that engulfed my esophagus. A new Kia, horn blaring, sped past; our famished group scattered into a schism of carnivores on one sidewalk and pescatarians across the other.

Our host was also the owner of the Sandunga Dance School that was based on the roof deck of his house. For the next six days we'd practice yoga in the morning and Salsa in the afternoon.

A few houses away from the dance studio was the neighborhood Santeria shop, in plain view. An elderly woman stood in the horizontal split doorway of the store looking at us as we removed our bags. The convoy of antique cars parked on the right side of the street took up the majority of available space allotted to the narrow roadway and sidewalks.

Sahara and her daughter were assigned to a house diagonal to the dance studio. Nivea and I were farther down the block next to the market that distributed rationed foods to the locals. We passed the local man selling pork to the long line of natives waiting for their share of eggs, cheese, and the like on the way to our home. Our house was bright orange with heavy wooden doors that adorned fancy carvings. What looked to be modest from the outside was magnificent on the inside.

The house was balmy, with natural ventilation and light. We walked into a large white living and dining room area that spread out to separate living quarters on the first and second floors. Each room had its own queen-sized bed, closet, and bathroom. I chose the bedroom on the first floor while Nivea chose to go to the second. A narrow staircase led three stories up to the second floor and rooftop deck where we'd sit for breakfast and dinner each day. In the middle of the staircase area was a solarium, allowing the sunrays to shine through and the natural vegetation to grow between the concrete.

It was paradise hidden behind an asphalt jungle. Sharon, a lone traveler, stayed in a home by herself farther down the street from Nivea and me.

Unpacked and rested, our first order of business was Salsa. Each of the ladies was assigned a dance partner for the entire week. Our dance partner would serve as instructor, guide, and escort to the nightclubs after dinner.

We began by learning the basic salsa step following as the men led. I stepped back with my left foot on one while my dancer stepped forward with his right, placed my right heel down on two, and brought my left foot back on three. We did the reverse on the right side as I stepped forward with my right on five, left heel down on six, and right foot back on seven.

We repeated this sequence, getting the feel for each other. 1-2-3-5-6-7, 1-2-3-5-6-7 replayed in my head as I wondered what happened to the disregarded four and eight. My dancer, a young stylish football player profiling a straightened mohawk, pulled me in closer.

"Small steps," he said in his limited English. "Women make small steps. Hips do the work." He courteously reprimanded me for stepping my long legs too far behind me. As I brought my legs in closer with each step, he nodded and smiled his approval. The basic step progressed to our first turn, left foot forward on one, pivot on two, and turn with the right.

My dancer and I communicated in lock step, my steps mirroring his. It was a different dynamic being led by such sure, masculine energy. His innate affection and take charge attitude functioned in concert. In the humidity of the evening, pheromones secreting in the hot air, I felt safer in the arms of a stranger than in those of the men I'd previously loved.

We showered and changed for our group's dinner at the San Francisco Restaurant. Our male companions didn't accompany us the first night. This was a meeting for ladies of the retreat only. Nivea dressed in a form-fitting yellow dress that accented her thick hour-glass figure. She let her pinned hair fall to her shoulders in sweeping tresses. Not one to wear a stitch of make-up, her dark skin glowed with unprocessed radiance, and her smile lit up the night.

She strutted down the narrow Santiago streets in her floral Louboutin stilettos waving "*Ola*" and "*Buenos Noches*" to the neighbors who sat on the sidewalks and front porches. She captivated the natives. Men and women alike were charmed in a ritual way. Enamored of her carnality, they waved back, shouting, "Celia! Celia!" as she passed them by. Nivea was the late, great Celia Cruz reincarnated.

After dinner, we enjoyed live music and dancing at the Casa Grande Hotel. High heels in hand, we traipsed down the hill to our houses. At the top of the hill, the younger people congregated around the local telephone company, as that was the only WIFI hotspot available in the town. A phone card with an access code granted an hour's access to the rest of the world.

The nights came alive in Cuba. Loud music and happy people filled the safe roadways. We quickly came to learn that our neighbors looked out for us at nights when we left and made note of when we returned in the morning. The overpowering sense of family enveloped us.

Each day, we'd wake up to our 8:00 a.m. yoga class under the sweltering sunrise. We'd go back to our respective houses for a breakfast of guava, mango, banana, and pineapples, fresh blended juice, warm hops bread with butter, omelets, and ham. We'd dance from ten in the morning until lunch time.

Our clique, the Fabulous Five, would go to Rumba Café for piña coladas and appetizers; I'd nap until dinner while the others went sightseeing. We'd meet at any of houses for the night's meal, dance at the Klaqueta Bar or Casa de la Trova with our dance partners, and stay on the hill during the wee hours of the morning to converse with family and friends back home. Not much of a phone person, I was happy for the week's break from American society.

What was interesting about being in Cuba was, we'd heard so many stories from the American perspective that referenced lack, lack of food, lack of luxury, lack of internet, lack of modernization. The country was the happiest we'd ever seen. For a country that suffered from scarcity, we received any amenity and luxury requested of our hosts and hostesses.

Nivea's charm enticed the local *hustle man* to provide us with extra luxuries such as black market cigars, clothing, perfumes, and marijuana. Our dinners were lavish, with huge spreads of organic fruits, vegetables, lobster, shrimp, pork, chicken, fish, beef, soups, rice, and beans. We wanted for nothing.

On our third day, we danced and ate lunch at Siboney Beach. It was a relatively cloudy day, but our dance partners catered to our every whim, making the day quite bright. While the others frolicked in the rocky waters, I asked our host for a distinguished courtesy.

"While we're here, would we be able to see a Babalawo?" Sahara and Nivea joined in on my conversation.

"Ah, yes," said our gracious host. "The man you're staying with is a Babalawo," he said, pointing to Sahara. "You can speak with him. He can do a ritual for you at the house. I'll organize it with him when we get back."

That afternoon we each met with the Babalawo, one of our dancers serving as the translator. He read the five of us for five dollars each. He didn't use cards. Instead, he used cowrie shells in a calabash. The shells are purported to be a portal through which the divination specialist can make contact with ancestors and a world of divine, infinite wisdom otherwise out of reach.

He tossed the shells on the sacred cloth and interpreted the message based on their position on the fabric. His message for me was straightforward; I was to remain calm, focused, and careful at work. I was advised not to argue. The most significant message of all was that I hadn't yet stepped into my role as a practicing high priestess. He advised that I wear white to be closely aligned with that vibration.

He went on to say that of all the orishas, I was the daughter of Osaín. Osaín is the orisha of wild plants, medicinal herbs, and magic. He's known to be a masterful spellcaster found in the feral, uncultivated areas of nature. All other orishas look to Osaín for assistance in their ceremonies because it's his knowledge of magic and plants that they rely on. His magic is said to be so powerful that no one can undo his spells.

The following evening, the Babalawo conducted a ceremony for each of us and our respective Orishas. I pleaded for Osaín to use his powerful magic to release me from Siete's spiritual tight hold once and for all.

The frequent travel weakened my immune system. I came home with a cold strong enough to rival influenza. Despite the vitamins I continued to take abroad, the room air conditioning was so cold at nights, my body responded with a head and respiratory cold. I was bedridden for a week.

Unable to sing, I decided to get my musical fix through film. Gwendolyn and I went on our habitual movie outing to see *Miles Ahead*, the biopic loosely based on the life of Miles Davis. I was drawn to one scene where Don Cheadle, in his portrayal of Miles, performed *Blue in Green* on the Birdland stage. I'd loved that song since I was in college. I'd memorized every single note and inflection of his muted trumpet. I wanted so badly to sing the song but didn't connect with any of the lyrics other artists had written.

One of the things I found myself at odds with in regard to the Jazz canon was the lyrical writing of many standards. I could never quite comprehend how musical compositions with such elitist connotations would be paired with hokey, infantilized lyrics. The instrumentation dared to venture into the depths of the auditor's gut, whereas the words danced superficially around the perimeter of the core. I needed to relate to the audience on a sophisticated level. My lyrics had to match the complexities the music conveyed.

I left the theatre inspired.

Saturday afternoon stays at the barbershop were normally painful. Phil, who was coincidentally cutting in a shop in Crown Heights, around the corner from Carlos, performed his craft meticulously slow. On this Saturday, however, I was preoccupied with Miles. I sat with headphones on my ears listening to the melody of *Blue in Green*.

I listened to the sounds his trumpet made. Heard the vowel sounds in each note. Saw the colors in the sound. Captured the syllables in each phrase to ensure I accounted for each chromatic sixteenth note. I played and rewound the song. Stop, played, and rewound until I had my own story to voice over Miles's chorus and solo.

In the span of an hour, I came up with my rendition of *Blue in Green*. Most love songs told the story about a love gained or lost. When the love was lost, it was almost always the other party's fault, and how many *I loved you, but you did me wrongs* have we heard? Too many to count.

I told the story of a woman napping next to her amour as she reconciled the anguish of the relationship within herself. I humanized the woman's thought process as she analyzed her warped, entangled affair with her resting beau who sought to both deify and destroy her in his waking hours. Perhaps it was my ode to Siete. There were many mornings I settled next to him, succumbing to a tension, yearning for a way out. With Miles's help, I'd initiated an escape.

Sleeping here

You lie so peacefully

I do not know where you end and I begin.

Caught in

This dream

Of make believe.

Even

When

I can

See through all of the lies you tell

You're a part of me

Connected are we.

You cause the sadness that is

My blue in green.

You are

My blue in green!

So I

Make peace with all the pain I feel inside me.

An extension of your heart that only beats and cannot feel.

We are

A broken melody

Song Incomplete

And here still I lie

With you

And kiss you softly.

Two kindred hearts in search of love so divine

But can't

Give love

Completely.

I

Envy your ability to sleep when

You

Are the cause of all of my hurtful memories.

You are my blue in green!

I practiced the song with Fay. This was going to be my song selection for the ending workshop series.

"Wow, Jacquii, this is the first song you've connected with immediately. Writing your own lyrics works for you. You're resonant and clear, but you're singing the song exactly as Miles played it. It has to sound musical. What story are you trying to impart through your lyrics?" Fay always knew how to push the development further.

"I want to tell the story of a woman processing her feelings and emotions toward her man as he sleeps."

"And who's she talking to?"

"She's talking to him as he sleeps."

"Okay, now I want you to speak the lyrics as you would if he was here sleeping. Jazz is a conversational art. You have to make people believe what you're saying. They need to be in the bed with you while you're speaking to him."

We dissected the theme by living the lyrics. While I was one step closer to bringing my feelings out, I hadn't yet learned how to be truthfully vulnerable in the music. No matter how much progress I'd made, Jazz was determined to be the genre that kept on teaching.

Tamia called in June.

Our relationship had become extremely strained over the years, branching along diverging channels. The poetic course of our lives brought

W. Somerset Maugham to mind when he wrote, *We are not the same persons this year as last; nor are those we love. It's a happy chance if we, changing, continue to love a changed person.*

There was no doubt we still loved each other; I just wasn't sure how much our transformed selves *liked* each other. We'd become distant and awkward in each other's presence. Neither of us extended the olive branch to discuss why. Instead, I retreated into myself, and she became the grim reaper's messenger, alerting me of all who'd died from the old neighborhood.

She called to tell me that one of our childhood friends from the old block had transitioned due to cancer. She and I were the same age. Mortality waved its red cape in front of our lives like a matador taunting the charging bull. I made the decision that, with the notion of authentic living being such an elusive abstraction, I'd seize life by the horns. I'd be the architect of my own existence.

Torrential rains poured from the skies on the afternoon of the service. It was almost as if the pluvial vault of heaven unbolted with fresh deposits of valediction, the earthy petrichor singeing the nose ever so slightly like a drifting aria.

The family was a religious clan who owned their own church. The funeral was a full-blown Sunday service complete with speakers, choir interludes, scripture readings, testaments, and sermons. Gwendolyn and I sat closer to the back watching the large church fill to capacity. I visually scoured the pews to see if I could find Milayo, the cousin I was closest with in the family.

Milayo had moved to Atlanta when we were teenagers, and her visits to New York were infrequent. She was a free spirit who sat at the opposite end of the family spectrum. She was daring, sexual, organic, fun-loving, and earthly. Her spirit exuded in any space even as a child. We were instantly drawn to each other as toddlers and maintained the bond through the passage of time no matter how many years and miles separated us. Tamia came to the service an hour after it started. She winked at me and blew a kiss as she looked for a seat up front.

When the service was done, we had the choice of attending the repast in the church basement, but the crowd was so devouring, I didn't have the spiritual strength to deal with all the energies coming at me. I wanted to locate Milayo; but I decided to forgo the gathering and went home to practice for my upcoming show, stopping on my way out to tell Tamia's nephew I'd speak with her another time.

My first hour-long set in New York was at the West Side Lounge on the upper West Side on June 19th. I sang the first set and Lyris sang the second. It was truly Lyris's show.

Lyris was another Jazz singer who attended the workshops with me. A self-employed psychologist by day, she'd been singing her entire life but wasn't sure if she wanted to make it a profession.

I was happy to sing the first set. The performance in Amsterdam and genesis of my songwriting evolution gave me additional confidence to get up in front of a crowd for an hour. I dressed in all white, as the Babalawo advised. It was an arduous undertaking to incorporate into my everyday life, so I started with performances.

The house was packed with my friends and family. My girlfriends from work, childhood, and my yoga class came out; Lucas came from Upstate. Keisha and her new husband sat in the booth to the left of Lucas. Gwendolyn was there with her friends. Trent came with his camera in hand to be my in-house photographer. Fay sat in the back observing her two students. I was fully loved and supported.

Barefoot and grounded, I started my set with Charles Mingus's *Eclipse*. It was my artistic manifesto of sorts. If you couldn't dig the eccentricity of Mingus, you wouldn't be able to dig me. The nerves set in through the first song selection, but I could hear Keish cheering me on from the audience.

The next song was *A Song for my Father*. Considering it was Father's Day, I dedicated the show to my father who, as an adroit drummer, was the first musician of the family, instilling his talents in both Lucas and me. With each song, I built the confidence to allow myself the freedom to let go, trusting in the magic of the moment. My shoulders started to shimmy. My improvisation was more daring. My voice opened up.

Through my entire eight-song set, my pitch was perfect. The audience reacted positively to my range and power, giving me a standing ovation. I ended the set with Oliver Nelson's *Stolen Moments* completely fulfilled and satisfied with my execution. In that instance, I knew, I was built for this.

The Saturday after the show I went to the barbershop still floating from the success of my New York City debut but slightly disappointed that Phil didn't make it. I walked two steps in, scouting out a seat when I looked up to see none other than Milayo Negesti sitting in my favorite chair.

"Milayoooo," I sang in circumspect shock at the coincidence.

"What's up, *mamacita*? How've you been? What are you doing here?" She ended her phone call, leaning in to kiss me on my cheek.

"Ok-ay. I live in Brooklyn. *This* is my normal barbershop. *He's* my regular barber," I said, pointing to Phil. "You live in Atlanta. What are *you* doing here? I looked for you at the funeral, but there were too many people and I had to practice for a show, so I left. I thought you went back home."

"I was there. I was in the front. I came in a little late. But *I'm* back home in New York. I came to this specific shop because my daughter wanted to get her hair braided, and one of my girlfriends recommended the hairstylist here."

"Talk about the magic of the universe. What are the odds of that happening?"

"Yep. I manifest greatness all day, every day, Love. You mentioned you had a show. What kind of show was it?"

"Oh, I'm a Jazz singer now. At least after work. But I do sit in and perform at open mics around the city as well."

"That's dope. I can see that songstress energy on you."

"So what are you up to now?" I asked.

"I'm an independent consultant. I work as a life coach. I deal with the tantric art of massage, energetic healing, empowerment coaching, numerology, and sacred crystal jewelry design. I was working in sociology after I got my master's degree, but the traditional approach to the work didn't quite fill me."

"That's next level. So many of us can use some healing arts right now."

"Girl, can't we ever. I talk about the importance of sex as a form of healing. Women around the world are sexually repressed and are being taught to harness that repressive energy. And *then* they wonder where the blockages are coming from. Girl, they're not activating their sacral and root chakras. Every ailment or form of dis-ease in our bodies is a form of energy blockage that has taken root and spread.

"Recurring bacterial vaginosis come from a lack of trust in our partners or ourselves. Whenever we approach the act from a place of mistrust, we make ourselves susceptible to infection, because the intentions going in weren't pure. And then we don't take the time to heal ourselves naturally. All infections and viruses can be treated naturally."

I was her attentive student, absorbing all she said.

"Do you hold classes or speak to large groups of women?" I was hatching a plan to have her speak at one of my girls' gatherings.

"I do."

"Okay, I'll organize something for my girlfriends." We exchanged phone numbers.

She excused herself to go to the restroom. She, a chocolate woman, stood at five feet, six inches. Her hair, dyed blonde, was close-cropped contrasting against the sheen of her skin. Her eyes and nose were small in comparison to her full lips. After two grown children, her body had snapped back into shape with no stomach bulges.

A collection of waist beads made out of crystals adorned her small waistline and sat over her wide hips and protruding behind. Her sashay oozed with sex as she floated to the back of the shop. A born sensualista, she had every man's attention in the room. Over twenty years later, she still captivated an audience.

After months of phone tag, calendar coordination, and working around Milayo's many speaking engagements, we finally held the first of the four-session Wellness Series in mid-September. The theme of the first session was *Getting to Know Yourself: Self-Love and Acceptance*. We had an intimate circle of six because many of the ladies, reluctant to do self-work, declined at the last minute. Milayo commenced the roundtable.

"Today we set out to answer two questions based on the principles of value and worth. Value; What do I expect from myself for myself? Worth; What do I expect from the world based on who I am? We're feminine by nature. Femininity is intuitive. However, we've been showing up with a lot of masculine energy. Feminine energy moves from the heart. Currently, we've been making logical decisions and not trusting the heart. Feminine is the state of being active and masculine is doing the activity. If we're too heavy on either side, it shows up as resentment or frustration.

"We have to learn to be and do less, as we're guided on a daily basis by our intuition. The way to develop our intuition is to listen. The way to listen is to inquire and be still because femininity births visions and thoughts. I want to stop to ask you all to tell me what you think femininity is."

Rhianne started. "I don't know what it means to be feminine anymore. I'm not going to be submissive until I can get what I want and the peace that I need. So if I have to be strong and feminine, and rolling my eyes like I'm not cooking for anybody--at home, of course, not in the workplace, that's just how I'll be. And that's just it."

Rhianne was my cousin through a pumpkin-vine family linkage. A year older and less complicated than I, she trained her girlish desires and intentions on manifesting a blissful union as a kept wife to a distinguished gentleman. After thirteen years, she was a dedicated mother of four, married to a tight-fisted, run-of-the-mill fellow who snuffed the optimistic gleam out of her eyes.

"Rhianne, can I ask you a question?" asked Sahara. "When's your birthday?"

"Why?" Rhianne said, shying away as she laughed.

"No, she sounds just like me before Cuba," Sahara answered. "You sound exactly like me. They're people who tell me I hate everything because I like to complain. I'm the one who's normally like, *I don't like you doing that. I'm not going to do that. This is how I need my life to be.* And when people tell me you're going to do this or that, I'm like, *Oh hell no! That's never going to be me.*

"I did it for so many years that I didn't even realize it. Before I went to Cuba, people would always tell me, *You're so negative.* My experience in Cuba changed me so much. And the word *submissive* doesn't have to do *anything* with a man. *Nothing* to do with a man."

"No, I'm not speaking about a man," Rhianne defended her position. "I'm just being realistic. And that's just what it is. I'm realistic. Two plus two equals four. It doesn't equal five or one, and that's just it!"

"I'd like each of you to tell me what you think the word submissive is," Milayo interjected, starting with me.

"Surrender."

"We're just responding to the word submissive?" Belle asked.

"Yeah," Milayo said encouragingly.

"Fear."

"Okay. That's an honest answer. Rhianne?" Milayo continued.

"I have *no* words," Rhianne chimed in, laughing.

"Giving of yourself and equally receiving," Halle contributed.

"Come back to me." Sidney still needed to process.

"Learning to shut the fuck up when necessary," Nivea quipped with conviction as the ladies fell out in amusement.

"For me, it's going to be the same as Jacquii," Sahara concurred. "It's surrender. And not in the sense of surrendering and being more feminine with a man. Surrendering to my masculine self. Surrendering to my masculine self to say that I don't always have to be this strong. I don't have to do this all by myself.

"Like, for instance, when we were in Cuba, dancing with our male partners. One of the ladies decided to depart from her role as the follow, to lead the man instead. And you can see he was totally confused. He didn't know what to do because she took his position away. He didn't know how to approach her. And although it was just a dance, the way he interacted with her from then on was totally different.

"Surrendering can also be that sense of, *I don't have to do this thing now, I can do it later.*"

"Agreeing to compromise is submission." Milayo brought the focus back to the collective. "Submission is an agreement. It's surrendering yourself. Surrender is surrendering your ego to the spiritual side, because the shadow self is the side of you that isn't good. Submission is receptive.

"We're the vessels that receive, as everything is internal. Embracing your receptivity allows you, as a woman, to receive with grace and gratitude. If you're feeling guilty about receiving your gifts or unwilling to receive, you block your feminine power. Why? The woman is the keeper of spirit. If the energy is blocked, spirit can't communicate with you. I want you all to write this; *today I'm planting a seed of new sensual beginning. I look forward to creating yumminess in all areas of my life moving forward.* Now I want you all to write your full name and date of birth. We're going to look at the meaning of the numbers in our names."

We were barely into the numerology exercise before the night came to an end. Our two-hour session went on for five hours. At midnight, we'd only still scratched the surface. We had a lot more to unpack within femininity and surrender before the larger group was ready for numerology.

I invested in Milayo's services outside the sister circle for private numerological studies. Like any great teacher, she gave me a reading commensurate with my numerical breakdown. She taught me how to work through each calculation as she took me through the process in the same manner as did her life coach, the omniscient Happy Hero*Power. As life would beget synchronicities with six degrees of separation, my metaphysical indoctrination was universally predisposed to the same guru via two distinct and unconnected students.

Over two phone calls, we calculated and analyzed my life path, my expression, my soul urge, my personality number, my pinnacles, and transits. I was fixated. I purchased every renowned numerology book there was for my own erudition, and taught myself the esoteric meaning of numbers. Using our birthnames and birthdates, I put myself and my relationship with Siete under numerological scrutiny.

I wrote a spiritual forensic report.

Spiritual Forensic Report								
Pythagorean Alphabet								
1	2	3	4	5	6	7	8	9
A	B	C	D	E	F	G	H	I
J	K	L	M	N	O	P	Q	R
S	T	U	V	W	X	Y	Z	

The Profile

Jacqueline Noelle Leveine

Life Path	Birth Card	Venus Card	Maturity Number
4+2+5 = 11	A♦	5♥	9

Destiny = 7

```
1 1 3 8 3 5 3 9 5 5   5 6 5 3 3 5   3 5 4 5 9 5 5 5 = 106
J + A + C + Q + U + E + L + I + N + E   N + O + E + L + L + E   L + E + V + E + I + N + E
1     3 8     3     5     5       3 3     3         4         5       = 43
```

Personality = 7

Siete Terrence Jackson

Life Path	Birth Card	Venus Card	Maturity Number
8+22+22 = 7	4♣	J♠	16/7

Destiny = 9

```
1 1 2 5 5 4 2 5 9 9 6 5 1 5 3 3 5 9 1 = 81
  +   +   +   +   +       +   +   +   +   +       +   +   +   +   +   +
1       2       4 2       9 9       5 1       3 3       9 1 = 49
```

Personality = 4

Why was I an attractive target for Siete?

I was his spiritual teacher. That's what the numbers demonstrated. We were joined together by the gravitational pull of my birthname and his birthdate. Siete was attracted to me because my name, whether it was spelled Jacqueline Noelle Leveine, Jacqueline Noelle, Jacqueline Leveine, Jacqueline, Jacquii Noelle Leveine, Jacquii Noelle, Jacquii Leveine, or simply Jacquii, was a seven destiny number. My name, revealing the key to arcane metaphysical secrets and universal ethics all encompassed in the number seven, is what I was destined to teach in this lifetime.

Siete's birthdate equates to a seven life path lesson. His birthdate dictated the skills and talents he was incarnated in this lifespan to learn and master. I being the teacher and he the pupil, when he was ready for spiritual enlightenment, I truly did appear. Thus, it makes sense that we'd be so strongly drawn to one another; he had a need that my soul was predestined to fulfill.

The Analysis

What governed the spiritual alliance between Siete and me?

I craved the freedom of conditional attachments. My A♦ birth card made it difficult for me to maintain a balanced, devoted relationship in tandem with my pursuit of material wealth. With *ten* fives in my name and a 5♥ in Venus, I purposely entertained liaisons that were detached geographically, by emotional unavailability or a third party.

Siete was the perfect candidate because he had a 4♣ birth card, and we Diamond women manage best with Clubs men. As a 4♣, his desire for closeness with a mate presented inner conflict. His restless nature deemed him unable to commit. With a J♠ in Venus, he was both amorous in his dealings with me as he was deceitful. His J♠ was drawn to my artistic abilities; but he had a penchant for criminal escapades, which motivated him to use me for emotional security and money.

Our affiliation, however, was sanctioned by a force way more powerful. Our connection stemmed from a past-life association that left some unfinished business to be completed in this time period. A romantic conundrum, he rejected me with open arms. For I reincarnated as a living example of integrity that was both challenging and unreachable for him even though his soul bespoke my teachings.

What was Siete's motive for the burglary and spiritual torment?

Siete's name is missing the numbers seven and eight. These deficits revealed themselves as karmic lessons. The eight karmic lesson personified an inherent weakness in the way he handled his financial resources although he amassed a great sum of money. Couple the eight karmic lesson with the seven, there was the lack of integrity and regard for the law.

The master number twenty-two appears twice in his birthdate, warning of illusions and delusions. It implied that he lived in a fool's paradise, dreaming, and was roused only when in danger; consequently, he exercised false judgment due to others' influence.

Coupled with his birthdate, the four personality proved that, on a lower frequency, he was easily wounded, prone to mental and emotional illness, vindictive when he felt slighted, and had an inner urge to rebel against rules, thus creating his own.

Siete was Mars in my twelfth house of karma and hidden enemies, which explained why the reader in St. Martin said there was something about me that brought out his bad side. We were either brothers or enemies in our past life. Thus, there was a lot of incomplete desire, passion, and adversarial energy between us.

What was the significance of the 2E apartment number?
Adding the two and the five of the E equals ... seven. While a seven home, on the higher side of the spectrum, is one that is tranquil and conducive to quiet reflection and retreat, on the lower side of that same spectrum, the seven vibration represents loss and endings as a result of theft. Since seven is the universal law, on a lower vibe that universal law is broken; therefore, the sacred home corresponding to a higher vibration seven is broken into and entered unlawfully on its lower vibration.
Why was I a victim of burglary twice?
My destiny number is 106/7, the karmic debt number 16/7 which is amplified by the zero strategically placed in the middle. With my 16/7 karmic debt, I broke the universal law in a former life. Because of my disregard for love or the law, and the consequent misery caused to others, I paid in this lifetime through my own undoing in professional matters. My lack of humility set me back several times when I should have been promoted. I also lost what I'd gained in material accumulation and investments due to the sudden and unusual circumstances surrounding both burglaries.
Will justice be served for the crime Siete committed?
Siete's maturity number is 16/7, so he too will have to bear the responsibility of mishandled love affairs in *this* lifetime. While the burglary case is a cold one for the 70th Precinct, that won't prevent the universe from upholding the law. From age forty-five onward, Siete will reap his karmic debt. He can evade man's law, but he can't elude spirit.

I enlisted Andrew's help to find a Yoruba grand priest who could give me a thorough spiritual bath. The psychic attacks seemed to resurge with a whole new rigor. No matter how far I'd traveled, his evil was indomitable. Biting and pinprick sensations continued in my bed when I tried to sleep at night.

I managed to get the biting to stop while I was in the living room by replacing all the furniture with which Siete was associated. I bought a new sofa, new paintings on the wall, and two new red bar stools to replace the old white ones. I know it sounds extreme that I'd change the paintings on the wall too.

There was a particular picture he'd taken on the day he and his friend visited my apartment in December 2012, where he sat on the then couch with the paintings as a backdrop. Four years into the future, he still used that picture for his social media profile. I presumed him to be taunting me, laughing at my ignorance as the unsuspecting dupe excluded from the joke.

Andrew asked a prominent Yoruba grand priest from Trinidad to give me the bath. The priest would be in New York to administer someone else's spiritual thanksgiving prayers and would extend his services to me during that time.

In dire straits, I asked the priest to make me a protective talisman that would shield me from future psychic attacks. The priest gave me the ingredients to buy for the baths. Like Andrew and I had done for my apartment, I'd be given two baths, one to remove the negative forces, another to bring in the positive. The list of ingredients included those we used in my apartment but was more intense and extensive. I'd shop for them later that evening. In the meantime, we drove to the jewelry store on Flatbush Avenue to see about the talisman.

"So," the Yoruba priest started with a calm, sagacious Trinidadian cadence, "I'm thinking I'll have the jeweler make a talisman from *The Key of Solomon*. You'll have one key on the front and another on the back. Are you familiar with the *Greater Key*?"

"Yes, my uncle introduced me to them when I was in my twenties," I said, becoming teary-eyed at my remembrance of Francis, Tamia's father. "It's been a while since I've read them, though."

The Key of Solomon is a Hebrew book of magic based on Kabbalistic mysticism. Built on a Judaist school of thought, it was written for King Solomon during the Renaissance. It's a powerful book to be employed only by those who fully understand its symbolism and application. To dabble in it with limited foresight could expose one to a lot of spiritual danger.

"Good, I'll use the fourth pentacle of Venus to attract anyone of your bidding, and the fourth pentacle of Mercury to acquire an understanding into all things hidden."

When we arrived at the jeweler, the priest made me read the powers related to each pentacle to ensure I was okay with it.

"It'll take a few months to make. You won't get it until the New Year." The jeweler managed my expectations.

"That's fine. I'll need time to pay for it anyway."

"Remember, it has to be consecrated before you use it," the jeweler added.

"I'll show you how to consecrate it before I leave," the priest reassured me. "I'll tell you what you need to know after tomorrow's bath."

I completed the shopping for my baths later that day with Andrew's help. The next day the priest bathed me in two rituals filled with prayer in languages known and unknown. He moved with the dexterity and grace of a man who'd studied his craft methodically. He had a paternal instinct that was endearing and kind.

"Don't worry, darlin'. The attacks will stop. You don't need to worry yourself much longer.

"Later tonight," he continued as he lit the frankincense and myrrh in my coal incense pot. "I want you to go to a quiet crossroads--not too close to your home because you'll have to avoid it for some time afterwards--and drop these old clothes and stuff in the middle.

"Put nine pennies into the bag before you drop it off. You have to pay the gods of the crossroads. And when you drop the bag in the crossroads, *don't look back!*"

I nodded my understanding and consensus. The priest departed, leaving me with the sanctification for the talisman and seven pages of *Psalms* to say on my train ride to work every morning.

One of the hardest feats in life is to find a quiet intersection in Brooklyn at any time of the night. Even when the night seems to be still, there's always someone or something lurking in the shadows. I was overrun with anxiety as I waited for the clock to strike 2:00 a.m. Unable to contain my composure, I hopped into my car with my bag, which now held my old bath clothes and nine shiny pennies.

I drove around the borough trying to choose a neighborhood for the drop. My spirit told me to go to Gerritsen Beach, as it was tranquil and predominantly inhabited by Caucasians; but I was deterred by the new neighborhood watch surveillance cameras that the residents might've had.

I drove around the area in my immediate neighborhood. Despite the priest's heeding, I thought the intersection ahead would be a good one. It was clear and still. When the light turned green, I opened my truck door and pushed the bag out with my foot.

The getaway wasn't as smooth as it should have been. One of the *advances* of the new Mercedes cars was the engine automatically shifted to the neutral gear once a door was opened while in motion. Having to now shift the gear from neutral back to drive, I sensed the headlights of a car coming up from behind and fumbled to accelerate through the intersection.

The headlights pulled back a little as if the driver was suspicious, almost hesitant to proceed. Wanting to see if he or she stopped to inspect or tamper with the drop, I caught myself instinctively looking in the rearview mirror for a split second. My clairaudience booming the words, *Don't look back!* caused me to rapidly avert my eyes to the windshield.

In that faulty retrospection laid my bag of supernatural burdens, choking with the beautiful hate of two people who once loved and now annihilated the other.

$$2017$$
$$4 + (2 + 0) + (2 + 0 + 1 + 7)$$
$$4 + 2 + 1 = 7$$

Seven Personal Year

Inner growth, sabbatical, self-awareness, self-discovery. No longer motivated by worldly pursuits, you'll find yourself analyzing your past motives and actions, and developing an intense need to be alone to give more time and attention to your own personal needs and desires. There'll be a need to get away from all the noise and confusion. This is a spiritual and intuitive cycle that will inspire you to pen your deepest truths, as secrets about yourself or others may rise to the surface.[9]

---

[9] (Strayhorn, 1997)

"Bittersweet is the moment when you leave me,
And I'm left with you on my mind.
Like an hour glass trickling quickly,
Our love is on borrowed time.
If we decided to bring this affair out of night,
Would you run look for shelter? Would you stay and fight?
Cause what's done in the dark always comes to the light!"

17

I BECAME DISHEARTENED WITH WORK AS A WHOLE. I BEGAN TO QUESTION the impact my existence had on the larger organization. I became more apathetic toward material things.

I stopped shopping for designer shoes and clothing. In truth, I no longer had the fervor to shop. Shopping was a pointless pastime that expended my limited time and money on filling a void still gaping wide open after the bank account was depleted and the clothing no longer glitzy. I marked a mental milestone to terminate the lease on my Mercedes Benz when it expired in 2018. The truck was feeling more like the overpriced liability it truly was than an accomplished luxury.

I tested the waters by growing my Caesar into a mohawk. When I felt the tides were still, I dyed my mohawk a bright fuchsia pink and had Phil cut tribal-designed patterns on the right side of my faded head.

I was becoming more inhibited at the work place because the construct of upward mobility was an imaginary one. I was physically present at work, but my mind was in the music. I sat at my desk in between meetings and projects listening to instrumental Jazz standards on Spotify for my demo recording.

This would be the year that I sacrificed travel for the promotion of my craft. To market myself, I reinstated my social media presence after being incognito for three years. I was tired of enduring a closed, closeted life when Siete was living his easily, in rare form on every platform there was.

I commissioned Fay to produce my first recording project. Together, we selected musicians for the album. I had a specific sound in mind, and I needed instrumentalists who could bring a combined sound of arrangement and free improvisation to life. I funded the entire project on my own. I figured if I wasn't willing to invest in myself, no one else would see the value in investing in me.

I occupied my time by writing lyrics to many more songs by Thelonious Monk, Horace Silver, Freddie Hubbard, Mal Waldron, and Miles Davis. The more I wrote, the more vulnerable I became. Exposing so much of myself in my art was uncomfortable. I scheduled the recordings for two consecutive eight-hour days a week before my 41st birthday. It would take months to sing the songs I'd written with plausible conviction.

My yoga practice was reduced to Sunday morning sessions only. Natalie had since expanded her business to include additional yoga instructors who taught classes while she worked her day job at the department. Thus, the Sunday restorative yoga classes were really restorative. I didn't have the physical strength to do the power classes every week like I did the year prior. I listened to my body. I didn't think it was physical deterioration. Rather, it felt like a physical realignment.

I meditated to Solfeggio frequencies to shift my own energetic field and enhance my psychic abilities. 440 Hz is the standard frequency for American music. There are frequencies below and above this standard that I wasn't hearing. For instance, 174 Hz is the frequency for the mind-body connection. 639 Hz is the healing frequency, 852 Hz the brain power.

I cut my cable services off. Besides losing my zeal for the yearly fight to restore the package promotions, I lost interest in the regular programming. In its place, I viewed spiritually uplifting videos on YouTube about harnessing motivation, being a more concentrated thinker, the behaviors of an empath, and spiritual synchronicities.

With the simultaneous multiplicity of these alterations, I noticed the synchronicities of the universe. I observed visual patterns of 11:11 during my day. Sitting at my desk at work, I'd be called to glance at my phone where

11:11 a.m. appeared on the screen. 11:11 was the universal call to take heed to ascending energies. It was a call to activations of the spiritual realms. Simply put, it was an awakening of the sleepwalking soul.

I'd see 111, 222, 333, 444, and 555 on clocks, license plates, or on the numbers of buildings. The messages were all around me. The videos I watched gave me more clarity into these repeated number sequences as being *Angel Numbers*. Each sequence having its own meaning, my angels, ancestors, or spirit guides as they're all called, were communicating with me through numbers.

I'd monitor my thought process at the time I'd see the number to understand what I was seeing. If I was anxious about something I had to do before I saw 222, I'd know the angels were telling me that I was on the right track, to remain patient and positive, and ask for their assistance, two being the number for cooperation, diplomacy, and peace.

Whenever I saw a new sequence, I'd research its meaning on my phone and add it to my notes so I could quickly cross-reference my thought pattern against the message behind the sequence. The number sequence wasn't always repetitive. I'd always see 524 on my clock before I had this awakening.

Five-twenty-four was the house number of my childhood home. I thought it was a reminder of that, but 524 means my angel guides are leading me toward new fortuitous opportunities and positive life changes. The five is the vibration of change, the two is positivity, and the four is the determination and diligence related to stability, much like their numerological derivations. Spiritually, I was in a new place. I gave myself permission to be alright with these changes.

The dreams began again. I dreamt of Collin often. In my dreams, he'd be hugging me with *love in his eyes*, as he'd often say. The dreams felt real. I hadn't spoken to him in so many years. By this time, the anger I harbored against him had long dissipated. Honestly, I don't know if I was ever really angry with him. I think I was more angry at myself. It was just easier to lash out at him than for me to accept responsibility for my part in the situation. I called Andrew to make sense of it all.

"Andrew, I keep dreaming about Collin. I think my spirit is trying to tell me that I need to make things right with him."

Hmm. Okay, he thought. "And what were the dreams about?"

I explained the contents of the dream with as much detail as I could recall.

"Yeah, sounds like something that needs fixing. But do you even know how to contact him?"

"I don't. I think Carlos told me he's working in a shop off Nostrand Avenue, not far from where his shop used to be."

"Well, Nostrand is a damn long street. The most you can do is walk a stretch of it in the general area to see if you see him in one of the stores."

"Really? Who has time for all of that? I'm getting overwhelmed just thinking about it." I felt stymied.

"Well, it's either you want to find him or you don't." I acknowledged that I did.

I attempted to do as Andrew suggested. I drove my car, though. I rode slowly down Nostrand inspecting any shop I saw on the avenue. I looked for any vehicle that resembled the car he drove when we were last together, even though I wasn't sure if he was still driving that particular car. I repeated this pattern for weeks when, obliquely off one of the corners, positioned in the cut, I spotted the awning of another shop. All it took was a left turn to see if this was indeed the one.

When the red light ahead switched to green, I stepped on the gas vigorously, straight through the intersection. There would be no left turns on that day or any other thereafter.

Milayo Negesti launched her 30-Day Relationship Challenge on the spring equinox. For thirty consecutive days a private group of women would come together from all parts of the country to work on their relationship with themselves. Each day we'd be given a new assignment, virtue and principle that nurtured self-healing and corresponded with the number vibration of the challenge day.

Nivea and I joined the private Facebook group as an ode to self-improvement. The first four days of the challenge were devoted to internal detoxification. We were preparing our bodies and spirit for a healthier state. Milayo urged us to ingest bitter herbs and diuretics to release the anger stored in our livers. She also warned that resistance may come, but advised that we push through, making note of the traumas and suppressed emotions that rose to the surface.

At lunchtime, I went to Tansey's shop to buy a yellow obsidian gemstone for the challenge. After I cleansed, dedicated, and programmed my crystal for renewed abundance and prosperity, I placed it in my bra for a closer connectedness to my solar plexus. I ordered my pendulum and divination deck on Amazon. Having no involvement with divination, I opted for a deck of cards that was self-explanatory, *Ask Your Guides*. I already had a deck of playing cards at home since I played Spades. I used those in the interim.

That evening I did my digestive detox. I purchased some Smooth Move tea because I didn't want to take the harsher Senna pods, and dandelion root tea was my everyday drink. The tea took some time to kick in. When it did, hours later, it griped my stomach to no end. Milayo did say that the griping would shift the energies in our solar plexus and sacral chakras. The pain made me jolt out of my rest in physical and emotional affliction. I was unprepared for the suppressed memory that came to surface.

What materialized was the physical abuse I'd endured from my brother Lucas as a child. We grew up in a home with a verbally and physically abusive father. His abuse was deep-rooted in alcoholism, the predisposed family trait of Leveine, a nine last name. The first thing our father did when he arose from sleep in the morning was drink.

His condition was so calamitous our mother forbade him from having any liquor in the house at all. Our living room bar was a festooned obstruction with empty shelves of dashed-away delights, dreams deferred, loud wrangling, and tears of despair. He took solace in cooking wine, which was the closest he'd get to a fermented beverage in our home.

Our father cast my brother aside when I was born. He took to me as if I was his only child. At five years of age, I noticed the toll our father's rejection had on my brother. Lucas sought with all his heart to win him over.

Eventually, my brother would come to me asking me to get his attention. When that proved futile, I snubbed my father's advances, thinking it would draw him closer to Lucas. Rather, he did away with us both, finding satisfaction from other women and children outside our home.

Lucas took his anger and hostility out on me. Every day, after we arrived home from school, the beatings would commence. He'd start senseless arguments in the same manner as our father when he was drunk. He hit me repeatedly. I tried to fend for myself as best I could. Six years my senior, he was physically stronger than I.

We'd fight every afternoon until my head ached. When I eventually ceded in tears, he'd stop and pamper me with head rubs and tea. This continued for about two years. I begged our mother not to leave me in the house with him alone. I begged her to stay home from work.

Every time I pleaded with her to shield me from his wrath, her eyes glossed over with an ache so deep of domestic disloyalties. She punished and beat my brother for every infraction he imparted upon me. Once he was healthier, his doling out of licks would increase with a renewed sense of purpose.

At forty years of age, our mother quit her job to monitor us as a homemaker. At eight years of age, I was finally safe. By then my brother had taken to the streets. The physical trauma was gone, but the emotional trauma took root. I rationalized his actions, attributing them to our father's misplaced devotions. I birthed a pathology of enabling my abusers.

The gravity of this suppression fell on me the second night of our challenge, its weight impenetrable. I thought about the way I related to Siete. The constant feeling of pity for his life circumstances. Feeling like I could explain his actions away. There were so many correlations between my dealings with these two men. In that moment of physical and spiritual detoxification I realized how my aversion to my brother was brought into being. I bawled a release, shuddering from the enormity of this realization.

I needed time to process all that was resurrected. I challenged my own thoughts. Was it fair for me to attribute my brother's actions to our father's? Until that point I thought it was my parents' will that birthed my soul. When in actuality it was my soul's purpose to choose my parents for specific life lessons.

Every time my brother and I shouted, *I didn't ask to come here!* to our parents, we were mistaken. Our souls in fact did. Our parents just created the vessel. With this being the case, was it reasonable or even accurate to ascribe all of our traumas to this current incarnation with our current biological family? A soul being as transient as it is, it seemed illogical to amass all our individual hurts, traumas, pathologies, learnings, and aptitudes in one lifetime.

This epiphany brought pressure to bear on me by resuscitating dormant samskaras. I'd previously learned that samskaras, an ancient Hindu concept meaning *to flow together*, were cognitive impressions embedded by all the thoughts, actions, and intents I'd ever undergone. Personal samskaras collected from past lives preconditioned my mind to respond in the same restricted manner recurrently, without the freewill to choose.

My mental and emotional unbalances such as anxiety, addiction, and obsessive compulsion were all examples of how samskaras stole my choices. These toxins were compiled layer upon layer until they became unconquerable. Below my normal consciousness, these memories were implanted as the root of all my compulsions.

I accredited my enabling demeanor, obsessive compulsion, perfectionism, and nervousness to this intellection. Thus, was Lucas's abusive behavior shaped by experiences in this lifetime, or was it also a samskara, inherited from past incarnations, wanting to be healed through interaction with our father, his spiritual likeness? It was definitely food for thought.

My brother had a karmic debt number of sixteen as his birthday, birthname, and life path, which meant he was also my spiritual student. He'd been guilty of having illicit, and possibly abusive, relationships in previous lifetimes. Therefore, his endless cycle of rises and falls was his burden to bear. After years of enduring his abuses toward me, I tired of my role as his teacher. I had my own crosses to carry, and I was taking corrective action to unhinge them.

On the seventeenth day of the challenge, I sat on the Lexington Avenue Express train line heading toward Utica, perusing my phone's Kindle library for a business prototype. Since seventeen denotes executive ability and possesses the financial success associated with its reduced number eight, we were tasked with finding an existing business model that we'd pattern our love lives after.

I came across a book based on Zappos' business model, *Delivering Happiness*. It was a framework based on ten core principles that deeply touched me when I first read them. The company had since revised its management team, and thus, its ideals. I still wanted to apply these ten core values to my love life business model.

I skimmed through the chapters, taking note of each principle in my phone. One, *deliver WOW through service*; two, *embrace and drive change*; three, *create fun and a little weirdness*; four, *be adventurous, creative, and open-minded*; five, *pursue growth and learning*.

The train stopped at the Atlantic Avenue station to let departing passengers out and arriving passengers in. The woman next to me was one of the departees. The seat to my left was vacant. To fill its space sat Felise. At least I thought it looked like her. I hadn't seen her in seven years, but I recognized her presence. I looked up from my phone out of my left periphery.

I turned back to my phone ... principle five, *pursue growth and learning*. I looked up from my phone again to look intentionally to my left. It was indeed Felise. On the congested NYC transit we sat arm to arm, skin to skin, years and worlds apart. She took her phone out of her bag to look at her photo library with a soft smile on her lips, eyes downcast on the subject of the digital photograph.

It wasn't awkward for me. In fact, I felt the calm obedience of a surrendered ego. The old me would've confronted her about her sudden, icy withdrawal. The new me allowed it to be what it was. It was undeniably growth and learning. Growth enough to accept that the invisible line of demarcation had been drawn. For whatever reason, she made her choice to jettison our kinship, and I was mature enough to respect that. Learned enough to know that the line didn't need crossing.

Again, my head pivoted to the phone. Six, *build open and honest relationships*; seven, *build a positive team and family*; eight, *do more with less*; nine, *be passionate and determined*; ten, *be humble*.

When the train doors opened at the Franklin Avenue station, I put my phone into my Gucci bag, brushed my fingers through my fuchsia mohawk, placed the heels of my feet back in my Ferragamo pumps, and exited the train without looking back.

A week later, I was in the studio with my hired band of professional musicians. It was the first day of my demo recording. The goal was to record eight songs in two eight-hour days. The instrumentalists were hard to schedule, so there wouldn't be another day for months when they'd all be available at the same time. We had to create and capture the magic in this very moment.

It was a foreign paradigm being the talent in the booth as opposed to being the talent behind the mixing board. I received my bachelor's degree in audio engineering from City College and was familiar with the recording process, but being isolated in a booth unnerved me. In my art, I relied mostly on energy--the energy of my bandmates, the energy of the audience.

The studio, on the other hand, represented a seclusion of my own artistic hype from which the other musicians drew. The permanence of it all scared me the most. Once I put it on the track and co-signed its release, it was set loose for public consumption, open to examination and speculation.

With all of these phobias floating in my head, my untrained mind caused the unreal to become actual, wreaking havoc on my body. My allergies flared up, my ears clogged, and my throat tightened. I was literally making myself sick. Fay was having none of it. The roster of music wasn't by any means easy, but she knew my capabilities. She knew I had been practicing with my musical director for months. She knew I was getting in my own way.

Fay had me run five of the songs a minimum of four times each. Most of the takes were still vocally rudimentary. The band, however, was killing. They came to complete the job they were hired to perform. They fed off the feeble energy I was giving them and created some among themselves. By the end of the first day, I was physically spent. Studio work required stamina, and I was sucking all the life out of my kidneys with false evidence that actually became real.

The morning of the second day in the studio, I meditated. I steamed with Eucalyptus. I did two hours of yoga. I ate well. I arrived early, carrying my essential oils into the booth with me; peppermint to open my lungs, eucalyptus to open my sinuses, and ylang ylang to build confidence.

I sang four songs four times each, repeating one of the songs from the day before. I supported the music as best I could, but my abdominal muscles weren't receiving the positive charge it needed to push forth crisp, mellifluous phrases. The sound was generally better than the day before, but I left feeling dissatisfied with my own performance. The saving grace was I could always scrap my vocals and practice over the instrumentals.

At the end of two days, Fay and I were sure I'd have to book another session to do overdubs. We booked another session for mid-July. It was a toilsome course, yet it demonstrated the fundamental condition of freedom--the freedom to err, fall, and get back up again.

By May, the clairvoyant dreams were happening with a greater intensity. They were about Siete this time around. I had dreams about us being in the same restaurant. He was seated at a bar table with his best friend, and I was sitting alone. He beckoned me to come to him while his friend pestered and mocked me, blowing salacious kisses. In the first dream I flipped them the bird and walked off. In every subsequent vision, Siete appeared by himself. All times he called on me to come to him.

The premonitions had me conflicted. Was I supposed to contact him, or was I being tested? Uncertain of what to do, I used the divination tools Milayo taught us to use in the 30-Day challenge. I took out my pendulum, summoning my angel guides.

"Ancestors and spirit guides, I call upon you to be with me in this moment. Please surround me with your love and awareness. Please encircle me in a ball of protection and shield me from any outside entities who may try to infiltrate. Spirit guides please show me 'yes'."

The pendulum swung vigorously to the left in circular motion.

"Thank you. Spirit guides, please show me 'no'." The pendulum swung to the right in a circular motion.

"Spirit guides, please show me 'I don't know'." The pendulum swung forward and back in a straight line.

"Spirit guides, am I having dreams about Siete?"

I already knew the answer but wanted to gauge the pendulum's accuracy--if it was really in tune with spirit. The pendulum swung to the left in a circular motion.

"Yes! Okay. Spirit, should I contact Siete?" Again, the pendulum swung to the left in a circular motion. "Spirit, will he be upset when I call him?" The pendulum swung to the right in a circular motion. "Spirit, will he be expecting me to call?" Again the pendulum swung in the direction of a 'no'.

Still uncertain, I took my deck of playing cards out. I shuffled the deck liberally, asking if I should contact Siete again. I shuffled and cut the deck four times before I stopped to pull the first card off the top. When I flipped the card over, there was the 9♥. The fact that the card was one of red suits indicated a 'yes'; however, this yes was a yes with an outcome of completion. The nine in numerology meant doing away with people or things that no longer served us.

I called Milayo and described my current dilemma.

"Milayo, my spirit is telling me to contact Siete."

"Okay. I think you should ignore your spirit this time." She wasn't convinced.

"Okay, but the messages have been frequent and intense."

"Let sleeping dogs lie. You don't need that energy back in your life."

She was correct about that. I disconnected the call and went about my days as normal.

A few days later, I received a message via Facebook. One of my older Maytime memories of Siete came up on my feed. In this memory, he was presenting at career day for one of his friend's kindergarten students. I didn't know whose classroom he was in. I just knew hosting career day was something he did every year. I had the option to ignore it, but I took to writing about being in a relationship with a narcissistic male. The post garnered much attention because I was passionate in my written account.

A little while after, I received a text from my colleague saying, *It's a small world. Guess whose classroom your ex is in?*

Turns out he was close friends with one of my co-workers. I did confirm that we were dating for quite some time, but she thought it was necessary to reach out to Siete to inquire on his end. He confirmed our relationship. I believe he told her that I was cool people, but unfortunately things between us didn't work out. She already had the full rendition of the story from me, which really made me question her motives.

The hornet's nest stirred, I knew it was only a matter of time before he reached out. I called Milayo again.

"Milayo, I think I need to contact Siete--seriously."

"Okay, since you're so adamant, come over to my house after work. We can do a divination together."

"Great, I'll see you tonight."

Later that evening, we sat in Milayo's boudoir. Laying on the carpet was a piece of paper with boxes sectioned off; *Call Siete Yes, Call Siete No.* I asked her to hold onto me as she did the divination herself because I didn't want to will her pendulum in any direction, but I wanted my energy to be connected to the reading. Holding the pendulum over the piece of paper, she began to ask her spirit guides if I should contact Siete. The pendulum swung heavily over the box that said, *Call Siete Yes.* She asked if I should call that night. Again the pendulum swung over *Call Siete Yes.*

"You see?" I said, convinced. "When I used my pendulum it said the same thing. I even used my deck of cards."

Her ears perked up. "Which cards? The playing cards?"

"Yeah."

"What card did you get?"

"I got the 9♥."

"So that means yes. But you know the 9♥ isn't a good relationship card, right? The 9♥ signals the ending of a relationship."

"I know."

"Well, get to ending this saga, mama. Make the call!"

Now that I had a unanimous and solidified answer from spirit, I suddenly got cold feet. I no longer wanted to make the call. I didn't know what I was going to say. I hadn't thought the plan through in great detail. The proposal sounded sexy when it was still an abstraction, but actualized, it was terrifying. I engaged in unrelated chatter for another hour.

Minutes after nine, Milayo centered my attention on the duty I came to carry out. "Stop with the side conversation, procrastination queen. You've been sitting here for over an hour now. It's almost 10:00 p.m. Make the call!"

I scrolled through my phone contacts under the letter H. I located a contact entitled *Hell No!*

I pressed the call button. The phone rang once ... twice ... three times. I was readying to let myself off the hook, literally, when I heard a click.

"Hello?" Hell No answered on the fourth ring.

18

"HELLO," I REPEATED.

"Hello?" he asked again. He couldn't believe it was me.

"*Hi.* Umm, I hope I caught you at a good time." My mouth was instantly bone dry. "I was calling because I know you've been trying to reach me for some time now. I wasn't quite ready to speak with you then. But I figured, three years later, I'd give us both a chance to clear the air so we can each move on."

"Well, I'd like that," he said, his smooth tenor voice bringing me back to the cozy space that once was. "I just walked in the door from work. Can I call you right back?"

"Yeah, sure." I was thrown off by the unanticipated break in conversation.

"Are you okay?" A hint of concern registered in his tone.

"Mm-hmm."

"Okay, I'll call you right back." He ended the call.

"He has a *nice* voice," said Milayo, eavesdropping. "What was the outcome?"

"Hard to tell. He said he'll call me back. He just got in from work."

The plan was for me to have a quick, strategically monitored phone conversation, but plans were simply premeditated follies designed to make God laugh. I waited another hour before I was convinced he wouldn't be calling back any time before night break. I retreated to my five-month-old bed for my first night of undisturbed shuteye in years.

May 23, 2017

The morning after text actually came in the night before, right before midnight, *Are you still up?*

I'd missed his late night effort to reconnect, but we tried again later on that evening.

Talking at cross-purposes, the call was one riddled with regrets, miscommunications, misunderstandings, misrepresentations, misconstrued emotions. It was almost as if we were two characters in the same chapter of two separate books.

He expressed his remorse for the loss of our unborn son. I reminded him of his threats against me if I did carry the baby to term. He denied the accusation stating that, *He didn't recall using those words specifically, but if he did make such a statement, he apologized.* His lack of accountability triggered the conversation's meandering onto a winding road of lexicology as I felt the need to observe the differences between the words sorry and apology, one being sincere, heart-felt sympathy, the other a frivolous formality of defense.

He denied that he dwelled in that informal, unfeeling space while I debated that he was devoid of emotion, his need to abbreviate the word *sorry* in his texts to *sry* [sic] being my key piece of evidence. He thought there was a chance for us to rebuild something tangible and different. I countered that we'd be a modern-day version of Mr. and Mrs. Smith; two wedded assassins with contracts out on the other, sleeping in the same bed with loaded semi-automatic pistols under our pillows, waiting to see who'd be the first to aim and shoot.

Finally, I changed the topic to get to the more persistent issue of his previous employment.

"So, I have to ask you a question, and I really want you to tell me the truth."

"Okay, I always tell you the truth."

"Hmm? Okay." I wasn't going to waste his willingness to engage my inquisitions on proving him to be a liar. "Did you leave your last job or were you fired?"

He chuckled to himself before answering.

"I wasn't fired, honey. I decided to revive my life and left the company at the start of this year. I wanted a fresh start in a new company that had more room for growth and allowed me more time to myself. That was one of my biggest regrets--my lack of time with you. If I had more time at home, I think our relationship would've fared better. I missed out on so many good things in my life because I was always at work. It's a big pay cut, but I'll sacrifice the money for more life." He texted an image to my phone.

"Wow, that's noble of you." I truly was shocked at his evolution.

The image was a screenshot of a lone text bubble in an otherwise empty thread addressed to his former boss. The text expressed Siete's need to branch out into something new. He decided he'd take some time to regroup with his family in the South, leaving the keys to the dealership and his company car in the safe. He thanked his ex-employer for his mentorship along the sales journey and left the job and partnership on the screen of his phone. There was no response.

"Why didn't he respond to your text?" I asked with genuine curiosity. "It seems odd that after all these years and how close the two of you worked together, he'd leave you hanging."

"I don't know. I guess he was still upset by how abruptly I left."

Flashbacks of the last reading with the Wall Street psychic came into my mind's eye: *He has nothing now. He's hit rock bottom. He's depressed. He's sad. He's lonely.* I wasn't sold. Still, I let the case rest. It took absolutely no effort to send a text message to an arbitrary contact titled with the name of a real person but belonging to a fictious or different number.

We ended the call on a positive and amicable note. When my delicate heart wanted to seep sorrow and pity, my intuition squelched those oozing emotions with a dose of raw reality, *Get it together, girl. Keep your head on this time. That shit was all a bunch of lies.*

June 6, 2017

"I had a show tonight at Club Bonafide in the city. It was amazing. The turnout was low this time, but the energy was great. It was more of a test set designed to gauge people's reaction to the songs I'm going to record on my demo."

Contrary to how I'd thought our interaction would play out, we continued to speak almost every night. It was our one thing to look forward to during the day--our private diversion and guilty pleasure.

"A show? You're performing now?" he asked, amazement in his voice.

"Yeah, I've been doing shows. I've done two in Amsterdam and two in New York City. I also do open mics once in a while when I build up the nerve to just go out and do my thing."

"Do you have any videos? Something I can see?"

"You know, I always get still photos from my audience. I never get videos unless I have someone filming, and Trent couldn't make this show. He's usually my camera man. I hope it means the audience is so intrigued, they don't want to be distracted with video."

I sent him a still of me singing mid-song in my white, floor-length halter top gown, face tilted to the left, the stage light illuminating my cheekbones and hot-pink mohawk.

"You look absolutely gorgeous. I'm so proud of you right now. I'd really like to hear something, though."

"Well, I can send you something I've written. Yeah, you're a lover of words yourself. I'd like to get your feedback on who or what you think this song is about."

I sent him the lyrics I'd written to Thelonious Monk's classic, *Monk's Mood*:

Standing bare before you,
Unconcealed in your view.
Scared of rejection or deep connection,
With you I'm whole and new.

You make my truths feel frail,
Beaten by storms of hail.
But in due time, my words gave you life
And now, my heart's free to set sail.

Men try to play
Hide and seek with self
Hoping you'd leave them alone.
Women will say
That they need your help,
And then go it all on their own.

I'm so glad you found me.
Compassion heard my plea.
He took one look in my lyric book,
An ode to vulnerability!

"Nice! You wrote this yourself?"

"Yeah, I did. I enjoy penning my own lyrics to instrumentals. It allows me to connect to the music more. But who do you think it's about?"

"Siete?"

"I knew you'd say that. You're so vain, I knew you'd think this song was about you." I quoted Carly Simon in jest.

"It's about my relationship with vulnerability. I'm singing to vulnerability, the actual emotion itself."

"Well, you did a great job, because I thought you were singing to the kid."

"It's called personification--giving an inanimate object or abstract notion human attributes. But this next song, however, *is* about you!" I sent him the lyrics and the instrumental version to *Blue in Green*. "I'd always watch you sleep and think these things to myself. I've always wanted to sing this song, and you gave me a reason to."

Siete took some time away from our banter to listen to the song with the written lyrics.

"The trumpet in this song took me someplace else. This song is so dope. And, I guess a *you're welcome* is in order since I was your muse. But you have to stop singing so many sad songs."

I thought, *I will when you stop giving me a reason.*

July 13, 2017

"Why are you home from work today? It's not a Friday." He knew I had a habit of taking Fridays off in the summer, but it was Thursday.

"I was supposed to be in the studio today laying the vocals over my demo again, but my allergies are acting the fool. I've been sick an entire week. I *have* been listening to season one of the *Serial* podcast you recommended, though. I've listened to the entire season in two days, every episode back-to-back."

"Damn, it took me a week to get through it all during my commute to work. I told you that podcast is fire. The narrator, Sarah Koenig is her name? She has a knack for storytelling. She draws you in with her calm demeanor. And the way she breaks down the details of the case is so succinct. You can't help but be drawn in by her thought process as she synthesizes the case."

"Well, my love, let's talk about this case. We're about to have a debate."

"Why a debate, queen?"

"Because I believe Syed to be guilty of murdering his girlfriend, Lee."

"*You* think he's guilty? I'm surprised *you* think he's guilty."

"Why are you surprised by that? Because he's Muslim? First of all, I've learned not too long ago that a lot of men, you included, can't deal with rejection. When his girlfriend Lee left, she didn't *just* leave him; she left to be with someone else. His friends said his emotions fluctuated between being cool and sad, to being enraged and plotting to kill.

There's the cryptic note in the back of his notebook where he himself wrote, *I want to kill*. Why write something like that *on paper* if you're not going to manifest it? The written word shows intent. Then his friend Wilds implicates himself in the crime saying that he and Syed *both* buried the body."

"I don't think he did it!"

Siete was convinced of his innocence.

"First of all, the cell phone records, which were supposed to have placed Syed at the scene of the crime when he was supposedly burying Lee's body, wasn't sufficient enough to substantiate the exact location. Then, his boy Wilds's story changed several times during his many interviews with law enforcement. And every time he gave another account, each testimony became more and more inconsistent than the first.

"What I think is, both of their parents were against the relationship because of their cultural differences. And her parents, being strict Asian people, must have found out about them and murdered her in a rage, framing the Muslim boyfriend."

"Nice theory. You're not going to get me to budge on this one. Hopefully, Syed gets an appeal so we can see how the case plays out again in trial. But I strongly believe that he's a psychopath who snapped."

Of all the cases, this one would be the one to resurface the nebulous circumstances surrounding our first split. The coincidence was uncanny. The forensic anomalies constituted it a classic case of whodunit, except Lee's perpetrator had been caught, tried, convicted, and incarcerated. I, on the other hand, was having a healthy legal debate with mine four years after the fact, and I still wasn't anywhere remotely close to the truth.

August 2017

"I went on your Instagram page today. First of all, your posts, with their graphic sexual imagery are thirsty. They make you appear to be one-dimensional. You were put on this earth to do some high-vibrational work, but you insist on hanging around low-vibrational people, engaging in low-vibrational dialogue.

"In any case, I went scrolling through the many years of your profile and I was heart-broken when I got to January 2015. I can actually see the stages of grief you went through when we broke up. When we first split, back in the summer of 2014, you were going through the *I Don't Give a Damn* phase because your posts were more on the indifferent side. Then around winter of 2015 your posts turned to the *Reminiscent* phase.

"There were a lot of sexual posts with women wearing short Caesar haircuts like mine and men looking like you. Then by March, you were all in the *I Want Her Back* phase. One post in particular brought me to tears, because I felt you aching in every word. It was the post with the quote from *The Chaos of Stars*. You know, the one that goes:

"And I'd choose you; in a hundred lifetimes, in a hundred worlds, in any version of reality, I'd find you and choose you.

"But what really got me was your caption underneath: *Sometimes I wish I could go back in life. Not to change things, just to experience a couple of things twice.*

"Your Instagram page for a whole entire year was in essence a shrine dedicated to me. And the thought of that made me sad. Because contrary to what you may believe, we were both grieving in our own ways. I just had to protect my spirit while I healed in my grieving process."

He wasn't happy he'd been exposed.

"Don't try to get up in *the god's* head. You don't know what I was thinking."

"Honestly, Siete? You really want to argue this with me? I know you! I ... know ... you! And your page was a dedication to me."

"Well, don't leave any comments or make anyone wise to what you know. A lot of my followers don't understand why I post some of the things I do. And your interference will show a part of me that I don't need others to see. It'll conflict with my brand."

"Well, it's a shame that you hide behind your social media handle. People have no idea who you truly are. And that *brand* is, once again, low-frequency. Elevate black man. You have it in you."

"I know." He sat on the side of the phone in deep cerebration. "I know."

He revisited our last thread. "I know there's no hope for us in this lifetime. I just don't see how it would be possible for us to get back together. You've painted me to be someone your family and friends will never want you to be around. It'll be hard to change that narrative."

"No, my dear, you painted that portrait of yourself. And yes, my mother and friends have all vowed to disown me if I ever get back with you."

"Damn! Disown? That's harsh. But I'll find you first. In our next life, I'll be sure to find you first."

"That's a sweet sentiment; I'll find you first."

In all honesty, I was touched by his motivation to recapture an unrequited love. Here he was, fully spiritually cognizant, laying the groundwork for another life's contract. His soul was desperately seeking to solidify yet another life's pact with mine.

Before meeting Siete, I threw the term *soulmate* around so flippantly, carelessly even. I automatically assumed that a soulmate union was one of ecstasy and nirvana, two like souls coming together to grow in parallel, nurturing and supporting the other through constant evolvement. Siete and

I were of the same soul family, so it made sense that he'd want to propel this bond into a next lifetime.

We came into each other's life to reflect the aspects of ourselves that needed the most development back to the other, which is why we saw each other so clearly. We'd come to see and experience each other through many varying perspectives; we'd been brothers, we'd been enemies, now we were lovers--well, ex-lovers.

Some soul mate configurations required the two people involved to incarnate over and over until they exhausted all of the relationship perspectives. As enticing as his offer for yet another perspective was, my soul was overtaxed. Siete had brought me the most suffering I'd ever experienced. He pushed me to the outer boundaries of growth's peak until I almost lost my balance, catapulting to my spiritual grave.

Prior to our romantic partnership, I wasn't the vibrational match for unconditional love. When we met, I was drawn to him, my soulmate, out of an attraction based largely on ego, shadow, karma, and subconscious agreements. The lessons within our present life's union were hardest because they were drawn from the lower frequencies of karmic debt, unmastered lessons, and unhealed wounds of the past.

When I first described our coming together, I said we each mirrored the other's reflection in our spirit. I wasn't aware then that we were reflecting the parts of ourselves that we liked least, that we imposed the most judgment upon each other--those suppressed parts of ourselves in great need of rehabilitation. After all, falling in love with Siete was a step closer to me falling in love with myself.

I had him to thank for my soul's expansion. Because of him, I allowed myself to feel everything as I regenerated my energy and power, sitting deeply in my own pain. Because of him, I broke my pattern of self-betrayal, lack of trust, dishonesty, and silencing my truth. Because of him, I was forced to bring these ailments to greater enlightenment by taking introspective alone time to tend to them affectionately.

Alas, I'd already received the message from spirit through the 9♥ that this was to be our last dance together. At this stage, I was approaching love, unconditionally, from my higher chakras of heart, throat, third eye, and crown.

September 21, 2017

"I feel so accomplished today. So alive."

"That's good to hear, queen. But what's so special about today?"

"Today, I went back into the studio and re-recorded seven of the eight songs on my demo. Originally, I was supposed to lay overdubs. But after painfully listening to the first takes, I sang every song over, two and three takes each of seven of the eight songs in three hours. I went in for business today. There was no game-playing.

"I'm satisfied with the outcome. I don't know how the world will receive it, but the tracks are laid and mixed. Now I'll put the project out for free on Bandcamp. I'm calling the album *Womban of Words*. Get it? My words are birthed from the womb?"

"Yep, I do. That's a dope concept. I'm glad you mentioned that, by the way. I'm thinking about building out my motivational speaking brand. I want to create another Instagram personality based on my motivational principles. Each day I want to create a one-minute video speaking about something enlightening.

"I need your help with curating the topics. Whatever topics you choose, I'll put my spin on them and convey to the world. The topic can't be about relationships, though. People don't know me as the *relationship guy*, so I won't have any credibility in that area."

"Nice idea. Finally some high-frequency communication."

I rummaged by brain for quick and dirty spiritual ideas.

"Why don't you use the *Seven Spiritual Laws of Success* as your springboard? You're the one who introduced it to me. You can do one law each day of the week, breaking down each principle into bite-sized segments that are accessible to the everyday person. I think that'll go over really well."

"You know what I'll do?"

"What?"

"I'll take the *Seven Spiritual Laws*, I'll record a video on each separate law for a full week starting on Sunday, adding my unique spin and interpretation."

"So, I like the way you take the same idea I just gave you and present it back to me like it's your own. Nice." We couldn't help but laugh at how ludicrous his last statement was.

There was the genesis of his positive alter ego. As promised, he started on Sunday launching the first spiritual Law of Pure Potentiality. He recorded it in his bedroom before he left for work each morning, specs placed intellectually over his eyes, appearing to be a true spiritual scholar. I agreed to send the hashtags for each video the night preceding the day's recording.

Our operation became so synchronized that I'd send him ideas and hashtags for the succeeding day's video at the same time he was preparing his mental script. He thought the synchronicities were spooky. I knew we were in spiritual alignment as I was fulfilling my spiritual obligation to ensure he was living in his purpose.

As the days progressed, the videos improved. He recorded some indoors, others outdoors. He recorded the first few in black and white, the last three in color. He moved with ease through the remaining six laws, ending with the Law of Dharma or Life's Purpose. He had hundreds of followers by the end of the first week. Born for this work, he was truly in alignment with his own dharma.

October 5, 2017

"You look the same. I'm glad you cut off that pink mohawk. It was cool, but your Caesar fits you much better." He paused to look at me. "You're pretty. Very pretty!"

"Why, thank you. But you keep telling me I'm pretty like you forgot." I laughed at the freshness of his words.

"Talking to you over the phone and seeing you over FaceTime is different than seeing you face-to-face."

I stared into his eyes, which seemed to have aged years since we last saw each other. He looked the same overall, but the crow's feet around his eyes were etched deeply into his skin, serving as tribal markings of a black man mixed with Caucasian blood. His were just aggravated by a hard life that consisted of deep squints that blocked the light of truth and feigned smiles which masked his pain.

It was an unseasonably warm day in early October at 75°. I took the day off to finally see Siete in person. We'd been throwing the possibility around for quite some time. I didn't have any reservations about seeing him. I had to look into his eyes for one last time to see if truth lived behind the light of his irises. We'd just driven from the barbershop where his growing beard was shaped and now sat in the diner over my Belgian waffle and his spinach and feta cheese omelet.

"So I bought a gift for you. Since you're speaking to people every day and recording your videos frequently, I figured I'd get you a blue kyanite pendant to wear around your neck."

"What's this? Kiya-what?" He took the pendant in his hand hesitantly, looking the crystal over to see if anything suspicious was engraved on it.

"It's blue kyanite. Crystalline kyanite really. It will help you find your true soul's purpose by allowing you to meditate easily. You said when you come home from work you need time to unwind. This crystal will help you channel that energy and open your closed third eye by showing you where you abused trust in the past.

"It'll also assist with your videos by allowing you to tap into intuitive communications and insights. So please don't look at it like it's some voodoo hex, because you're the one dabbling in witchcraft and black magic. Not me!"

"Well, I didn't know what it was. And I'm not doing any witchcraft. That's what you do."

"No! My dear. That's what *you* do!"

I was adamant to drive that point home with him. I had to make him aware that I was mindful of everything he was up to. He looked at me with a glint of amusement in his eyes.

"Anyway, you can replace your dog tag pendant with this. It has to be around your neck to activate your throat chakra, which resonates with the color blue."

We sat and conversed some more about my work with crystals. I told him about my experience with moldavite. How I'd dreamt of speaking with extraterrestrial ancestors who felt too vividly real to be figments of my imagination. We left the diner after about an hour and headed back to his place for a stint.

Sitting in his bedroom, we sat while he looked at ESPN, feeling a bit awkward and out of place. I looked out his window onto the street where the front of his apartment building faced.

"You took a long time to come out to greet me when I first pulled up. I know you were standing here, looking out of this window to see where my truck was parked and if I brought any of my goons with me."

"I really didn't. When you came, I was still in the supermarket buying toiletries. I came upstairs through the back entrance because it's closest to the store. I wasn't even thinking that you'd set me up. We've been speaking to each other too often on the phone for me to think you still held animosity toward me."

"Hmm. That's true. But you were still scared," I kidded him.

"But what we have to decide now is what we want to do. Are we staying as friends or are we going to see if we can make this work one last time? And I have to let you know, before you answer, I'm not hiding anything this time. I'm taking you to all of my family functions. I'm taking you around friends. And I expect the same from you. I won't be the side man."

His absoluteness made me pause. There was loaded meaning in his last sentence.

"What do you mean by that? Side man?"

I was thrown, but his senses perceived that I'd recognized more than a measure of truth in his words.

"I'm saying, I won't be your side man! I won't be the man you really love, staying in the background while you parade the man you're with, the one with whom your friends and family are comfortable and knows, around." His eyes were fixed pointedly on mine without a flutter, his speech direct and calm.

I didn't speak about the man I was with much. In fact, I hadn't mentioned him at all in this narrative. We'd been together for two years, meeting at a Taco Tuesday event in 2015, a full year after Siete and I split. I wasn't ashamed of my affiliation with my current beau. It just wasn't earthshaking. It served its purpose while allowing me ample freedom to roam the world and other life possibilities.

An alliance derived more from a place of refuge than rebound, we each needed someone with whom we could lick and heal our past wounds. Most of our time together was spent at night, in the unspoken safety of a sleepy embrace. The fact that Siete even knew of its existence further verified that he'd been lying about his flirtations with the occult.

Needless to say, with my fellow in the way of his wanting, we could only be friends from a distance.

November 2017

"Today I've come to a major realization. It's final for me. I'm leaving my job. I can't do this anymore."

"Wow. What happened that made you decide this?"

"Well, you don't know because I've been keeping my work at the job once I get home. But with this promotion to deputy executive director, my work has largely become community-based, requiring me to assist superintendents with school consolidations and closures. It's all-consuming. I swear it sucks the life out of everything in its path.

"Anyway, tonight we had a hearing about two transfer schools in District 23 that are consolidating. A transfer school is an alternative school for young adults who are over-aged and under-credited. Many of the students are in their early twenties. The problem is, although the schools are in the same community school district, the schools are geographically located in two distant neighborhoods. One school is in Crown Heights, the other in Brownsville."

"Oh? So they just want to start a gang war, huh?"

"See how easy that was for you to figure out? And you're not even a resident of Brooklyn. But you understand the underlying social ramifications of such a decision.

"What has me so disturbed by all this is the fact that these young adults were speaking from their hearts tonight, with tears in their eyes, saying if the merge happened, they'd stop going to school. They were crying for their identity, their teachers, their sanctuary--another stable structure in their lives being ripped from them.

"And while they were speaking to the department's officials many of them, Caucasian and young of course, were on their phones checking email, or looking at them with blank stares, reading from a pre-drafted script with robotic, logistical retorts. For these people it was all a formality. They're literally climbing up the career ladder on the backs of black and brown children.

"When those young adults were speaking, I couldn't help but clap in support of their oppositions. I used to get my hair cut around the corner from that school when Carlos's shop was still there. I'm in this neighborhood. I'm a face that's recognizable. How could I stand and look those young adults in the eyes and tell them I didn't hear or care about what they were saying? How? For what? A higher position and bigger paycheck? No! I'm not doing it! Come June, I'm out!"

"I understand how you feel. It's a bit of a tightrope navigating the political interests of the job and maintaining your personal integrity.

"Well, what I can say is you've always been the impulsive one in our relationship. Not saying you haven't given this idea much thought, but you move based on your impulses. You make quick decisions, live in the moment, and that seems to work for you. Where I take my time to think and rethink every decision I make, you make movements on a whim. You've been successful in your career, so I have no doubt you'll be successful in this next phase of your life, whatever you decide to do."

"Thank you. That means a lot to me. I'm going to pursue my singing career. I know it'll be challenging, but I'm willing to do it. You're just going to have to put me on your health insurance as your domestic life partner because that's the one area I haven't yet figured out. You owe me anyway."

I laughed to add some levity to my heavy heart.

"Don't worry. I got you."

We laughed, silently speculating about the possibilities.

"The next six months will be slated to my crafting a careful and responsible exit strategy. I just have to maintain my composure and not sabotage myself in the interim."

December 2017

"I saw your post on Instagram today. You're reading *The Alchemist* again?"

I knew he was an avid reader. The best gift to buy Siete was a good book.

"I read it often. It's one of my favorite books. In this new phase of my life, I just wanted to see what I'd find that can help me on this journey. I had it on my desk, and one of my co-workers who stopped by saw it and asked if he could read it. Now it's circulating around the office."

"It took me some time to get into the book at first. I guess the simplicity of the story turned me off, but when I took my time with the words, there are a lot of hidden gems in the story that I couldn't quite relate to at the time. The main premise of the story is the thing that one strives for most is always there, right in front of you to begin with."

"That's one takeaway, but you missed the point that it's just one big love story. The best quote in that entire book is: *So I love you because the entire universe conspired to help me find you.*"

Metamorphosed by time, he'd forever be the hopeless romantic. For all roads in Siete's future led back to us. We continued with our spiritual conversation on alchemy. He introduced me to the videos of Dandapani, Hindu priest, who facilitated a talk titled *The Energy Alchemist*. We watched the video over our phones.

The talk delved into the transference of energy and ways to direct, manage, and invest it in the things that mattered most in one's life. He demonstrated the power of directing one's awareness and energy to fulfilling his or her life's purpose through the application of willpower. He spoke about using willpower and the power of concentration to focus awareness on manifesting things most desired.

What resonated with me most was Dandapani's notion of the subconscious mind filled with experiences that had negative emotions attached to them. He lectured on the importance of removing the negative emotions associated with those subconscious experiences by writing them on a piece of paper where the experience moves from the subconscious to the conscious mind. The emotion comes out of the experience flowing through one's hand onto the piece of paper, and the paper is then crumpled and burned, transferring the energy to heat.

"This is deep. You should write down all of the anger and animosity you feel toward me regarding our breakup and burn the paper. It might help you heal faster."

"Yep. I'll do that." He was willing to begin the process of detachment.

"Speaking of energy transference, I want to pass something by you to get your take on the situation." I shifted gears.

"Okay, what's up?"

"I sat in on my vocal coach's set last Thursday. To sit in means the main act, my vocal coach, gave me an opportunity to perform during her set. I performed a song called *Fire Waltz*. We started with a wicked free improvisation, but when I began to sing the actual song, I was a bit off-key because I couldn't hear the bass player clearly. I'm used to practicing with the pianist, and there wasn't any in this ensemble, so the bassline was foreign to me.

"Anyway, I found my key and rocked the audience for the remainder of the song. The crowd loved it. My vocal coach even came over to tell me how great my performance was.

"Later on in the week, however, she sent me a congratulatory email. She started out saying the performance was great, I gave the musicians clear and quick direction, and the crowd received me well. Then, she launched into a litany of critiques, mostly about semantics. I didn't thank her for the opportunity, I didn't thank the establishment, I shouldn't have given the two band members solos during her set because of time constraints, I took too long to come off stage, I placed the mic in the stand and not back in her hand.

"The email threw me a bit because these are all logistical items that she could've discussed with me when we practiced together. I feel like I should print that email and burn it."

"I really don't understand her point. What is she really talking about here? Did you rock? Or did you not rock? That's all that matters. Why were you nervous when you started? That's the real reason you began in a different key!" He knew me too well.

"Just the thought of being in front a crowd unnerves me."

"Honey, I always tell you no one in that audience can do what you do. Yes, some people can sing, but they can't sing like you. Once you stay rooted in that reality, there's nothing to be afraid of. Just do what you do without thought."

"But it's not the same as public speaking. I have to be cognizant of my control, my breathing, my key, making sure each note is in tune and not flat or sharp. It's a lot to think about."

"Yeah, I get it. But that sounds like some sucker shit."

His words remained with me. They'd become my mantra before every performance thereafter.

First Week in January

"Did you read the outline I added to the Google Doc earlier today?" I asked.

"I saw that you added to the document. The email notification came across my phone, but I didn't get a chance to actually look at what you wrote."

"Are you close to your computer now? Open it and let's look at it."

Siete had been writing his book since we met. He scrapped his original approach because, seven years later, he'd amassed more spiritual knowledge that would make a greater impact on his writing. He just didn't know how to open. I urged him to start at the beginning of his flow of thought.

I wouldn't commit to writing his book for him, but I did create a shared Google Doc for him to start his writing process. I made an agreement to edit his work as he progressed. Not knowing how to create a working outline, I drafted one for him at work in a matter of minutes.

"You have the Doc open?"

"Yeah, I'm reading what you've written now."

"Good, so let me navigate you through the structure of the outline. Your book is based on eight principles, so it's relatively formulaic. First, start with a preface or introduction that explains why you're embarking on this journey. Where were you in your life when you felt the need to create these eight steps to greatness? Why were they important to your development? Don't go into them, though; just provide the reader with background into who you are.

"Then each chapter begins with a short quote, you introduce one principle at a time. Relate the principle to a real-life story of a person you've either worked with, conducted business with, or one of your direct reports, demonstrating how the principle is applicable. Then you end the chapter with methods of application for the reader so it's a functioning read and practical workbook that the reader can use immediately.

"Don't save the exercises until the end because it'll be ignored by the majority of readers. Repeat this methodology for the remaining seven principles until you get to the conclusion. Use the conclusion to summate your own findings along your personal progression, using these eight standards."

"Thanks so much. I guess the part I'm most concerned about is being careful not to write how I speak."

"Yeah, I know. You're getting caught up with the grammar, more specifically. The pages you've written thus far are good. They're very good actually. You don't realize that your gift is your speech. When you speak, you invite people to listen to you. Look at the influence you've had at this new job. It would behoove you to write the way you speak because it's an extension of what makes you great. Don't worry about the grammar; I'll correct it as you go along."

"Thank you. That's a compliment coming from you because you're a great writer. But there's one written piece of yours that isn't so great."

What written work is that? I thought for a second. "Oh, you're talking about the breakup letter I sent you?"

"It makes me mad every time I read it."

"As it should. That was a clever piece of writing. I purposely worded it in that manner to use your own words against you. That letter was a classic. It should go down in the book of world records for being the *Best Breakup Letter Ever Written*."

"Never! It was based on unfounded accusations."

"No, it wasn't! Everything in that letter was factual."

"Are you *kidding* me? Do you still feel that way? Are we back at *this* juncture?"

"I don't believe we ever left, black man."

"I don't believe you still feel this way about me. Otherwise, you wouldn't have reestablished the friendship that we have now."

"No, not quite. I believe in the power of forgiveness. I still believe in my heart of hearts that you were behind the burglary. I do."

"I don't want your forgiveness," he pleaded. "I don't want to be forgiven for something that *you think* I did. I want to be exonerated for a crime *I know* I didn't commit."

"I can't do that, Siete. For me to say that you were innocent would be me going against my spiritual gifts. My spirit showed me, clearly I might add, that you were involved. If I were to forsake my gift of clairvoyance, I'd run the risk of losing it altogether. And I'd rather take the risk of losing you than losing that. Honestly."

"Well, if that's how you feel, I don't want to be friends with you anymore."

"*You* no longer want to be friends with *me*," I reiterated incredulously, my ego bracing to rare its ugly little head.

"No! I don't."

"Okay, then ..." I arrested my primitive drive. "Bye ..." My voice cracked at our bond's finality. We hung up. I removed myself from our shared Google Doc, deleted his number and texts, severed our social media connections. He was now on his own. The 9♥ had played its hand.

There it was, my underwhelming coup de grâce. It was far from the showdown of my long anticipated finale. I permitted my ego to acquiesce to his force of hand because I believed his moment of self-vindication cemented my peace of mind for the remainder of this life and lives to come. He, being the instigator, had no more reason to retaliate.

Our soul contract was broken. I freed myself from the karmic cocoon, weightlessly, emerging a goddess emancipated.

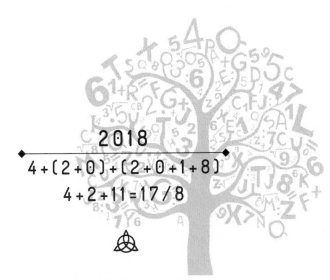

2018

$$4 + (2 + 0) + (2 + 0 + 1 + 8)$$
$$4 + 2 + 11 = 17 / 8$$

Eight Personal Year

Achievement, career, major moves, power, births. Consider this your "power year" cycle—the chance to do and achieve something big in your life. You develop a deeper maturity and a deeper sense of destiny in yourself and in events about to happen.[10] The blessings you seek are about to manifest as you move forward with your heart's desire, because thought without action is just vain imagination.[11]

---

[10] (Strayhorn, 1997)
[11] (DannyTarot, 2020)

"I love music! In the colors of life I hear,
Pouring down the canals of my ear,
A sweet whisper so sincere.
I love music! In the flowers that bloom every spring,
In lusty lullabies passing birds dare to bring,
In harmonies lovers sing ..."

19

I SAT ON THE MOUNTAINTOPS OF ILHABELA, A BEAUTIFUL BEACH ISLAND 124 miles from São Paulo, Brazil. Watching the winds blow on the waves of the azure seas, it was winter in August at a comfortable 75°. A pandemonium of green parrots flew above me. They gurgled, trilled, whistled, and squawked their happy good morning hellos as the hummingbirds sucked nectar from the hibiscus plants. Orchids sprinkled the air with sweet jasmine.

My hostess's black cat sat perched a few yards away, keeping a watchful eye on me as my guardian with a mission from my ancestors to ensure my safety. The yellow and white butterflies encircled my crown with messages from my spirit guides that I was in the right place, serving my life's purpose as I sat to write this story. I was sitting down to the tale of the modern-day woman, the altitude making me light and ethereal.

I had no idea what this would turn out to be, nor had I known this would be the story called forth when I sat down to write. Sequestered for three weeks in this tropical paradise called Casa Na Ilha, I was situated in an artists' residence with other creators who dared to probe the artistic cavities of their minds without daily tedium and disruptions. How did I arrive at this point, you ask? Well, the tale is a rather auspicious one.

It was April 27th, an exact week after my forty-second birthday. It was a rainy Friday. I was feeling particularly nostalgic because I'd just turned the license plates to my Mercedes Benz in to the Atlantic Center Department of Motor Vehicles after returning the truck the day prior. I stayed in the Fort Greene area waiting for Lyris to meet me for dinner.

We had originally planned to meet at the Blue Moon Café on Fulton Street, but when I walked into the establishment to put our names on the waiting list, I was greeted by a boisterous after-work crowd and deafening cacophony. Knowing Lyris the way I did, I knew the setting would alter her mood instantaneously upon entry. So I told her to meet me at the Thai restaurant farther down the block.

When she arrived, we sat in the only available seats by the window of the restaurant's entrance. We were discussing the two-hour *Woman Reborn* set I performed for my birthday the week before, reflecting on the growth I'd demonstrated since I first started out in 2012. I confided my plans to leave my seventeen-year career at the department of education. To Lyris's subsequent question, *What will you do?* I expressed my desire to go somewhere warm, serene, and surrounded by nature to sit and write.

As we were conversing, a young lady sitting at the table next to us overheard our conversation. She kindly excused herself for ear-hustling before she shared her own experience as an artist who once worked as a teacher. She left her job to explore the unknown through exciting artist residencies found on a website called ResArtis. She advised that I investigate the site as I embarked on the next phase of my life.

The next afternoon, I scouted the site for a residency that made sense for me and the experience I wanted to create as part of my artistic maturation. I found Casa Na Ilha and it all came together. The application was due on the Monday, giving me a day to gather my samples of work and answer all four questions. I forfeited sleep to submit my completed application late Sunday at midnight.

I received my acceptance letter that Tuesday, the day following the admission deadline. The synchronicity of it all amazes me every time I retell the story. The likelihood of changing restaurants at the last minute, meeting this young lady, and finding Casa Na Ilha was pure alchemy. It was as if the universe was assuring me that the more I relinquished my attachments to material things, the more gifts I'd receive toward my life's fulfillment.

With concretized plans to go to Brazil for a month, I handed my letter of resignation in to my superiors in mid-May. The work climate had about-faced to the worst, just as The Priest of Ochun had prognosticated. The work became less meaningful and less structured as the micromanagement of minutiae spiked to anxiety-raising levels. While I wasn't the one under siege, most of my time on the way out was spent towing the fine line of maintaining a stellar professional reputation and safeguarding my vulnerable team.

On June 29th I humbly walked out of Tweed Courthouse unceremoniously, with no flamboyant after-work celebration, no words of wisdom for my co-workers who remained, and no forwarding email address.

On the peak of this mountain, I sat cranking out one or two chapters a day for twenty-one days straight with a one-day break each week. The words poured out of me. I didn't get in the steady flow's way because there'd be no way to recreate this exact environment with these exact conditions back home in Brooklyn.

A month after I returned home to New York, Tamia called. This time she called bearing news of life. She called to tell me that a month earlier, while I was writing in Brazil, she was at a girlfriend's house hanging out when she fell asleep. She dreamt that she was gambling at a casino and won a windfall of cash. When she came to, she relayed her dream to her friend and her friend's fellow, who then decided that they should indeed go to the casino to see if the dream was a prophecy demanding to be actualized.

On the way to the casino, her girlfriend's fellow called his friend who was familiar with the road and knew the fastest route to take. His friend agreed to go on the gambling excursion with the small entourage under the condition that someone else drive back home in the morning. Tamia consented to being that designated someone. When they arrived to pick up his friend, Tamia was astonished to discover that it was none other than Collin.

349

Collin took his place in the driver's seat first before he turned to see who he was chauffeuring in the back seat. Once he rested his eyes on Tamia, it was as if his heart poured open with eight years of inexpressible affectivities. Tamia said for the entire drive to the casino he spoke about him and me. He spoke of our late-night beach hangs. He laughed at our stakeout. He spoke of our arguments. He spoke of my meanness toward him when I started to rise in occupational stature. He spoke of our unborn child whose loss he still mourned. He spoke of our parting.

Now, separated from his wife, single, and on his own, he shared that I was the one who'd gotten away. To the credit of a misleading Facebook post I'd written saying I was leaving New York to *reside* in Brazil, Tamia declared that I'd made a new life abroad, implying that our time had passed.

I asked her for his number to do what I didn't have the courage to do the year before. Once three weeks had passed and I still hadn't received the number, I ventured onto Nostrand Avenue by foot and made the definitive left turn.

There he was smiling knowingly of his earth angel who'd whispered in my ear on his behalf. I've been fortifying my friendship with Tamia ever since. Collin and I are rebuilding our love daily by grounding ourselves in the present moment.

I close this chapter in December. As I added the finishing touches to this story, I had the forethought to have my talisman fashioned from *The Key of Solomon* melted and made into something else. The pendant was inviting entities to rape and sodomize me in my sleep when it should've been shielding me from psychic intrusion.

Because the consecration petition the Yoruba priest gave me included the general command, "I now invite thee. I now incite thee," without addressing a specific deity, it opened the portal to random spirits with diabolical agendas.

On the nights I'd sleep without underwear, I'd greet the dawn in my empty bed, with my vagina or anus feeling as though it belonged to a plundered rag doll. I knew it was a male spirit because he revealed his face in my dream.

The room was dark. I was in my bed. When the spirit finished having his way with me, he walked toward the door, his face illuminated by the dim, hallway light. He was a tall, middle-aged, light-skinned male. He wore an ivy cap, which he tipped, winking at me on his way out.

Though, on this particular morning, the sexual encounter didn't end. I felt the presence of him inside me while I strained to navigate throughout my day. I wanted to slither out of my skin in defenseless repulsion. I took another spiritual bath to exorcise it.

My spiritual godmother stripped me naked. She bathed me with white corn kernels and rum while lashing my body with branches of bay leaves. She lit a cigar and blew it on my back against a white plate. When she was finished, she showed me the dish and said, "You see this? This is a dick!"

On the smoked porcelain was the likeness of a phallus.

"Don't worry," she said, consoling me. "This happens more often than you think."

I took the pendant and chain to Tansey to have it weighed and tested, only to discover that the chain was 14-karat gold, but the pendant was likely silver.

Incensed, I took the jewelry back to the original jeweler who tested it himself to prove that it was undeniably 14-karat gold. My thought was to melt the chain and create one in yellow gold that replaced the fourth pentacle of Venus with the fourth pentacle of the moon for protection against evil sorceries. To do so would require me to spend additional money on top of the exorbitant price I'd already spent to first make it. Unable to accept the words of the jeweler as gospel, I took the pendant to the Diamond District where it was proven to be 10-karat gold and not the 14-karat I'd paid for.

Back in the jewelry store on Flatbush Avenue, I argued with the jeweler for a return on my investment since he dishonored our agreement. In his thievery, he made the most telling revelation. He said that the talisman had stopped working because I'd lost my faith. Although the pentacles themselves possessed some degree of magic, it was *my* belief in their mystical powers that gave them its true potency and might.

It wouldn't matter if I had the pendant blessed in a synagogue, temple, or church. Without my internal belief the pendant was rendered purposeless. I knew that the talisman hadn't stopped working, but rather, it was working toward the wrong intent. No longer wanting the talisman nor chain in my possession, I sold both back to him, cutting my losses and preserving my dignity.

At this crux, I felt like the little shepherd boy in *The Alchemist*, on a desperate pilgrimage to search for knowledge of all spiritual treasures unseen. What I failed to realize was *I am* my own precious metal energetically charged for protective programming. All intuitions, spiritual guidance, psychic protection, prophecies, and miracles originate from within.

I took the long course in search of a complex love filled with complex half-truths when my own truthful path with heart was right here all along. What I wanted, I already had. Every incident I'd experienced, and every person I'd met until now, led me to this pivotal moment of my transcendence.

Hence, I'm in love with *me* forevermore because the entire universe conspired to help me find my own authentic voice, and my voice was divinely commissioned to communicate the missive of universal love. What this means for me, or what lies ahead? I haven't a clue; but for once in my life, the unknown is exhilarating.

Perhaps the greatest love story ever told was my own.

Made in the USA
Middletown, DE
15 August 2022

71427669R00213